BRITISH POLITICS

UPDATE 1999-2002

Roy Bentley

Peter Dorey

David Roberts

Causeway Press

Acknowledgements

Cover design	Caroline Waring-Collins (Waring Collins Ltd)
Page design	Caroline Waring-Collins (Waring Collins Ltd)
Grapic origination	Derek Baker
Graphics	Tim Button
Reader	Wendy Janes

The editor and authors are grateful for any comments. Please contact us:

by post: Causeway Press, PO Box 13, Ormskirk, Lancs, L39 5HP
by tel: 01695 576048
by e-mail: stevel.causeway@btinternet.com

Picture credits

Austin 70, 89; Steve Bell 35, 67b, 73, 80; Peter Brookes 30; Joe Cummings 60; League Against Cruel Sports 50; Nicola 15, 16; PA Photos cover (all), 2, 3, 4, 13, 25, 37, 47, 49, 51, 53, 62, 63, 64, 65, 66 (both), 67t, 72 (both), 74, 77; Chris Riddell 5, 8, 9, 10, 11, 29, 48, 92; Martin Rowson 52, 86; David Simmonds 12.

Every effort has been made to locate the copyright owners of material used in this book. Any omissions brought to the attention of the publisher are regretted and will be credited in subsequent printings.

British Library Cataloguing in Publication Data
A catalogue record for this book is available from the British Library.

ISBN 1 902796 49 7

Causeway Press Limited
PO Box 13, Ormskirk, Lancs, L39 5HP

© Roy Bentley, Peter Dorey, David Roberts & Steve Lancaster
First impression, 2002

Printed and bound by LEGOPRINT SPA, Italy

Contents

Contents contd

1 What is politics?

1 The fuel blockade of September 2000

In protest against the high levels of tax levied on fuel in Britain (particularly compared to fuel duties elsewhere in Europe), a relatively small group of lorry drivers and farmers instigated, in early September 2000, a 'spontaneous' blockade of Britain's oil refineries. The result was that, within five days, the protestors nearly brought Britain to a standstill as garages ran out of petrol and panic-buying emptied supermarket shelves. In spite of the chaos and inconvenience their action caused, the 'People's Fuel Lobby' (the ad-hoc umbrella group set up during the protest) enjoyed substantial support among the British public. The government was portrayed in the tabloid press as being arrogant and out of touch, particularly when ministers made it clear that they would not surrender to those 'holding the country to ransom'.

The fuel protest was enthusiastically supported by William Hague and the Conservative Party (backed by anti-Labour newspapers such as the *Daily Mail* and the *Daily Telegraph*) - quite a U-turn for a party and its press supporters who normally attack trade unions which engage in direct action and who invariably demand that ministers 'stand firm' and not give in to 'mob rule'. Hague made much of lower levels of duty on the continent. He also claimed that the fuel protests represented the moment when the British people had finally realised the extent to which New Labour was taxing them by stealth.

Within a week, the fuel protestors had called off their action, but issued the Blair government with a 60-day ultimatum - either announce a cut in fuel duty in the November pre-Budget speech, or face renewed blockades. In November, the Chancellor offered just enough concessions and initiatives to avert a repeat performance. There was only a token protest by a handful of disgruntled lorry drivers and farmers when the 60-day deadline expired.

In the immediate aftermath of the fuel protests, the Blair government's popularity plummeted. Several opinion polls conducted during the second half of September showed that the Conservatives had secured a lead over Labour for the first time since September 1992, with one poll revealing that the Conservative Party had surged ahead to an 8% lead. With expectations of a general election within the next 12 months, the Conservatives were understandably jubilant. Labour ministers, however, were furious that neither the oil companies nor the police had taken action against the protestors. Certainly, some ministers felt that they had been placed in a no-win situation by the fuel protests since, while they were denounced as arrogant for not offering concessions, they also knew that, if they had adopted a more conciliatory stance, pro-Conservative newspapers would lambast them for 'caving-in' at the first sign of trouble.

Significance of the protest

Although the taxation adjustments made in November were relatively small, the fact that concessions were made indicates that the government had been shaken by the protest. It also suggests that the balance of power does not always rest with the established authorities. The highly disruptive and effective tactics of the fuel protestors show that pressure groups can exert power and that governments can be forced to make some adjustments to their policies. As a result of the fuel protest, it is likely that the option of collecting additional revenue through higher fuel taxes will be off the agenda for some time.

It should also be noted that, although the 'People's Fuel Lobby' might well have been successful without support from the mass media, the Conservative Party and the wider public, the support it did receive from these groups enabled it to exert significant pressure on the government.

Nevertheless, the fact that the 'People's Fuel Lobby' was an unelected body raises questions about the use of power in a democracy. Is it right that a self-appointed, unelected pressure group can almost bring the country to a halt?

Finally, it should be noted that, although the Labour government suffered a temporary loss of support, its position in the polls soon recovered and it went on to win a second landslide in the general election of June 2001.

Adapted from Anderton 2000, Dorey 2001 and McNaughton 2001.

Figure 1.1 Fuel protestors
This photo shows fuel protestors driving in convoy in September 2000. In addition to driving slowly along motorways, causing congestion, they picketed oil refineries, causing many garages to run out of fuel.

2 Anti-capitalist demonstrations

The late 1990s witnessed the emergence of a global anti-capitalist movement. Those opposed to capitalism believe that the pursuit of profit and wealth involves the exploitation both of people and of the world's natural resources. With escalating globalisation, the anti-capitalist movement is particularly worried about the growing power of large multinational businesses.

The anti-capitalist movement is unlike a conventional pressure group in that it has no identifiable single hierarchy or leadership and no established headquarters. It consists of a loose collection of dissatisfied people and groups including environmentalists, socialists, anarchists and those demanding debt relief for Third World countries. A visible focus of the anti-capitalist movement has been a series of mass demonstrations held in major cities including Seattle (USA), Gothenburg (Sweden), Prague (the Czech Republic) and Genoa (Italy). Several of these meetings have been organised to coincide with meetings of the leaders of the world's most economically powerful countries (such as the G8 summits).

Figure 1.2 May Day, 2001
Police confront demonstrators on 1 May 2001.

London, 1 May 2001

The first day in May is International Labour Day and, around the world, is often a day for mass protests and demonstrations. Anti-capitalist demonstrations were held on 1 May 1999 and 2000, resulting in damage to property estimated at several million pounds. In 2001, the British government and the London authorities were determined to prevent a repeat performance. As part of a media campaign, the Metropolitan Police Commissioner warned newspaper executives that there was a dangerous anarchist threat and that the police would adopt a 'zero tolerance' policy. On the day, 6,000 police officers were on duty, including dog units and police helicopters. Would-be peaceful protestors were advised to stay away. Some protestors claimed that, before the event itself, the police systematically harassed and intimidated them.

In contrast to the high-profile media campaign of the police chiefs, the public relations campaign of the protestors was conducted primarily on the internet. The Wombles (White Overall Movement for Building Liberation through Effective Struggle) set up websites which showed a mock Monopoly Board constructed 'as an ironic symbol of anti-capitalism and an excuse to tour London causing chaos'. The intention was to direct this 'chaos' especially at premises of large multinational corporations which, the protestors alleged, were engaged in dangerous or exploitative global activities (for example, McDonald's, Tesco and Barclays Bank).

On 1 May 2001, the estimated 5,000 protestors in central London (see Figure 1.2) were fewer than had been expected and fewer than in the previous year. This time they were outnumbered by police and representatives of the media. Those who did attend were penned in for a number of hours by riot police, denied access to food, water or toilet facilities and, effectively, prevented from expressing their views. As a result, most of the protestors' planned targeted activities could not take place.

Interpretations

Much of the subsequent press reporting of the May-Day protest concentrated on the methods used by the police - hailing them as a great success. Similarly, in the House of Commons, there were cross-party congratulations for the way in which the police handled the event. Certainly, the actions of the police in London were far less harsh than those used in Genoa less than three months later. In Genoa, one demonstrator was shot dead by the police and there were reports of numerous incidents of police torture and severe beatings of arrested protesters.

Naomi Klein offers an alternative interpretation. She argues that, by portraying planned peaceful protests as potentially violent outbursts, the authorities exercise a major form of control. For many would-be protesters, this functions as a form of self-censorship. The media campaigns frighten them into staying at home. Noreena Hertz, who witnessed the London May-Day demonstration in 2001, agrees. In their eagerness to protect property rights over the right to freedom of expression, she argues, the police and the media, backed by politicians of all major parties, acted undemocratically.

Adapted from the *Observer*, 8 and 29 April, 6 May and 29 July 2001, the *Guardian*, 23 March 2001, Hertz 2001 and Klein 2000.
See also *British Politics in Focus*, Second Edition, pp.177-81.

References

Anderton (2000) Anderton, A., *The Student's Economy in Focus 2000/01*, Causeway Press, 2000.
Dorey (2001) Dorey, P., 'The Conservatives in opposition, 1997-2000' in *Lancaster (2001)*.
Hertz (2001) Hertz, N., *The Silent Takeover: Global Capitalism and the Death of Democracy*, Heinemann, 2001.

Klein (2000) Klein, N., *No Logo*, Flamingo, 2000.
Lancaster (2001) Lancaster, S. (ed.), *Developments in Politics*, Vol.12, Causeway Press, 2001.
McNaughton (2001) McNaughton, N., 'Populist movements - a new development in the politics of pressure', *Talking Politics*, Vol.14.1, September 2001.

1 Contemporary liberalism

Figure 2.1 Charles Kennedy

The election of Charles Kennedy (see Figure 2.1) as Leader of the Liberal Democrats has meant an ideological shift away from that adopted by his predecessor, Paddy Ashdown, towards that held in the early 1990s.

Until the mid-1990s, liberalism in Britain, as represented by the Liberal Democrats, was widely understood as a 'middle way' ideology, one which sought equidistance between the Conservatives on the one hand and Labour on the other - in the hope of attracting votes from disillusioned supporters of both parties. Liberalism also rejected the traditional left-right ideological model, believing it to be inaccurate and largely irrelevant to the needs of contemporary British society.

As the 1997 general election approached, however, the Liberal Democrats formally abandoned equidistance, and moved much closer to New Labour - an ideological shift championed by the Liberal Democrat Leader, Paddy Ashdown. When Charles Kennedy replaced Paddy Ashdown as Leader in August 1999, the closer links with New Labour were, at first, retained, but it was no secret that Kennedy was less enthusiastic about 'Lib-Lab' cooperation than Ashdown had been. Then, following the 2001 general election, the Liberal Democrats began to review their stance on a number of issues and, at the same time, loosened their ties with the Blair government as part of a strategy to challenge the Conservative Party as the most credible or attractive opposition to New Labour. This process, quite understandably, produced debates among Liberal Democrats over the contemporary meaning of British liberalism. Although Liberal Democrats reject the traditional left-right ideological model, it is apparent that some have wanted to challenge New Labour from the left (in the hope of attracting disillusioned Labour voters), while others favour a move rightwards (in order to attract moderate Conservatives).

Kennedy, meanwhile, clearly believes that liberalism can be refashioned in a manner which can attract disillusioned Labour and Conservative voters alike. This suggests that he believes the left-right ideological model is outdated or over-simplistic and he favours a return to equidistance. In other words, under Kennedy, there has been an ideological shift back to the position held in the early 1990s.

The Liberal Democrats' 2001 general election manifesto confirmed belief in:

- the decentralisation of political power and decision-making
- constitutional reform
- social justice and equality, including opposition to all forms of discrimination against individuals and minorities on the grounds of race, ethnicity or sexuality
- improved public services, funded partly by private investment and public-private partnerships, and partly by a reform of taxation (including higher taxes for those on the highest incomes)
- recognition that the state, the market, and the voluntary sector, should be seen as partners in many areas, not as rivals or adversaries
- environmentalism
- a strong commitment to Europe and internationalism.

Adapted from Liberal Democrat 2001, the *Observer* 10 June 2001 and the *Guardian*, 21 January, 11 February, 28 February and 11 March 2002.

See also *British Politics in Focus*, Second Edition, pp.24-26.

2 What is contemporary conservatism?

When William Hague won the Conservative Party leadership contest in June 1997, he initially sought to articulate a 'compassionate conservatism', one which proclaimed to be more 'socially inclusive' or tolerant of minority groups and alternative lifestyles. This indicated a move away from the Thatcherism which had intellectually dominated the Conservative Party for the previous two decades, with many commentators anticipating a revival of the older 'One Nation' Toryism which had prevailed prior to the Thatcher years.

However, by 1999, this 'socially inclusive' conservatism had failed to make an impression on the electorate and Hague reverted to a hard-line conservatism, more akin to the authoritarian populism of Thatcherism. This switch revealed the party's uncertainty as to what it actually represented at the end of the 20th century.

Following a second crushing defeat for the party in the 2001 general election, Hague's successor, Iain Duncan Smith, faced an unenviable task.

The initial indications suggest the adoption of a three-pronged approach:

- a continued hard-line, populist stance against asylum seekers, the European Union (especially the euro) and the 'nanny state'
- a more compassionate stance towards poorer and 'most vulnerable' sections of society
- attacks on the Blair government's failure to deliver improved public services.

Adapted from Dorey 2001, Dorey 2002 and the *Guardian*, 15 May and 8 June 2002. See also *British Politics in Focus*, Second Edition, pp.28-31.

3 New Labour, the Third Way and social democracy

According to critics, notably Roy Hattersley, New Labour and the 'Third Way' have increasingly betrayed the party's former social democratic principles. Since 1997, he argues, the Labour government has embraced a Thatcherite agenda.

While critics like Hattersley certainly do not hanker after the commitment to extensive state control and regulation of the economy espoused by Old Labour, they do believe that New Labour has become just as dogmatic and doctrinaire as Old Labour in its professed belief that only the private sector can provide answers to economic questions. Hattersley has described the government as being 'submerged in…fantasies about the…efficiency of free enterprise' (see Figure 2.2).

Hattersley has also maintained his criticism of New Labour's education policies, particularly the government's increasing emphasis on specialist schools, which he considers to be a revival of selection similar to that in the days of the old 11-plus examination. In pursuing such an education policy, Hattersley claims, New Labour is abandoning the social democratic commitment to comprehensive education and, as a result, ensuring that children from poorer backgrounds will effectively be denied genuine equality of opportunity and social mobility.

Ultimately, Hattersley insists, the pursuit of the Third Way has left New Labour and the Blair government without any distinctive intellectual framework with which to judge issues. Even a government priding itself on its pragmatism and on its rejection of outdated ideologies needs some firm principles with which to make decisions and determine the merits of the various options available to it. Instead, New Labour and the Third Way have, according to Hattersley, given Britain a vacuous 'philosophy-free politics', leaving the government without a clear or coherent sense of direction.

This criticism began to bite. In 2000, Anthony Giddens (whose book *The Third Way* was largely responsible for popularising the term) felt it was necessary to respond to criticism by restating and updating his case. By the beginning of 2002, a (then) senior New Labour minister, Stephen Byers, was able to concede publicly that 'some of the softer edges of the Third Way have been shown to be flaky'.

Such was the apparent uncertainty among New Labour ministers about the meaning of the term 'Third Way' and the

Figure 2.2 New Labour and Big Business
Critics argue that New Labour favours the private sector and gives in to the demands of Big Business far too easily.

direction in which it was taking them that a mini-conference was held at the Prime Minister's official country residence, Chequers, during early summer 2002 to discuss what the term meant and how it could be revitalised. Organised by Peter Mandelson and attended by Tony Blair, Bill Clinton, various Cabinet ministers, left-of-centre academics, policy advisers and Blair's personal pollster, Philip Gould, this 'summit' sought to re-establish the principles of the Third Way, particularly in the context of a conservative revival in much of Europe and the United States as well as the rise of the extreme Right in France and parts of northern Britain. At a previous meeting at Chequers in March 2002, the Health Secretary, Alan Milburn, warned ministerial colleagues that New Labour was in danger of being viewed as 'a value-free zone' and as a group of mere technocrats and administrators rather than as politicians in touch with the views and values of ordinary British people. This, he argued, was likely to increase public disenchantment with politics and mainstream politicians and either result in further apathy or an increase in support for populist demagogues lurking on the political extremes.

Adapted from the *Guardian*, 5 July 1999 and 14 January 2002, Giddens 2000, the *Observer*, 4 June 2000, the *Independent*, 9 March 2002 and the *Times*, 10 June 2002.

See also *British Politics in Focus*, Second Edition, pp.34-37.

References

Dorey (2001) Dorey, P., 'The Conservatives in Opposition, 1997-2000' in *Lancaster (2001)*.
Dorey (2002) Dorey, P., 'Policies' in *Garnett & Lynch (2002)*.
Garnett & Lynch (2002) Garnett, M. & Lynch, P. (eds), *The Conservatives in Crisis*, Manchester University Press, 2002.
Giddens (2000) Giddens, A., *The Third Way and its Critics*, Polity, 2000.

Lancaster (2001) Lancaster, S. (ed.), *Developments in Politics*, Vol. 12, Causeway Press, 2001.
Liberal Democrat (2001) *Liberal Democrat Manifesto: For a Liberal and Democratic Britain: Freedom, Justice, Honesty*, Liberal Democrat manifesto, 2001.

1 The general election of June 2001 (Great Britain)

Party	Total no. votes	MPs elected	% total votes cast	Party	Total no. votes	MPs elected	% total votes cast
Labour	10,740,168 (13,551,381)	413 (419)	42 (44)	**Scottish Socialist Party**	72,279 (-)	0 (-)	0.3 (-)
Conservative	8,352,845 (9,590,565)	166 (165)	33 (31)	**Socialist Alliance**	60,496 (-)	0 (-)	0.2 (-)
Liberal Democrats	4,815,249 (5,243,322)	52 (46)	19 (17)	**Socialist Labour**	57,536 (52,110)	0 (0)	0.2 (0.2)
SNP	464,314 (620,434)	5 (6)	1.8 (2.0)	**BNP**	47,129 (35,833)	0 (0)	0.2 (0.1)
Plaid Cymru	195,892 (161,030)	4 (4)	0.7 (0.6)	**Liberal**	10,920 (44,989)	0 (0)	0.0 (0.1)
UK Independence	390,575 (106,028)	0 (0)	1.5 (0.3)	**Pro-Life Alliance**	9,453 (18,545)	0 (0)	0.0 (0.1)
Greens	166,487 (63,991)	0 (0)	0.6 (0.2)				

(i) This table shows the results of the general election of June 2001 in Great Britain (1997 figures in brackets).

	Labour	Con	Lib Dem	SNP/Plaid	Other		Labour	Con	Lib Dem	SNP/Plaid	Other
London (n/c)	47 (-2)	31 (-1)	18 (+3)	N/A	5 (n/c)	**Yorks/Humb**	49 (-3)	30 (+2)	17 (+1)	N/A	4
South-East (-1)	32 (n/c)	43 (+1)	22 (+1)	N/A	4 (-1)	**North-West**	52 (-2)	28 (+2)	17 (+2)	N/A	3
South-West (-1)	26 (n/c)	31 (n/c)	39 (+2)	N/A	4 (-2)	**North**	56 (-5)	25 (+2)	17 (+4)	N/A	3

(ii) This table shows the regional share of votes in percentages, rounded to the nearest whole number (change from 1997 in brackets).

Adapted from Dorey 2002 and Butler & Kavanagh 2002. See also *British Politics in Focus*, Second Edition, p.70.

2 Main features of the general election of June 2001

- The lowest turnout was in Liverpool Riverside @ 34.1%.

- The highest turnout was in Winchester @ 72.3%.

- The smallest majority was in Cheadle, won by the Liberal Democrats by 33 votes.

- In Wyre Forest (Kidderminster), a retired consultant, Dr Richard Taylor, stood as the Kidderminster Hospital and Health Concern candidate, in protest at the closure of Kidderminster Hospital's accident and emergency unit. He overturned a Labour majority of nearly 7,000 to win with a majority of over 17,000 votes. Furthermore, the 28,000 votes he polled was greater than the number received by the incumbent Labour MP in 1997.

- In Oldham West, the British National Party Leader, Nick Griffin, polled over 6,500 votes and the BNP came fourth. The BNP also came fourth in Oldham East and in Burnley.

- The UK Independence Party could claim to be England's fourth most successful party, having obtained 1.5% of votes cast. The UK Independence Party's intervention also contributed to the loss of four seats previously held by the Conservatives (Cheadle, Guildford, Mid-Dorset & North Poole, and Dorset South).

- The Green Party came fifth in England, with ten of its candidates saving their deposits, and the party obtaining 0.6% of the votes overall. In Brighton, the Green Party candidate polled 9% of the vote.

- Arthur Scargill stood as the candidate for his Socialist Labour Party against Peter Mandelson in Hartlepool, but received less than 1,000 votes, representing a share of just 2.4%.

- In St. Helens, where Conservative defector Shaun Woodward had been hastily (and controversially) adopted as the Labour Party's candidate, the Socialist Alliance candidate who stood against him polled just under 7% of the vote, while in Coventry North-East, the Socialist Alliance's candidate, Dave Nellist (formerly a Labour MP for this constituency), secured just over 7% of votes cast, enough to retain his deposit.

- In Scotland, the Socialist Alliance's 'sister party' the Scottish Socialist Party, retained no less than ten of its deposits, nine of these in Glasgow constituencies. In Glasgow Pollock, the party polled 10% of the vote, and pushed the Liberal Democrats and the Conservatives into fourth and fifth place respectively. It also came third in the Glasgow Shettleston constituency.

Adapted from Butler & Kavanagh 2002. See also *British Politics in Focus*, Second Edition, pp. 68-71.

3 Seats changing hands and turnout

Conservative gains (9)	Liberal Democrat gains (8)		Sinn Fein gains (2)
Castle Point *(Labour)*	Cheadle *(Con)*	West Bromwich West *(Speaker)*	Fermanagh & South Tyrone *(UUP)*
Galloway & Upper Nithsdale *(SNP)*	Chesterfield *(Labour)*	Ynys-Mon *(Plaid Cymru)*	West Tyrone *(UUP)*
Isle of Wight *(Lib Dem)*	Guildford *(Con)*		
Newark *(Labour)*	Ludlow *(Con)*	**Plaid Cymru gain**	**DUP gains (3)**
NW Norfolk *(Labour)*	Mid Dorset & North Poole *(Con)*	Carmarthen East & Dinefwr	Belfast North *(UUP)*
Romford *(Labour)*	North Norfolk *(Con)*	*(Labour)*	East Londonderry *(UUP)*
Tatton *(Independent)*	Romsey *(Con)*		Strangford *(UUP)*
Taunton *(Lib Dem)*	Teignbridge *(Con)*	**Speaker gain**	
Upminster *(Labour)*		Glasgow Springburn *(Labour)*	**Ulster Unionist gain**
	Labour gains (3)		North Down *(UKUP)*
	South Dorset *(Con)*	**Independent gain**	
		Wyre Forest *(Labour)*	

Table (i) shows the seats changing hands at the 2001 general election. Winners in 1997 are shown in brackets.

Ten Highest Turnouts (GB) %		Ten Lowest Turnouts (GB) %		Ten Smallest Majorities % Votes		
72.3	Winchester	34.1	Liverpool Riverside	0.1	33	Cheadle *(LD)*
71.8	Brecon & Radnorshire	39.1	Manchester Central	0.1	53	Fermanagh & S. Tyrone *(SF)*
71.5	Monmouth	39.7	Glasgow Shettleston	0.1	48	Perth *(SNP)*
70.9	Hexham	40.1	Glasgow Maryhill	0.2	74	Galloway & U. Nith. *(Con)*
70.7	Eastwood	41.6	Salford	0.3	153	South Dorset *(Lab)*
70.7	Northavon	41.7	Leeds Central	0.4	128	East Antrim *(UUP)*
70.5	Devon W & Torridge	42.7	Manchester Gorton	0.4	235	Taunton *(Con)*
70.4	Carmarthen E & Din.	43.0	Liverpool Walton	0.5	269	Orpington *(Con)*
70.3	Somerton & Frome	43.6	Glasgow Kelvin	0.7	358	Braintree *(Lab)*
70.2	North Norfolk	43.7	Glasgow Springburn	0.7	338	Weston-S-Mare *(LD)*

Table (ii) shows the ten highest and lowest turnouts and the ten smallest majorities.

Adapted from Butler & Kavanagh 2002. See also *British Politics in Focus*, Second Edition, pp.68-71.

4 The 2001 general election – Scotland

Labour is the dominant party in Scotland, but its main challenger for votes is not the Conservative Party, as in England, but the Scottish National Party (SNP). In addition, because of the way in which their support is distributed geographically, the Liberal Democrats in the past have done much better in terms of winning seats in Scotland than their overall share of the vote would suggest. So, in Scotland there is a rather complex four-party system, even though one of the four is clearly dominant. In 2001, a new ingredient was added by the decision of the Scottish Socialist Party (SSP) to contest every seat. In advance of the election, the indications were that the 2001 election would be an 'as-you-were' election. In the event, although only one Scottish seat changed hands, the election results in other respects were anything but uneventful. As in the rest of Britain, the 'big story' was the drop in turnout. The decline in Scotland (-13.2%) was greater than in Wales (-11.9%) or any region in England except the North West (-14.6%). Within Scotland, the greater the share of the vote Labour had in 1997, the greater the drop in turnout. Nonetheless, the decline in turnout did not benefit or harm any party in a systematic way. In terms of voting support, the only gainers were the Liberal Democrats and SSP. The SNP's vote surprisingly declined by 2%. The decline in the five seats vacated by SNP MPs was noticeably greater (down 9.1% on average), but the

	1997		2001	
Party	Votes %	Seats	Votes %	Seats
Conservative	17.5	0	15.6	1
Labour	45.6	56	44.0	56
Lib Dem	13.0	10	16.3	10
SNP	22.1	6	20.1	5
SSP	-	0	3.1	0
Others	1.9	0	0.9	0
Turnout	71.3		58.1	

Note: The Speaker is counted as a Labour candidate in 2001.

Figure 3.1 Election results in Scotland in 1997 and 2001 *This table shows the general election results in Scotland in 1997 and 2001.*

overall fall in SNP support may be a first indication that Scottish voters are broadly satisfied with the current devolution settlement. The decline in the SNP's vote allowed the Conservatives to gain a seat - the only seat to change hands - and to come within 48 votes of also taking Perth.

Adapted from Denver 2001.

See also *British Politics in Focus*, Second Edition, pp.68-71 and 291.

5 The 2001 general election – Wales

While the 2001 general election in Wales saw few seats change hands, there was a 28% turnover of MPs. As elsewhere, there was a drop in turnout. At just under 62% it was slightly above the national average, however. The big question in 2001 was whether Plaid Cymru would make further gains (following the 1999 Assembly election) or whether Labour would reassert its dominance. The result shows that 7 June 2001 was Labour's day. Although the share of the vote declined, Labour clearly reaffirmed its dominance over vote share in Westminster elections.

Adapted from Bradbury 2001.

Note: *the 2001 general election result in Northern Ireland is given in Chapter 8, Section 8.*

Party	1997			2001		
	Votes	%	Seats	Votes	%	Seats
Conservative	317,127	19.6	0	288,623	21.0	0
Labour	885,935	54.7	34	666,956	48.5	34
Lib Dem	200,020	12.4	2	189,254	13.8	2
Plaid Cymru	161,030	9.9	4	195,893	14.3	4
Others	54,932	1.0	0	31,598	2.3	0

Figure 3.2 Election results in Wales in 1997 and 2001
This table shows the general election results in Wales in 1997 and 2001.

6 An impossible dream?

It is 24 June 2005. At 8 am, Marjorie Wilby drops her two children at their local children's centre in North London. Then she takes the tube to King's Cross where she immediately boards a high-speed train to Newcastle. An extra carriage has been laid on because internet bookings were high. The 186 mph train is clean, comfortable and leaves on time for its one hour, 55 minute 300-mile journey. Meanwhile three-year-old Robbie is enjoying free daycare supervised by trained teachers. Jane, his seven-year-old sister, leaves the children's centre for the primary school on the same site at 9 am, accompanied by all the other children whose parents dropped them off on the way to work. At 10.22 am, Marjorie arrives in Newcastle, three minutes early. She visits her mother, Mo, in the newly refurbished city hospital. Mo has had a hip replacement. She went straight to hospital when she needed attention, saving an unnecessary visit to the GP. She was seen at the time of her appointment and booked in for surgery within four weeks. Marjorie covers the three miles to and from the railway station in 15 minutes. Few people bother to use cars in the city centre. Bus fares are so low - because use is so high - that almost nobody dodges them. At 2 pm, Marjorie is back on the train to King's Cross. By 4.30, she can pick up the children from their free after-school and homework club. Then, at 5 pm, a policewoman comes round, exactly as promised. She apologises that it took three weeks to prosecute the thief who stole Marjorie's wallet at the shopping centre. With the Magistrates' Court now working seven days a week, she insists that such delays are very unusual and produces a letter of apology from the Crown Prosecution Service.

Implausible? All this happens already in other developed countries and Tony Blair has promised to give Britain 'world-class' public services too - not within a generation or a decade, but within the lifetime of one Parliament. If, by the time of the next election, Tony Blair fails to achieve what many regard as an almost impossible dream, his extravagant promise will return to haunt him.

Adapted from the *Observer*, 24 June 2001.

See also *British Politics in Focus*, Second Edition, pp.71-78.

7 The position of Tony Blair in the spring of 2002

To accuse the Blair government of being indistinguishable from a Tory government is preposterous. The tax system is manipulated to help the poor, not the rich. A national minimum wage has been introduced. And a host of reforms - changes in the age of homosexual consent, reform of the House of Lords, a ban on fox hunting - have been placed on the public agenda in a way that would be unimaginable under the Tories. But there are three problems at the heart of Blair's leadership. First, New Labour was always a marketing concept, an attempt to rebrand the party. But because brand and image are so important, New Labour is particularly vulnerable to sleaze. Second, Blair has never put down any deep roots in his party. He has no instinct for its heartbeat and no affection for it. And third, many of Blair's own inner beliefs remain obscure. These weaknesses will become more important in the months ahead. The polls show Blair's personal ratings slipping below those of his party - always dangerous for a Leader (see Section 8 below). It is true that Labour has never overthrown a Leader while in office. But Blair has changed the party and Thatcher's fate shows that winning elections does not make a Leader fireproof. The atmosphere is

Figure 3.3 Blair's popularity falters *This cartoon was first published in May 2002.*

WE DON'T UNDERSTAND IT, TONY, IT'S AS IF THE PEOPLE **DON'T CARE** HOW MUCH YOU'VE PROMISED TO DO FOR THEM AND WHAT A GOOD FRIEND OF GEORGE BUSH YOU ARE!

reminiscent of the late 1980s, right down to the whisper that the Prime Minister has gone slightly mad.

Adapted from the *New Statesman*, 25 March 2002. See also Chapter 12 below and *British Politics in Focus*, Second Edition, pp.71-78.

8 The British public's view of Tony Blair

After the failure of the 'demon eyes' campaign before the 1997 general election, the Tories' advertising company M&C Saatchi came up with another idea. Forget the eyes, go for the smile. The firm tested it on focus groups and found that there was something unsettling about the smile. Blair just didn't seem trustworthy. They proposed an advertising campaign exploiting this, but John Major vetoed the idea because he didn't want to get personal with Blair. Five years later, after the longest political honeymoon of modern times, two landslide victories and unprecedented personal ratings, there is some evidence that the Saatchi view is now becoming the nation's view. At a recent focus group, participants were asked to sum up their impression of Blair. Two phrases summed up the consensus - 'he's always up to something' and 'he's not straight'. To go more deeply into the question, the *New Statesman* commissioned a survey. This went beyond the usual headline questions about trust. It showed that more than two-thirds of people believe that Blair 'often twists things to tell people what they want to hear' and under a third see him as 'basically straight and honest'. Women in the 30-50 age range and ABC1s were more inclined to give him the benefit of the doubt, but only just. Some of the results are no more than mildly troubling. Although just over half the respondents agree that 'Blair does not really know where he is heading', as many as 44% think that he 'has a long-term vision for Britain'. Other results are disturbing, however. Ask people in the Prime Minister's Office to pinpoint the public mood and they often use the word 'disappointment'. That is borne out by the poll. The biggest group of voters is disappointed in Blair (40%) and, while a mere 4% is proud to have him as Prime Minister, 20% (rising to 25% in the over-50s) are angry that he is Britain's Leader. What must worry Downing Street is the softness in the support for Blair among Labour voters. Of those who voted for the party in 2001, 42% think Blair twists things, 25% think that he doesn't know where he is heading and 33% are disappointed in him. This is not a crisis, but it does suggest that we are heading to a shift in the balance of power -

Which of the following statements comes closest to your views?	
(i) Tony Blair often twists things to tell people what they want to hear	**67%**
Tony Blair is basically straight and honest	**28%**
(ii) Tony Blair does not really know where he is heading	**51%**
Tony Blair has a long-term vision for Britain	**44%**

Which of these best describes your overall attitude to Tony Blair as Prime Minister?	
I am disappointed with his record and feel he could do better	**40%**
I sympathise with the problems he faces and feel he is doing his best	**35%**
I am angry that he is our national Leader	**20%**
I am proud that he is our national Leader	**4%**

Leaving aside your views of Tony Blair as a person, do you think that, since he became Prime Minister, his actions have ...?	
Made little difference to your family's quality of life and standard of living	**52%**
Worsened your family's quality of life and standard of living	**28%**
Improved your family's quality of life and standard of living	**19%**

Figure 3.4 Survey results *This table shows the results of a survey conducted in June 2002. A sample of 1,003 people were asked the questions. The percentages do not add up to 100% because of don't knows.*

between the party and Blair and the people and Blair. This will affect everything he wants to do - such as delivering improvements in public services or holding a referendum on the euro. These things ultimately depend on trust - in him. Blair himself is confounded by his image. A man who rarely loses his temper, he finds it hard to understand why anyone would doubt his integrity. According to his friends, it came to a head during the 'Black Rod fiasco'. He was 'hurt, angry and humiliated' by suggestions that he would want to muscle in on the Queen Mother's lying-in-state. He is similarly upset by the brooding, intellectual powerhouse of a Chancellor contrasted with the lightweight, unprincipled Prime Minister who would say anything to look good. Blair prides himself on winning people over, but this can lead to accusations that he is two-faced. During the controversy over hunting, the journalist John Kampfner interviewed leading members of each of the three factions (the anti-hunting, pro-hunting and middle way group). Each of the three had been to see Blair and each of the three came away with the impression that Blair supported their approach.

Adapted from the *New Statesman*, 17 June and 1 July 2002.

See also Chapter 12 below and *British Politics in Focus*, Second Edition, pp.71-78 and 409-12.

Figure 3.5 Blair - spinning out of control?
This cartoon was first published in June 2002.

9 The economy, 1999-2002

The Blair government's record on the economy in the period 1999 to 2002 stood in the starkest contrast to that of previous Labour governments. The Blair government was able to contest the 2001 election boasting the lowest levels of unemployment since the mid-1970s, the lowest rates of inflation since the early 1970s, and the lowest interest rates for 30 years.

The Budget of 2000 introduced a new 10% income tax band on the first £1,500 of taxable earnings. The next band up was reduced to 22%. The top rate remained at 40%. The government offset these reductions in direct taxation by various increases in indirect taxation, the so-called 'stealth taxes', such as the 1% increase in National Insurance contributions in the 2002 Budget. It was partly a backlash against increasing indirect taxes which prompted the fuel protests of September 2000 (see Chapter 1, Section 1). Those protests aside, however, the government began to win the 'tax-and-spend' argument, after years of being forced on the defensive by the Conservatives over the issue of funding public services.

Adapted from BoE 2002, ONS 2002a, ONS 2002b and ONS 2002c. See also Chapter 15 below and *British Politics in Focus*, Second Edition, pp.72 and 518-21.

10 The NHS

During the 2001 general election campaign, the Labour leadership claimed that only a Labour government could 'save the NHS'. After the election, however, the government struggled to make progress. By the summer of 2002, the NHS was the policy issue about which the British public was most concerned and where disappointment with New Labour was most pronounced.

Having adhered to the former Conservative government's spending plans for the first two years after election in 1997, the Chancellor, Gordon Brown, announced in 2000 that public expenditure on health would be increased at an average annual rate of just over 6%. It was intended that, by 2004, public expenditure on health would match that of many of Britain's European neighbours.

However, in typical Third-Way style, the increased expenditure was linked to a variety of targets and performance indicators which were not only intended to provide an improved system of health care for the British people, but also to make it clear where - and how effectively - the additional sums were being spent. Labour's 2001 election manifesto promised 20,000 extra nurses and at least 10,000 additional doctors, as well as 'fast, high-quality treatment' of patients.

The government placed the modernisation of Britain's health infrastructure - ie the hospitals themselves - at the forefront of its controversial Public-Private Partnership initiative, insisting that, while a hospital may be built by a private consortium, the crucial point remains that treatment remains free at the point of delivery.

The 2002 Comprehensive Spending Review announced that health expenditure as a proportion of GDP was to be

Figure 3.6 Injecting resources into the NHS
This cartoon was first published in April 2002, shortly after Gordon Brown had announced an increase in spending on the NHS in his Budget Statement.

increased from 7.7% in 2002 to 9.4% in 2007-08 (a rise from just over £50 billion to over £70 billion). In addition, a new target was introduced to reduce the waiting time for an NHS operation to a maximum of three months by 2008.

Adapted from Dolowitz 2001, Proud 2002, the *New Statesman*, 22 April 2002 and the *Guardian*, 16 July 2002.

See also *British Politics in Focus*, Second Edition, pp. 72-73.

11 Law and order

New Labour's promise to be 'tough on crime, tough on the causes of crime' appeared to be bearing fruit, with recorded crime falling in overall terms during 1999 and 2000, in spite of some increase in specific types of crime. However, in 2002, it became clear that crime was once again beginning to rise, particularly crimes involving violence.

Throughout the period 1999 to 2002, the government was, on the one hand, criticised by its opponents for being 'soft on crime' (a charge always levelled against Old Labour) and, on the other, denounced for making policy 'on the hoof' or of being authoritarian, when it did announce tougher measures. Some of the measures announced were rejected as yet more 'spin', rather than genuine policies for reducing crime and punishing criminals.

A further problem which the government encountered on several occasions was that certain headline-grabbing initiatives were denounced as unworkable in practice - such as Blair's apparently impromptu suggestion that drunken yobs should be fined on-the-spot. Other proposals, such as cutting child benefit payments to parents of delinquent children, or cutting housing benefit to nuisance families or neighbours, were similarly condemned for being administratively unworkable as well as likely to increase financial hardship (which would encourage a recourse to crime).

Adapted from Morris 2001 and the *Guardian*, 12 July 2002. See also Chapter 18 below and *British Politics in Focus*, Second Edition, pp.74 and 639-42.

12 Education

During the period 1999-2002, there was a strong emphasis on raising standards in primary schools, particularly with regard to literacy and numeracy skills. Both primary and secondary schools continued to be subject to a plethora of performance indicators and targets, with 'failing' schools subject to direct intervention. There was also an increasing promotion of 'specialist' or 'beacon' schools, whose teaching of the National Curriculum would exist alongside the development of a particular expertise, such as sport or Information Technology. The plan is to create at least 1,500 such schools by 2006. These schools are permitted to select 10% of their pupil intake, leading to fears about the re-emergence of grammar schools via the back-door. The government also clamped down on truancy and hinted that parents who assaulted teachers might be imprisoned.

The 2002 Comprehensive Spending Review announced that total expenditure on education would increase from £45 billion in the 2002/03 financial year, to £58 billion by 2005/06, representing a 6% increase each year, although the money would be linked, as ever, to reform and improved performance.

Adapted from McCaig 2001, Smithers 2001 and the *Guardian*, 16 July 2002. See also *British Politics in Focus*, Second Edition, p.74.

13 Europe and foreign affairs

The Blair government's stance on Europe has continued to be dominated by the question of whether Britain should join the single European currency. The government is formally committed to British membership, but only when the economic conditions are judged to be favourable - as determined by Gordon Brown's five economic tests - and public approval has been provided via a referendum. With opinion polls continuing to show a clear majority opposed to British membership, and most newspapers very hostile too, the government has continued to stall, insisting that neither the time, nor the economic conditions, are yet right.

Supporters of immediate British membership have grown increasingly frustrated with the government's prevarication, pointing out that public opinion is unlikely to become more favourable until ministers, particularly the Prime Minister, state the case more confidently and provide stronger leadership.

Other European issues that have concerned the government are plans for enlargement and proposals for a military Rapid Response Force, seen by some as a dangerous forerunner to a European Army (see Chapter 4, Section 2). Also controversial has been Blair's insistence on the need for further 'labour market flexibility' within the EU. Trade unions equate such 'flexibility' with a reduction in employment rights and protection, longer or more unsocial working hours and possible cuts in pay, particularly if it also entails a greater role for the private sector.

When the Republican, George W. Bush, was elected President of the USA in 2000, it seemed, at first, as if Britain's 'special relationship' with the USA might cool. The terrorist attacks in the USA on 11 September 2001, however, resulted

Figure 3.7 The euro and the five economic tests *This cartoon, produced in May 2002, plays on the supposed rivalry between Gordon Brown and Tony Blair. At the time when this cartoon was produced, Edward Balls was Gordon Brown's Chief Economic Adviser.*

in a strengthening of British-US ties, as the two countries took the lead in the international 'war against terrorism'. As well as providing total support for America's subsequent bombing of Afghanistan, Blair was, initially at least, a strong supporter of the USA's reported plans to launch a military attack on Saddam Hussein's Iraq.

Adapted from Deighton 2001, Hill 2001, Buller 2001 and the *New Statesman*, 28 January 2002. See also Chapter 6, Section 12 and *British Politics in Focus*, Second Edition, p.75.

References

BoE (2002) Bank of England: www.bankofengland.co.uk/mpc/decisions
Bradbury (2001) Bradbury, J., 'General election 2001: Labour holds on in Wales', *Politics Review*, Vol.11.2, November 2001.
Buller (2001) Buller, J., 'New Labour's foreign and defence policy' in *Ludlam & Smith (2001)*.
Deighton (2001) Deighton, A., 'European Union policy' in *Seldon (2001)*.
Denver (2001) Denver, D., 'General election 2001: Scotland is different', *Politics Review*, Vol.11.2, November 2001.
Dolowitz (2002) Dolowitz, D.P., 'The provision of services: transformation for justice' in *Geddes & Tonge (2002)*.
Geddes & Tonge (2002) Geddes, A.P. & Tonge, J. (eds), *Labour's Second Landslide: The British General Election 2001*, Manchester University Press, 2002.
Hill (2001) Hill, C., 'Foreign policy' in *Seldon (2001)*.
Ludlam & Smith (2001) Ludlam, S. & Smith, M.J. (eds), *New Labour in Government*, Macmillan, 2001.

McCaig (2001) McCaig, C., 'New Labour and education, education, education' in *Ludlam & Smith (2001)*.
Morris (2001) Morris, T., 'Crime and penal policy' in *Seldon (2001)*.
ONS (2002a) Office of National Statistics: www.statistics.gov.uk/themes/economy/Articles/PricesandInflation
ONS (2002b) Office of National Statistics: www.statistics.gov.uk/themes/labour-market/unemployment_claimant_count
ONS (2002c) Office of National Statistics: www.statistics.gov.uk/pdfdin
Proud (2002) Proud, L., 'The National Health Service, *Talking Politics*, Vol.14.3, April 2002.
Seldon (2001) Seldon, A. (ed.), *The Blair Effect - The Blair Government 1997-2001*, Little Brown and Company, 2001.
Smithers (2001) Smithers, A., 'Education policy' in *Seldon (2001)*.

1 The Human Rights Act and parliamentary sovereignty

Under the terms of the 1998 Human Rights Act, judges have the power to rule that Acts of Parliament are incompatible with the European Convention on Human Rights. The courts, however, are not able to strike down laws that are judged to contravene the convention. Instead, it is up to Parliament to amend laws that judges declare are incompatible. The Human Rights Act:

- makes it unlawful for a public authority - a government department, local authority or the police - to breach rights laid down by the convention, unless an existing Act of Parliament means that the authority was unable to have acted differently
- allows anyone who feels that their rights under the convention have been breached to take their case to a UK court or tribunal, rather than waiting to go to the European Court of Human Rights in Strasbourg
- lays down that all UK legislation must be given a meaning that fits with the rights laid down by the convention, if that is possible. If a court says that is not possible, it is up to Parliament to decide what to do.

The Human Rights Act came into effect in October 2000. Some commentators argue that the passing of the law did not undermine parliamentary sovereignty because the ultimate decision, in a case of conflict, still lies with Parliament and not the courts. Others, however, do not agree. Richards and Smith, for example, take a broader political, rather than a legal, view. They argue that the passing of the Human Rights Act, taken together with other developments such as Scottish and Welsh devolution and the independence of the Bank of England, amount to a significant series of 'structural constraints' on parliamentary sovereignty. They point out that, in January 1999, Jack Straw (the then Home Secretary) signed the Sixth Protocol of the European Convention on Human Rights, part of which abolishes the death penalty in the United Kingdom. This means that future governments will not be in a position to reopen the debate on the death penalty without first overturning the entire European Convention on Human Rights. This suggests, Richards and Smith argue, that, in reality, clear and discernible structural constraints have now been placed upon Parliament by the signing of the convention. In other words, parliamentary sovereignty has been breached.

Adapted from Home Office 2000, Peele 2001, Richards & Smith 2001 and Evans 2002. See also *British Politics in Focus*, Second Edition, pp.87-91.

2 The euro and the constitution

In January 2002, 12 members of the EU relinquished their national currencies and introduced the euro. The UK was not among them (Denmark and Sweden also opted out), but the introduction of the euro sharpened the debate in the UK about whether or when Britain should also follow suit.

For many in the Conservative Party, opposition to the euro is a constitutional as well as a political matter. Anti-European Conservatives worry about the

Figure 4.1 *This cartoon appeared in the Guardian on 1 March 1999.*

transfer of powers from British to European institutions (the setting of interest rates would be transferred from the Bank of England to the European Central Bank, for example). The transfer of powers is seen as a sign of loss of national sovereignty.

A further and related constitutional concern to Eurosceptics is that the adoption of the euro would take the UK a step nearer to a federal Europe. A federal Europe would entail federal control of armed forces, something which is not implied by the adoption of the euro. The Eurosceptic Bill Cash, however, sees moves in Europe towards the formation of a rapid reaction force as the start of 'an embryonic integrated European army'. This he regards as just as dangerous to Britain's democracy as a single currency. But, he argues, both are part of a broader question

about who governs us - the British people through their elected representatives or the unelected, unaccountable bureaucrats and judges of the EU institutions?

The official position of the Labour government is that any decision to join the euro is an economic matter, there being no constitutional bar to entry. The question will be put to the electorate by referendum when 'the time is ripe', and this is to be determined by the Chancellor's five economic tests. Many commentators, however, argue that the decision is ultimately a political one because the Chancellor's five tests are open to wide interpretation.

Adapted from Watts 2000, Pinder 2001, Cash 2001, Buller 2001 and Kane 2002.

See also *British Politics in Focus*, Second Edition, pp.88-90 and 521-25.

3 The Scottish Parliament

On a low turnout of 58%, the first elections for the Scottish Parliament were held in May 1999. Labour won 56 of the 129 seats, becoming the party with the most seats. But, as no party achieved an overall majority, Labour entered into a coalition with the Liberal Democrats (the Scottish Parliament is elected using a version of the Additional Member electoral system, making coalition governments likely to become the norm). Labour's Donald Dewar was appointed Scotland's first First Minister but, following his death in October 2000, he was succeeded by Henry McLeish. McLeish resigned in November 2001 after a row over office expenses. He was replaced by Jack McConnell.

Figure 4.2 *This photograph shows the Scottish Parliament in operation.*

The existence of a coalition government raises an issue of constitutional concern. Following the May 1999 election for the Scottish Parliament, a formal coalition was arranged between Labour and the Liberal Democrats. Yet the Liberal Democrats had won only 17 seats, coming fourth behind Labour, the Scottish Nationalists (SNP) and the Conservatives. Despite this, the coalition agreement gave the Liberal Democrats two out of the 11 Cabinet posts and two junior ministerial positions. More significantly, the formal coalition entailed political compromises enshrined in the coalition document *Partnership for Scotland*, designed to last for the four years up to the next election. The document included compromises over spending plans for education and health, replacement of student tuition fees, a rural affairs policy, land reform and freedom of information. On all of these issues, the policies were not exactly what either Labour or Liberal Democrat electors had voted for.

After examining the role and powers of the Scottish Parliament, Russell Deacon and his colleagues pose further questions about the Parliament's effectiveness in meeting the high democratic ideals which surrounded its establishment. Although these authors recognise it is, as yet, too early to answer such questions fully, they suggest that the questions can be used in the future to test the extent to which these ideals are being met. The questions they ask include:

- how involved has the public been in the Parliament's work?
- how many pieces of legislation come from backbenchers rather than the government?
- how effective is the committee system in terms of holding government to account and generating reports and legislation?
- given the control exerted by party leaderships does the Parliament actually operate by consensus?

Adapted from Deacon et al. 2000 and Lynch 2001.

See also *British Politics in Focus*, Second Edition, pp.94-98.

4 The Welsh Assembly

The Welsh Assembly does not have the primary legislative or tax-varying powers of the Scottish Parliament and its establishment, if judged by the close referendum result in 1997, was not greeted with the same degree of enthusiasm by the people of Wales. After the first election for Assembly members in May 1999, no party had an overall majority but Labour took 28 of the 60 available seats. At first, Labour opted to operate with a minority administration with Alun Michael as Leader. In February 2000, however, Michael resigned following the tabling of a vote of no-confidence. He was replaced by Rhodri Morgan who formed a coalition with the Liberal Democrats.

There is some concern that, in the long term, the Welsh Assembly and executive may be seen as nothing more than a Welsh council writ large. This may be confirmed by its having followed a local government rather than the parliamentary model in its procedures. It is also like a local authority in some other respects. For example, its officials are accountable to all members of the Assembly, just as local government officers are accountable to all members of their councils. By contrast, Scottish civil servants are accountable to ministers on the Scottish Cabinet, just as civil servants in Whitehall are accountable to particular government ministers. The adoption of local government procedures may, therefore, make the Welsh Assembly appear more like a council than a Parliament.

Adapted from Elcock and Parks 2000. See also *British Politics in Focus,* Second Edition, pp.94-98.

5 An evaluation of devolution in practice

In the short time since the devolved assemblies were set up, Welsh and, in particular, Scottish devolution has been the cause of embarrassment to central government on a number of occasions. The Scottish Parliament, for example, has made decisions which are in direct conflict with those made by central government - on provision of care for the elderly (in Scotland, financial support is given to elderly patients in nursing homes, in England it is not), on student finance (in Scotland, students do not have to pay tuition fees, in England they do) and on teachers' salaries (in Scotland, they are higher than they are in England). In addition, broader issues, some with at least potentially constitutional implications, have arisen and are the subject of debate. Five are particularly important (see Box 4.1 below).

It is possible, however, to exaggerate the impact which Scottish and Welsh devolution has made. Some commentators argue that Scotland, in particular, has always had a strong degree of autonomy and that devolution provides legitimacy for something that was happening anyway. Also, it is important to point out that the Scottish Parliament and Welsh Assembly are still in their infancy and, in the words of Ron Davies former Secretary of State of Wales at Westminster, 'devolution is a process, not an event'. The way the process will unfold is uncertain. It will depend on the experience of governments at central and devolved levels, on the way the parties behave and on the reactions of voters.

Box 4.1 Devolution and constitutional issues

1. Finance

The majority of the funding for the Scottish Parliament, and all of it for the Welsh Assembly, comes from Westminster. The actual amounts are worked out according to the 'Barnett formula' which has ensured that per capita expenditure is higher in Scotland and Wales than in England. This has led to accusations that the people living in the devolved areas continue to be subsidised by English taxpayers. Any attempt to redress the balance, however, is likely to cause an outcry since the formula has been applied for over 20 years.

2. The West Lothian question

MPs representing Scottish constituencies at Westminster can vote on all matters affecting England but MPs representing English constituencies have no say on devolved matters affecting Scotland. This long-debated anomaly shows no sign of being resolved but it could cause considerable problems in the future. If, for example, there was a Conservative majority of MPs in England and a Labour government had to rely on the support of Scottish MPs to remain in power at Westminster, the West Lothian question would become acute and it would be likely to cause considerable controversy.

3. Coordination with the centre

Although, following the Scottish and Welsh elections in 1999 and the UK general election in 2001, Labour is currently the largest party in all three assemblies, conflict between the two tiers of government could be significant. If and when this situation changes, the Judicial Committee of the Privy Council would be the arbitrator for unresolved disputes and this committee's intervention would involve entry into uncharted constitutional waters.

4. Intra-UK differences

The Scottish Parliament has the power to create legislation and its executive has the power to make policies which apply only to Scotland. This, indeed, is a fundamental reason for devolution. But this degree of autonomy can conflict (and has already done so on a number of issues) with the principle of equal treatment for all UK citizens, irrespective of where they live. Some commentators argue that this undermines the idea that Britain is a unitary state.

5. Devolution to the English regions

The devolution of powers to Scotland, Wales and Northern Ireland raises the question of similar developments in the English regions. In May 2002, the government announced that English regions will have the opportunity to decide whether they want their own regional assembly. Commentators have identified three problems with regional devolution. First, most parts of England do not form 'natural communities' with their own distinct regional identities. Attempts to divide England for the purpose of devolved government could, therefore, produce artificially created regions. Second, with the partial exception of some areas in the north of England, there is little evidence of much enthusiasm for or interest in the prospect of English regional devolution at the present time. And third, the government announcement in May 2002 made it clear that, if English regions decided on regional assemblies, there would only be a single tier of government. In other words, county councils in the region would be abolished.

Adapted from Denver 2001, Richards & Smith 2001 and Butler 2002. See also *British Politics in Focus*, Second Edition, pp.99-100.

6 Northern Ireland - developments 1999-2002

Following the referendums held on both sides of the Irish border in May 1998 and the election to the Northern Ireland Assembly in June 1998, Ulster Unionist (UUP) Leader David Trimble became First Minister designate with Seamus Mallon of the SDLP as his deputy. The new executive was to be set up in March 1999, but problems over the decommissioning of weapons halted the process. The Ulster Unionists refused to serve in an executive which included members of Sinn Fein unless the IRA took steps to decommission their weapons (under the Good Friday Agreement, Sinn Fein would have two members on the executive because it won 18 seats in the June election). Sinn Fein, on the other hand, argued that, under the Good Friday Agreement,

Figure 4.3 *This cartoon was published on 7 August 2001. IRA decommissioning began two months later, in October.*

decommissioning was not a precondition to the setting up of the executive.

The stalemate continued until 6 September 1999 when Senator George Mitchell began a review of the Good Friday Agreement's implementation. This was a review rather than a renegotiation. He engaged in one-to-one meetings with all the parties, encouraging them to talk to each other and involved the British and Irish governments when necessary. Following the review, all parties agreed to work in the executive and the Northern Ireland Assembly came into operation on 2 December 1999. The UUP, however, agreed to work in the executive only on the understanding that the IRA began decommissioning its arms within a few weeks. When, at the end of January 2000, there was no sign of decommissioning, David Trimble prepared to resign and collapse the process. In order to prevent this collapse, the Secretary of State for Northern Ireland, Peter Mandelson, introduced legislation suspending the Northern Ireland Assembly and reimposing direct rule from Westminster.

The Assembly and the executive were reinstated in May 2000, following a statement from the IRA that it agreed to start the process by which its arms would be put 'completely and verifiably...beyond use' by allowing international inspectors access to its arsenal. The British government also announced a year's postponement of the deadline by which decommissioning should be completed. These developments, however, did not put an end to the difficulties. Over the following 15 months, disagreements and disputes continued and, in August 2001, the UUP rejected an agreement between the IRA and the decommissioning body for IRA arms to be put permanently out of use. Again, the Northern Ireland

Secretary (now John Reid) temporarily suspended the devolved government. By doing so, he effectively allowed a six-week period to resolve the issue.

In October 2001, the conflict over decommissioning reached crisis point. Devolved government in Northern Ireland came close to collapse but, on 23 October 2001, the IRA announced that it had actually decommissioned some of its weapons and that members of the independent disarmament body had witnessed it doing so. This was seen as a major breakthrough, setting the peace process back on track.

According to press reports, the IRA's decision was a response to developments in the USA. Irish republicans had long received financial support from Irish-Americans. But, following the arrest of three IRA suspects in Columbia for training guerrillas associated with cocaine smuggling, this support came under threat. Then, the al-Qaida attacks in New York and Washington on 11 September altered the perspective of Americans sympathetic to the republican cause. In response to a changed political landscape, the IRA made its 'historic move'.

Although hailed as a major breakthrough, a start to the decommissioning process did not immediately resolve all the problems facing the government in Northern Ireland. Only a tactical deal between Trimble and the Alliance Party in November 2001, for example, ensured that he was re-elected as Northern Ireland's First Minister and that the Assembly and executive were not thrown into a further crisis.

Adapted from the *Observer*, 7 May 2000, the *Guardian*, 24 October 2001, Elcock & Parks 2001, Hunter 2001, Lomas 2001, McDonald 2001 and Totten & Collomb-Robert 2001.

See also *British Politics in Focus*, Second Edition, pp.102-08 and 612-17.

7 Northern Ireland – an evaluation

Viewing developments over the three-year period following the Good Friday Agreement, some commentators feel there are good grounds for optimism. Implementation of the Agreement has seen the introduction of new institutions and practices of devolved government, with a high level of public support. These same writers are well aware, however, of the many other problems that remain to be solved. As well as continuing the decommissioning process, the reform of the police service in Northern Ireland is a controversial area, as is the Bloody Sunday Inquiry. Issues such as these still have the capacity to perpetuate divisions in the province. At the same time, sectarian conflict at street level continues. Violence has not ended with the introduction of devolved government.

Looking at devolution in Northern Ireland from a constitutional point of view, Richards and Smith argue that the setting up of a Northern Ireland Assembly has undermined the principle of parliamentary sovereignty since the Assembly has become the prime source of authority in respect of all devolved responsibilities. In addition, they argue, the setting up of the North/South Ministerial Council and the British-Irish Council, also established by the Good Friday Agreement, raises further questions about the notion of territorial sovereignty within the UK because these institutions have introduced non-Westminster elements into the policy process.

Adapted from Lomas 2001, Richards & Smith 2001 and Totten & Collomb-Robert 2001.

See also *British Politics in Focus,* Second Edition, pp.102-08 and 612-17.

8 The monarchy – the golden jubilee

Writing on 5 June 2002, the *Guardian's* leader writer accepted that the Queen's golden jubilee celebrations (held on 3 and 4 June) were more successful than either the organisers had feared or critics had hoped. This success, however, was by no means inevitable. Even in the early spring of 2002, the programme of celebration was a considerable gamble. The royal visit to Australia had not been particularly successful. The set-piece parliamentary celebrations passed almost without notice. When the Queen travelled to the South-West, crowds weren't huge and the atmosphere was muted. Things improved as she travelled round the country. Even so, as late as May 2002, the palace was uncertain about whether the jubilee holiday weekend would be a great occasion or a great embarrassment. In the end it was a success. But, the uncertainty, the sense of risk, the genuine fears that Britain might be indifferent or even hostile, were real. They did not come out of nowhere. They came out of a decade of rejection of the kind of monarchy that had evolved under Elizabeth II. There are three main reasons why the jubilee was a success, however. First, national respect for the Queen crosses the boundaries of the monarchy/republican debate. She is not the divisive figure her husband and eldest son are. Second, the jubilee calendar was cleverly planned, enabling the thanksgiving of 4 June to proceed on the back of a wave of popular pleasure that was unleashed by the previous three-day party. And third, people enjoy ceremony and celebration. For many, the first four days of June were a free party. This party was much more inclusive than events in the past. In the past it was

Figure 4.4 *This cartoon was produced in August 2001 and looks forward to the Queen's golden jubilee year. Actually, there were two royal funerals in the first half of 2002 - those of Princess Margaret and of the Queen Mother.*

their show, not ours. This time we were all invited. While the jubilee gives food for thought to those who seek radical change in the way Britain is governed, it should also make those who think all is well with the UK guard against complacency. The jubilee would have been impossible if there had been no public respect for the Queen. But that respect is not easily gained and less easily transferred. When the Queen goes, much of the respect will go with her and the objections to the system will remain. Unless proper thought is given to changing the monarchy, this golden jubilee will be seen as a fool's paradise.

Adapted from the *Guardian*, 5 June 2002.

See also *British Politics in Focus,* Second Edition, pp.108-12.

9 Constitutional reform

The Labour Party's 1997 general election manifesto contained a number of pledges to implement constitutional reforms. These pledges are outlined in Box 4.2 below and an assessment made of the steps taken to implement each of them between May 1997 and September 2002.

Box 4.2 The Labour government and constitutional reform

Pledge	Action
To abolish the right of hereditary peers to sit and vote in the House of Lords.	*The House of Lords Act 1999 removed the right of all but 92 hereditary peers to sit and vote in the House of Lords. A 2001 White Paper revealed plans to remove remaining hereditaries as a final stage in the reform process.*
To set up a special select committee in the Commons to review its procedures.	*This select committee was set up by the government on 21 July 2001.*
To hold a referendum on the voting system for elections to the House of Commons.	*Such a referendum has not been held.*
To draw up a Freedom of Information Act.	*A watered-down Freedom of Information Act was passed in 2000, but the government delayed its introduction until 2005 (see Chapter 19 of this book).*
To hold referendums and, if they supported the idea, to set up assemblies in Scotland and Wales.	*Referendums were held in 1997. The Scottish Parliament and Welsh Assembly are now in operation.*
To hold a referendum and, if it supported the idea, to set up a strategic authority and mayor for London.	*The referendum was held in 1998. The Greater London Assembly and the Mayor were elected in May 2000.*
To incorporate the European Convention on Human Rights into British Law.	*The 1998 Human Rights Act incorporated elements of the Convention (see Section 1 above).*
To hold a referendum on whether to join a single European currency.	*To be held 'when the time is ripe' (see Section 2 above).*

See also *British Politics in Focus*, Second Edition, pp.112-18.

10 Electoral reform

Labour's 2001 manifesto promised a review of the new voting systems the government had introduced since 1997 and stated that: 'A referendum remains the right way to agree any changes for Westminster'. Compared to the commitment to a referendum in the 1997 general election manifesto, this was a clear climb down. As a result, in September 2001, the Liberal Democrats withdrew from the joint Cabinet Committee. Electoral reform for Westminster has clearly become a low priority for the Labour government.

Adapted from the *Guardian*, 4 January 2001 and 21 January 2002. See also *British Politics in Focus*, Second Edition, pp.112-18 and 231-34.

References

Beetham (2001) Beetham, R., *The Euro Debate: Persuading the People*, The Federal Trust for Education and Research, 2001.

Buller (2001) Buller, J., 'New Labour's foreign and defence policy: external and support structures and domestic politics' in *Ludlam & Smith (2001)*.

Butler (2002) Butler, R., 'The state of British governance', *Talking Politics*, Vol.14.2, January 2002 (summary of lecture given by Lord Butler of Brockwell to the Politics Association Conference in September 2001).

Cash (2001) Cash, B., 'Valid consent, not mere persuasion: a referendum on European government' in *Beetham (2001)*.

Deacon et al. (2000) Deacon, R., Griffiths, D. & Lynch, P., *Devolved Great Britain: the New Governance of England, Scotland and Wales*, Sheffield Halham University Press, 2000.

Denver (2001) Denver, D., 'The devolution project', *Politics Review*, Vol.14.1, September 2001.

Elcock & Parks (2000) Elcock, H. & Parks, J., 'The English imperium reversed? Devolution sought and (partly) achieved?' in *Lancaster (2000)*.

Evans (2002) Evans, M., 'Human Rights and Freedom of Information' in *Lancaster (2002)*.

Home Office (2000), *Human Rights Act: An Introduction*, Home Office Communication Directorate, October 2000.

Hunter (2001) Hunter, J., 'Centre party move breaks Ulster peace deadlock', *Observer*, 4 November 2001.

Kane (2002) Kane, F., 'Nul point in this eurovision contest', *Observer*, 6 January 2002.

Lancaster (2000) Lancaster, S. (ed.), *Developments in Politics*, Vol.11, Causeway Press, 2000.

Lancaster (2002) Lancaster, S. (ed.), *Developments in Politics*, Vol.13, Causeway Press, 2002.

Lomas (2001) Lomas, B., 'The Good Friday Agreement: termly report', *Talking Politics*, Vol.14.1, September 2001.

Ludlam & Smith (2001) Ludlam, S. & Smith, M.J. (eds), *New Labour in Government*, Palgrave, 2001.

Lynch (2001) Lynch, P., 'Scottish devolution and coalition government', *Politics Review*, Vol.11.2, November 2001.

McDonald (2001) McDonald, H., 'Trimble: Good Friday deal is certain to fail', *Observer*, 29 July 2001.

Peele (2001) Peele, G., 'The Human Rights Act', *Talking Politics*, Vol.14.1, September 2001.

Pinder (2001) Pinder, J., *The European Union: A Very Short Introduction*, Oxford University Press, 2001.

Richards & Smith (2001) Richards, D. & Smith, M.J., 'New Labour, the constitution and reforming the state' in *Ludlam & Smith (2001)*.

Totten & Collomb-Robert (2001) Totten, K. & Collomb-Robert, N., *The Northern Ireland Question: Towards a 21st Century Solution?*, Sheffield Halham University Press, 2001.

Watts (2000) Watts, D., *Britain and the European Union: an Uneasy Partnership*, Sheffield Halham University Press, 2000.

1 Class fragmentation and post-modernism

Post-modernists argue that class no longer has any real significance. For example, it no longer makes sense to generalise about the middle class because there is a huge range of different experiences that middle-class people have. Instead of class, post-modernists emphasise that people have very different lifestyles and that these are a matter of choice. An individual's identity is not based on class but on a range of factors including age, ethnicity, gender as well as personal choices such as musical taste, clothes or even support for a particular football team. In addition, people soak up the images of different cultures around the world that are offered continuously through media advertising, news and entertainment. In other words, globalisation also diminishes class identity.

Adapted from Griffiths & Hope 2000. See also *British Politics in Focus,* Second Edition, pp.127-31.

2 Class division remains

Over the past two decades, changes have taken place in the class structure especially the growth of the middle class and decline in the working class. There has been a big increase in professional jobs - for example, accountancy - and the creation of new 'white-collar' jobs - for example, in call centres. In contrast, the number of miners has fallen from 750,000 after the Second World War to less than 10,000 today. Important class divisions remain, for example, in access to higher education. Class remains a defining characteristic in people's lives and can be seen objectively (for example, in differences in income and wealth) and subjectively (how people feel about class). Figure 5.1 shows the results of a survey carried out for the television programme *World in Action*, broadcast in 1997.

Statement	% who agree
I am conscious of living in a society divided by class	75
Britain is more divided by class today than it was in 1979	50
The class system is harmful	70

Figure 5.1 Class consciousness
This table shows the results of a survey carried out in 1997.

Class is not something that is simply produced economically. It is performed, marked, written on minds and bodies. We can spot it a mile off even in the midst of our wish for it no longer to be there.

Adapted from Roberts 2001 and Walkerdine et al. 2001. See also *British Politics in Focus,* Second Edition, pp.127-31.

3 Gender and the home

The modern father is being squeezed by social pressure to become more involved in family life while continuing to fulfil expectations of being the main breadwinner. These findings emerged from a study by the Joseph Rowntree Foundation. Researchers interviewed family members in Rochdale and found that the vast majority of them believe that the man's main role is that of 'provider' - men should go out to work to support their family but had little or no obligation to perform domestic tasks. This was despite the fact that the women interviewed had a paid job in more than 40% of the households.

A further study by the Office for National Statistics in 2001 discovered that the average British male spends three hours a day watching television and listening to the radio, 45 minutes cooking or cleaning and 13 minutes caring for children. The average British woman spends 22 minutes less per day on television and radio, 93 minutes more on housework and 23 minutes more looking after children. These figures are lifetime scores, averaging the daily routines of all adults over 16 including weekends and periods of unemployment and retirement. Overall, the figures suggest a continuing gender inequality in the home in both leisure pursuits and domestic labour (see Figure 5.2).

Adapted from the *Guardian,* 16 June 1999 and ONS 2001.

See also *British Politics in Focus,* Second Edition, pp.131-36.

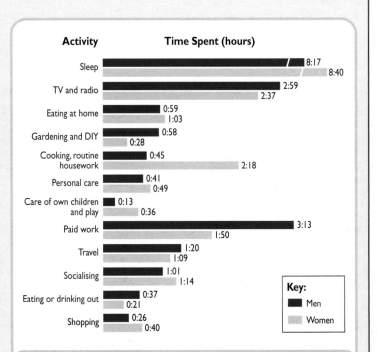

Activity	Time Spent (hours)	
Sleep	Men	8:17
	Women	8:40
TV and radio	Men	2:59
	Women	2:37
Eating at home	Men	0:59
	Women	1:03
Gardening and DIY	Men	0:58
	Women	0:28
Cooking, routine housework	Men	0:45
	Women	2:18
Personal care	Men	0:41
	Women	0:49
Care of own children and play	Men	0:13
	Women	0:36
Paid work	Men	3:13
	Women	1:50
Travel	Men	1:20
	Women	1:09
Socialising	Men	1:01
	Women	1:14
Eating or drinking out	Men	0:37
	Women	0:21
Shopping	Men	0:26
	Women	0:40

Key:
■ Men
■ Women

Figure 5.2 *This chart shows the way in which British men and women used their time in May 1999. It shows the average time in a day spent on an activity by men and women over the age of 16, including those retired, unemployed and working part time.*

4 Gender and work

According to a survey conducted by the London School of Economics in 2000, during the course of a typical woman's working life she can expect to earn £250,000 less than a man. Contrary to popular belief, this gender gap in earnings is not primarily caused by taking time off work to have children. According to the report, the main reasons are that women are concentrated in lower-paid sectors of the job market and they are paid less than men for doing the same work as men (even 25 years after the Equal Pay Act!). The survey also reveals that there is a greater pay gap for women working part time. Full-time women workers earn on average 84% of men's wages but female part-time workers only receive 58% of the rate per hour for male full-time workers. Figure 5.3 shows how much less women earn than men over the course of their lifetime.

The Equal Opportunities Commission (EOC) has blamed employers for the pay inequality and discrimination women face in the workplace. An EOC survey found that women were commonly denied access to bonuses and performance-related pay, while more than 10% reported that part-time employees, mainly women, were illegally excluded from pension schemes. However, the Confederation of British Industry (CBI - the main employers' organisation) rejected these findings, claiming that there was little evidence that employers were operating unfair pay structures. The CBI argued that the main cause of pay inequalities is occupational segregation - women are more likely to work in lower-paying sectors of the labour market.

The EOC's annual report for 2001 highlighted the disparity between the high performance of women in school and university compared to the chances of reaching the top in their field of work. In addition, the EOC reported on 8,900 complaints of possible discrimination at work, including 1,800 cases on pregnancy and maternity issues, 1,500 on working hours, 1,400 on equal pay for like work and 700 on sexual harassment. These figures are likely to be an underestimate of the gender inequalities in the workplace as many workers are not aware of their rights and may be reluctant to pursue legal cases even if they are.

Adapted from LSE 2000, the *Guardian*, 21 February 2000 and 9 January 2001 and HMSO 2002.

See also *British Politics in Focus*, Second Edition, pp.131-36.

The three categories of 'typical women'	Ms Low-skill Left school with no qualifications. Works as a shop assistant. Marries at 21. First child at 23 and second at 26. Takes nine years out of the labour market and works part-time for a further 28 years.	Ms Mid-skill Has GCSEs and works in a clerical job. Marries at 26. First child at 28, second at 31. Out of the labour market for just two years and works part-time for a further 12.	Ms High-skill Is a graduate and a professional. Marries at 28. First child at 30, second at 33. Works part-time for just a year, working full-time for the rest of her working life.
Earnings forgone, in three categories			
The female forfeit - how much less the woman would earn in a lifetime than a man with similar qualifications, even if she had no children.	£197,000	£241,000	£143,000
The mother gap - how much less the woman would earn in a lifetime than a woman with similar qualifications but no children.	£285,000	£140,000	£19,000
The parent gap - how much less the woman would earn than a man with similar qualifications - ie the female forfeit and mother gap combined.	£482,000	£381,000	£162,000

Figure 5.3 The pay divide

5 Race riots in Oldham and other northern towns and cities

Labour's 2001 general election manifesto claimed that: 'Labour believes that Britain can be a model of a multicultural, multi-racial society...now is the time to build the inclusive society in tune with British values'. Events in some northern towns and cities just before and just after the 2001 general election cast doubt on whether such hopes can be realised. In April 2001, rioting took place in Bradford after rumours of racist attacks on Asians. This was followed by violence in Oldham in May after a National Front march in the town which was ostensibly held to protest against alleged attacks on whites by Asians. There were also media reports that Asian youths had established 'no go' areas for whites in parts of Oldham. The tension in the town increased when the British National Party - a party which supports the voluntary repatriation of non-white immigrants to their lands of ethnic origin - fielded candidates in the June 2001 general election. In Oldham West and Royton, Nick Griffin, the Leader of the BNP, achieved 16.4% of the vote and, in Oldham East and Saddleworth, the BNP achieved 11.2% of the vote.

The second area where racial tension erupted was in Burnley in July 2001. After a number of racial attacks, over 200 white youths marched on a predominantly Asian area of the town. They were met by more than 100 Asian youths who threw bricks and set alight a local pub. In the June election, the BNP had picked up 4,151 votes, some 11.2% of the total votes cast. Such events were unprecedented in Burnley. The town had no history of racial violence.

Sporadic racial violence took place in other northern cities following the riot in Burnley, but the third and most serious rioting took place in Bradford in August 2001. Hundreds of Asian youths and white youths fought pitched battles as the police attempted to control the situation.

Adapted from Labour Party 2001 and the *Guardian*, 10 July and 12 December 2001. See also *British Politics in Focus*, Second Edition, pp.136-41.

6 Is Britain a racist society?

A report on race relations in Bradford, written by a panel headed by Lord Ouseley, the former Head of the Commission for Racial Equality, and published in July 2001 found that: 'Relations between different cultural communities should be improving, but instead they are deteriorating. There are signs that communities are fragmenting along racial, cultural and faith lines. Segregation in schools is one indicator of this trend. Rather than seeing the emergence of a confident multicultural district where people are respectful, people's attitudes are hardening and intolerance is growing'.

Reports on the riots in Burnley and Oldham painted a similar picture of segregated communities and 'white flight' from inner city areas. In addition, the report on Oldham noted that, although Asians made up 11% of Oldham's population, they only constituted 2% of the council's workforce. In Burnley, extreme poverty, drugs, squalid housing and criminal gang activity had been seized on by white racists who blamed the ethnic minorities. White fears led, subsequently, to the election of three BNP councillors in the local elections in May 2002.

This picture of disadvantage and discrimination is not confined to a small number of northern cities. The Cabinet Office's own research notes that, throughout the country, African-Caribbeans, Pakistanis and Bangladeshis are disadvantaged in the labour market and often face prejudice and discrimination.

Among the white population, the 2000 British Social Attitudes Survey found 'a sharp increase in the numbers of "Little Englanders" who do not identify themselves as British and tend towards racist and xenophobic views'. These figures (see Figure 5.4) are reflected in a negative approach to asylum seekers and concern expressed about immigration

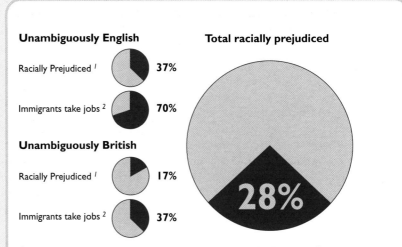

[1] Those who say they are "very or a little prejudiced against people of other races".
[2] Those who strongly agree or agree "immigrants take jobs away from people who were born in Britain".

Figure 5.4 Racism in Britain
These piecharts show the results of a survey published in November 2000. In all, 28% of people said they were 'very or a little prejudiced against people of other races'. Whilst this figure rose to 37% amongst those who defined themselves as 'unambiguously English', it fell to 17% amongst those who defined themselves as 'unambiguously British'.

by voters in the 2001 general election. A MORI opinion poll held just before the 2001 election on the 17 May revealed that asylum/immigration was one of the few areas where voters preferred Conservative policy to Labour and the issue ranked above transport in terms of importance to the electorate.

Adapted from BSA 2000, the *Guardian*, 8 November 2000, 10 July 2001 and 12 December 2001 and Cabinet Office 2001.

See also *British Politics in Focus*, Second Edition, pp.136-41.

7 Corporate Britain and black and Asian consumers

Corporate Britain is coming to grips with the complex realities of a multi-ethnic society. Needless to say, its motives are not exactly altruistic. It wants a bigger share of the c.£15 billion in after-tax income said to be in the hands of black and Asian consumers. Some big companies have realised that they need to change recruitment policies to attract the new customers they are seeking. HSBC, for example, set out to woo the South Asian business community with a banking service specifically tailored to their needs. Coincidentally or not, almost 50% of the staff on the bank's 12 special teams have South Asian backgrounds. Similarly, Lloyds TSB increased its intake of graduates with ethnic minority backgrounds from 4% to 19% in three years. Recent figures reveal intriguing trends in spending power. On a household to household basis, Indians, Chinese and African Asians all have average incomes higher than the white population. It is true that Pakistanis and African-Caribbeans

have lower incomes, but young black Brits are seen as style gurus.

Since 1998, there has been a sea change in attitudes within the advertising industry. Recent TV advertising campaigns for washing powder and washing up liquid, for example, have used blacks and Asians. Everyday products are seen to be promoted by ordinary black women and their families, not by icons or sports stars, and those appearing in the adverts are not just background faces in a crowd. Bruce Haines, President of the Institute of Practitioners in Advertising, points out that: 'One of the powers of advertising is to normalise things. The fact that it has embraced multiculturalism, particularly through the TV, means that viewers soon won't even think about it as being unusual'.

Adapted from the *Guardian*, 31 October 2001.

See also *British Politics in Focus*, Second Edition, pp.136-41.

8 Poverty and inequality

Since coming to power in 1997, Labour has introduced a number of reforms designed to help the poorest. These include the working families' tax credits, increased benefits for children in out-of-work families, and the national minimum wage. However, these reforms have been described as 'redistribution by stealth' because Labour feared criticism from Conservatives that middle-income Britain would be taxed to pay for the improvements.

Alongside these reforms have come other measures which seem designed to make life harder for the poor - abolition of lone parent benefit, cuts in disability benefit and tightening up on claimants for a range of benefits.

From 1997 to 2001 the numbers of those in poverty has remained broadly unchanged while the gap between rich and poor has actually widened. This is mainly because the incomes of those in work have risen significantly whereas benefits have not. The Institute of Fiscal Studies shows that the net income of the poorest fifth of society has grown by 1.4% annually whereas the income of the top fifth grew by 2.8%.

New Labour's unwillingness to pursue more radical measures to help the poor by taxing the rich more extensively was revealed in an interview by Jeremy Paxman with Tony Blair during the course of the 2001 general election campaign. Blair refused to say whether it was acceptable that inequality had widened under Labour. Instead, he argued that there was no point trying to tax high earners more, saying that 'you'd probably end up driving them abroad' and that 'it is not a burning ambition of mine to make David Beckham earn less money'.

Ruth Lister, Professor of Social Policy at Loughborough University, has argued that the Labour government sees the answer to social exclusion and poverty as lying not in money but in opportunity - through paid work, education and training. In return for providing people on benefits with opportunity, the government requires them to accept responsibility and imposes harsh sanctions on those who fail to comply.

Adapted from Glennerster 2001, the *Guardian*, 25 May 2001 and news.bbc.co.uk/vote 2001.

See also *British Politics in Focus*, Second Edition, pp.142-47.

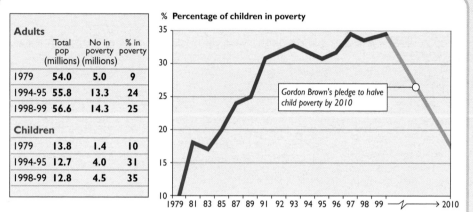

Adults	Total pop (millions)	No in poverty (millions)	% in poverty
1979	54.0	5.0	9
1994-95	55.8	13.3	24
1998-99	56.6	14.3	25
Children			
1979	13.8	1.4	10
1994-95	12.7	4.0	31
1998-99	12.8	4.5	35

% Percentage of children in poverty

Gordon Brown's pledge to halve child poverty by 2010

Figure 5.5 The growth in poverty
The table shows the number of people and percentage of the population living in poverty between 1979 and 1999. The graph shows the growth in child poverty and its projected fall. Poverty is defined as below 50% of average income after housing costs.

9 Boardroom salaries and workers' pay

A survey by *Management Today* in July 2001 revealed that British Chief Executives took home an annual salary package of £509,000 and that their pay rose by 29% between 1999 and 2001. These figures were well above pay levels for Chief Executives in other European countries. Vodafone, for example, paid its Chief Executive - Sir Chris Gent - more than £13 million in cash and shares. In contrast to these high rates of pay for senior staff, manufacturing employees in Britain are the lowest paid in the developing world. The average manufacturing wage is just £20,475 compared to £26,124 in Germany, £31,603 in America and £36,779 in Japan.

Adapted from the *Guardian*, 28 July 2001. See also *British Politics in Focus*, Second Edition, pp.142-47.

10 The Labour government and the 'underclass'

The continuing problem of long-term unemployment in certain parts of the country, social problems of delinquency and drug use, homelessness and the continuing rise in single-parent families have all contributed to a continuing debate about the existence of an 'underclass'. There is a concern that cycles of deprivation are passed from one generation to the next creating a permanently marginalised and excluded section of society. This section of society suffers multiple deprivation and is socially marginal, living outside mainstream society. It is claimed that this underclass is dependent on state welfare, develops a culture of fatalism and is surplus to the requirements of the economy.

New Labour has chosen to focus on the need for social inclusion for people in this position. In its 2001 general election manifesto, Labour claimed: 'Before 1997 social exclusion was ignored. We have a new approach - improving the quality of mainstream services, preventing people falling between the cracks, and reintegrating them into society'.

Labour has targeted five priority areas: (1) homelessness (2) teenage pregnancies (3) truancy and school exclusion (4) the 10% of teenagers not in education, training or work and (5) neighbourhood renewal for deprived neighbourhoods.

Adapted from the *Sunday Times*, 13 February 2000, Glennerster 2001 and Labour Party 2001. See also *British Politics in Focus*, Second Edition, pp.142-47.

11 The debate over the term 'underclass'

While there is little disagreement that a minority of the population has failed to derive benefits from improved living standards experienced by the rest of the population, there is a debate about the usefulness of the concept of 'the underclass'.

Arguments in favour

Charles Murray, a key American writer on the underclass, asserts that there are three key indicators: (1) dropout from the labour force among young males (2) violent crime and (3) births to unmarried women. In each case, he claims that the official statistics show that there has been an increase since 1990 (see Figure 5.6). Murray argues that these groups have developed a separate culture from the rest of society - most notably a refusal to take responsibility for their own welfare - and this should be seen as a threat to the rest of society. The government's own Social Exclusion Unit has noted that there are 44 local authority districts which contain 85% of the country's most deprived wards, with two-thirds more unemployment, 1.5 times the underage pregnancy rate, 1.5 times more lone parent households, extremely low educational attainment and mortality ratios 30% higher than elsewhere.

Arguments against

First, there is no agreement among the proponents of the underclass thesis on either the composition or the scale of the underclass. If the supporters of the thesis cannot agree among themselves on who exactly is a member of the underclass then this suggests there is a major flaw in their argument. Second, the underclass thesis makes links between categories of people and types of behaviour that do not necessarily stand up to scrutiny. For example, there is not necessarily a link between single parenthood and crime. Third, those who support the thesis have very different explanations for the causes of the creation of the underclass. Some authors argue that the underclass has a separate culture - a different set of values - from the rest of the population, while other authors argue that the underclass is separate because members of it have less materially than other classes in society. There is little evidence that the poor have a different set of values to the rest of society. Research for the Policy Studies Institute shows that members of the groups labelled by some commentators as 'the underclass' generally have the same basic beliefs as the rest of the population, for example wanting the best for their children or wanting to find work. In addition, studies have shown that, in reality, many of those characterised as being in the underclass move in and out of work at different points in their life cycles. Since the mid-1990s, with relatively low rates of unemployment, many of those previously characterised as being in the underclass have found work, suggesting that it is not possible to characterise the underclass as being a permanent grouping. Finally, by blaming the poor for their own condition, the underclass thesis diverts attention away from the real causes of poverty - the insecurity of work in the capitalist system and the low rates at which benefits are paid.

Adapted from Heath 1994, Pilkington 1999, Clarke 2000, *Sunday Times*, 13 February 2000.

See also *British Politics in Focus*, Second Edition, pp.142-47.

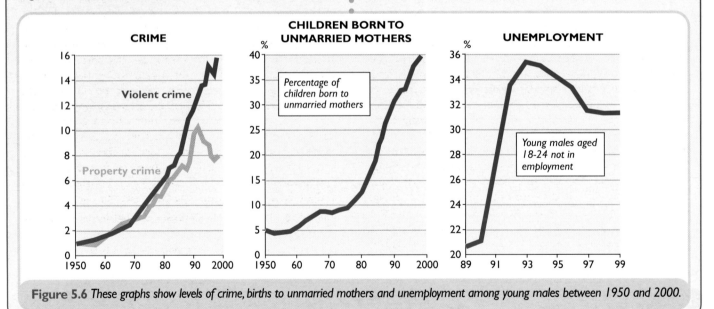

Figure 5.6 *These graphs show levels of crime, births to unmarried mothers and unemployment among young males between 1950 and 2000.*

12 Has Labour delivered for the unions?

Trade unions hoped that the return of Labour to power in 1997 would mean a significant improvement in their position. In reality, however, Labour's 1997 general election manifesto only promised minor changes to employment law and workplace rights. Most of these changes were implemented, but often in a watered-down fashion after pressure from employers. For example, the national minimum wage was implemented but at a much lower level than the rate proposed by the Trades Union Congress (TUC), and union recognition rights were much more narrowly drawn than the unions wanted. In addition, New Labour left in place all the major restrictions on the powers of the trade unions introduced by the Conservatives. As a result, the unions argued during the 2001 general election campaign that there was 'unfinished business'. Labour made even fewer promises on employment rights in its 2001 general election manifesto than it did in 1997, though there was a promise of a return to full employment as a key goal.

Adapted from Labour Party 1997, *Labour Research*, June 2001, Taylor 2001 and Labour Party 2001. See also *British Politics in Focus,* Second Edition, pp.147-50.

13 Union membership

	Number of members (thousands)	Percentage change in membership since previous year
1990	8,835	
1991	8,602	-2.6
1992	7,956	-7.5
1993	7,767	-2.4
1994	7,530	-3.0
1995	7,309	-2.9
1996	7,244	-0.9
1997	7,154	-1.2
1998	7,152	0.0
1999	7,257	1.5
2000	7,321	0.9
Change since 1990	-1,514	

Figure 5.7 Membership of unions
This chart shows the membership of unions between 1990 and 2000 and the percentage change in membership since the previous year.

Union membership declined between 1980 and 1998 and then began to rise again. In 1998, it stood at 7.152 million. By 2000, it had risen to 7.321 million (see Figure 5.7). Despite the modest rise in trade union membership since 1998, less than one third of the workforce belonged to a trade union in 2001. Within the overall figures, there are significant variations between different groups of workers. For example, on average, 60% of public sector workers are unionised compared to only 19% in the private sector. There has also been a change in terms of the social class of union members. Whereas a majority used to belong to the working class, in 2001 a majority were white-collar employees (ie belonged to the middle class). The highest union density within specific occupational groups was among professional employees (50%) and the lowest among sales (11%). Perhaps the most worrying figure for the future of unions is the fact that only 19% of 20 year olds are union members. In commenting on the figures, John Monks, General Secretary of the TUC, admitted that the unions were 'running fast to stand still' and would need to recruit new members as well as 'reach out to the many who have yet to see that unions are relevant for their job'.

Adapted from Taylor 2001 and TUC 2001.

See also *British Politics in Focus,* Second Edition, pp.147-50.

14 Unions and links with New Labour

Trade union discontent with the Labour Party reached new heights in 2001 both during the election campaign and at the TUC conference. In particular, the Labour government's plans to involve the private sector in the reform of public services caused a great deal of controversy. There are two main reasons for this. First, the unions have traditionally maintained an ideological commitment to the public sector. And second, the public sector has supplied the bulk of union members. Private sector initiatives, many union supporters believe, would result in a drop in union membership. At union conference after union conference in 2001, demands were made from the delegates for the unions to review their funding of the Labour Party and even their affiliation to the party. In the case of the GMB, a major public sector union, a decision was taken by the union executive after the 2001 general election to cut the level of funding given to the Labour Party by £1 million over four years. The money will be used instead to campaign against the private

sector's involvement in schools and hospitals. The leadership of Unison which pays £1.36 million per year to the Labour Party also agreed to review its links with Labour and to campaign against Labour's proposals. In the case of the Transport and General Workers Union, there was even consideration of an alliance with Liberal Democrats in the campaign against private sector involvement in the public sector. In an attempt to minimise the criticism, Tony Blair held a series of meetings with trade union leaders, though he made it clear that he has a mandate from the general election to deliver change in the public service. The Labour Party began life as the parliamentary wing of the trade union movement. New Labour might bring about an historic break in the relationship between the party and the unions.

Adapted from Taylor 2001, the *Observer*, 1 July 2001 and the *Guardian*, 18 July, 2001.

See also *British Politics in Focus,* Second Edition, pp.147-50.

References

BSA (2000) National Centre for Social Research, *British Social Attitudes Survey* (No.17), National Centre for Social Research, 2000.
Cabinet Office (2001) Performance and Innovation Unit, *Improving Labour Market Achievements for Ethnic Minorities in British Society*, Scoping Note, Cabinet Office, July 2001.
EOC (2001) Equal Opportunities Commission, *Annual Report*, EOC, 2001.
Glennerster (2001) Glennerster, H., 'Social policy' in *Seldon (2001)*.
Griffiths & Hope (2000) Griffiths, J. & Hope, T., *Stratification and Differentiation*, Hodder and Stoughton, 2000.
Labour (1997) *New Labour - Because Britain Deserves Better*, Labour Party manifesto, Labour Party, 1997.
Labour (2001) *Ambitions for Britain*, Labour Party manifesto, Labour Party, 2001.
Labour Research (2001) 'Has New Labour satisfied unions?', *Labour Research*, Vol.90.6, June 2001.

LSE (2000) London School of Economics, *Women's Incomes Over a Lifetime*, Women's Unit, Cabinet Office, 2000.
ONS (2001) Office for National Statistics, *Social Focus on Men*, HMSO, 2001.
Roberts (2001) Roberts, K., *Class in modern Britain*, Palgrave, 2001.
Rowe (2000) Rowe. M., 'Asylum Seekers in the UK', *Politics Review*, Vol.10.2, November 2000.
Seldon (2001) Seldon, A. (ed.), *The Blair Effect: The Blair Government 1997-2001*, Little Brown and Company, 2001.
Taylor (2001) Taylor R., 'Employment Relations Policy' in *Seldon (2001)*.
TUC (2001) Trade Union Congress, *Union Membership Holds Firm as Unions Win Women*, TUC press release, 22 June 2001.
Walkerdine et al. (2001) Walkerdine, V., Lucey, H. & Melody, J., *Growing up Girl: Psychosocial Explorations of Gender and Class*, Palgrave, 2001.

1 The Nice Treaty

The most recent revisions to the Treaty of Rome were made in the Treaty of Nice, finalised in December 2000. The central element of the Treaty was an agreement to expand the European Union by admitting new countries (see Section 3 below). The governments of all member states were committed to the Treaty, but the government of the Republic of Ireland was later prevented from signing by the Irish voters in a referendum (see Section 2 below). Critics argue that the Nice Treaty was a missed opportunity because members failed to review the workings of the institutions of the European Union.

Changes to qualified majority voting in the Council of Ministers

Under the system operating in 2002, each minister has a number of votes proportional to the population of their member state and at least 62 out of the 87 possible votes are necessary for a proposal to be carried. The Treaty of Nice agreed to the changes listed in Figure 6.1. They are to be introduced from January 2005 when new member states join the EU. In addition, to be successful, a proposal will have to be supported by a majority of member states and those states in favour will have to represent at least 62% of the population of the EU. Although, under the Nice Treaty, policy areas where qualified majority voting applies will increase, national governments will still be able to veto decisions in key areas such as taxation.

Adapted from the *Observer*, 30 May 2001 and McCormick 2002. See also *British Politics in Focus*, Second Edition, pp.157-61.

Member state	Current votes	Current number of citizens per vote (millions)	Reallocation of votes under Nice Treaty	Number of citizens per vote (millions)
Germany	10	8.21	29	2.83
UK	10	5.95	29	2.05
France	10	5.86	29	2.02
Italy	10	5.76	29	1.99
Spain	8	4.92	27	1.46
Netherlands	5	3.16	13	1.22
Greece	5	2.10	12	0.88
Belgium	5	2.04	12	0.85
Portugal	5	2.00	12	0.83
Sweden	4	2.22	10	0.89
Austria	4	2.02	10	0.81
Denmark	3	1.77	7	0.76
Finland	3	1.73	7	0.74
Ireland	3	1.23	7	0.53
Luxembourg	2	0.20	4	0.10
Total	87	4.31*	237	1.58*

* Average

Votes for new member states will be:

Poland	27	Romania	14
Czech Republic & Hungary	12	Bulgaria	10
Lithuania & Slovakia	7	Latvia, Estonia, Slovenia & Cyprus	4
Malta	3		

Figure 6.1 Qualified majority voting under the Nice Treaty

2 The Irish referendum

In the Republic of Ireland all important constitutional changes, such as a European treaty which affects Irish sovereignty, require the approval of a referendum. Following the Nice Summit in December 2000, the Irish government moved rapidly, confident that the Irish people would accept its recommendation of a Yes vote. The result of the vote asking the Irish people to approve their government's signing of the Nice Treaty is shown in Figure 6.2. The referendum result can be seen in both positive and negative terms:

The positive viewpoint

Those who fear the excessive power of the European Union and the so-called 'democratic deficit' have been encouraged by the fact that one of the EU's smallest members has been able to thwart the will of the great powers. Furthermore, this was the voice of the Irish people, not its government. Enlargement of the EU requires the unanimous consent of all member states. The result of the referendum shows that, in such cases, national sovereignty can be retained and asserted.

The negative viewpoint

There are suspicions that the referendum was seriously flawed.

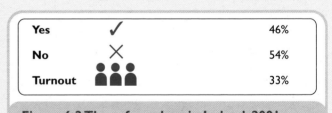

Yes	✓	46%
No	✗	54%
Turnout		33%

Figure 6.2 The referendum in Ireland, 2001

Some commentators have argued that people were not voting on EU enlargement at all, but rather expressing a general dissatisfaction with both the Irish government and EU institutions. It has also been claimed that many of the voters simply did not understand the issues and voted emotionally rather than rationally. Some commentators suggest that turnout was so low that the vote lacks validity. Critics agree that the referendum undermined the authority of the elected Irish government which negotiated the Nice Treaty in good faith.

Adapted from *Talking Politics* 2001. See also *British Politics in Focus*, Second Edition, pp.157-61.

3 European enlargement

The expansion of EU membership into eastern Europe is the key issue in EU external relations. Once an exclusive club of six members, in 2002, the EU had 15 members. Following the drawing up of the Nice Treaty, the number is due to rise to 20 and could then rise to 25, 27 or more. Enlargement promises not only significant economic and social change in eastern Europe, but a substantial reordering of the balance of power within the EU.

Ten central and eastern European countries are on the shortlist for the next round of European expansion:
- the Czech Republic, Estonia, Hungary, Poland and Slovenia (with which negotiations began in 1998)
- Bulgaria, Latvia, Lithuania, Romania and Slovakia.

All ten states applied for membership in 1994-96 and the general assumption is that the first wave of new members will join in 2004-05. It is most likely that this first wave will include the Czech Republic, Hungary and Poland and, possibly, Estonia and Slovenia.

In order to prepare these states for membership, the EU agreed 'pre-accession strategies' with all ten, and began publishing reports every year on the progress each country was making towards aligning their national laws and standards with those of the EU.

Several applicant countries complained in the late 1990s that much more was being expected of them prior to accession than had been the case with earlier entrants. Furthermore, they were being expected to wait longer.

There are strong political and economic arguments in favour of eastern expansion. EU membership:
- is likely to underpin the democratic transition for these states in the same way as it did for Greece, Portugal and Spain
- will open up new investment opportunities
- will put these states into a strategic relationship with the West that could be useful if relations with Russia deteriorate.

The promise of eastward expansion has also forced a reappraisal of the EU decision-making process which has been adjusted regularly since 1958 but is still founded on a club of six countries. Under the Treaty of Nice (see Section 1 above), arrangements were agreed for a redistribution of seats in the European Parliament, a revised weighting of votes in the Council of Ministers, and a rethinking of the balance of national representation in the Commission.

Adapted from McCormick 2002.
See also *British Politics in Focus*, Second Edition, pp.169-71.

4 The Convention on the Future of Europe in Brussels

On 28 February 2002, former French President, Valery Giscard d'Estaing, opened the Convention on the Future of Europe in Brussels. This body contains representatives from EU members as well as from those candidate countries which are due to join the EU in the next few years. The aim of the Convention is to discuss and make proposals on the future shape of the political institutions of the European Union. This is expected to take around 18 months. The Convention has been compared to the American Convention of 1787 which met in Philadelphia and, effectively, created the USA. This claim is exaggerated, however. The Convention is unlikely to come up with a full-blown federal system, though d'Estaing himself, its Chair, promises some radical proposals.

German delegates do wish to see progress towards a federal system and this is supported by some members of the French team. Britain and the Scandinavian countries, on the other hand, will resist federalism. Peter Hain, Minister for Europe and Head of the British delegation, insists that the EU should remain a union of independent states. Where Hain is radical, however, is in his insistence that the institutions of the EU should become much more democratic. The Commission is his main target. He sees it as unrepresentative, unaccountable and too secretive.

In the months to come many new arguments will be deployed in Brussels. This is the most serious attempt yet to reform and develop the European Union. The Convention may prove to be a ground-breaking body, but it may also turn out to be a damp squib. With over twenty countries and many different political groupings represented, the possibilities for consensus are limited.

Adapted from *Talking Politics* 2002.
See also *British Politics in Focus*, Second Edition, pp.169-71.

Figure 6.3 Peter Hain
Peter Hain, the UK's Minister for Europe, insists that the EU should remain a union of independent states. At the same time, he wants the institutions of the EU to become much more democratic.

5 The Common Agricultural Policy (CAP) – (1)

In July 2002, the European Commission announced plans to reform the Common Agricultural Policy (CAP) by placing a limit on payments to farmers and implementing a switch from an obsession with food production to policies which promote rural development. In 2002, half of the EU's entire budget was spent on the CAP, a system which was devised to boost production after the Second World War and which resulted in 50 years of intensive livestock farming and the heavy use of chemicals and pesticides in crop production. It was the CAP which was responsible for the lakes of milk and wine and mountains of unwanted beef, butter and grain produced by members of the EU. Research by the Organisation for Economic Cooperation and Development suggests that the CAP has driven up prices by 44%, with milk 70% more expensive than it should be and sugar 94% higher. The new proposals from Franz Fischler, the Agriculture Commissioner, would switch cash support to high-quality food produced in systems which improve animal welfare and the countryside. They would also mean that, in theory, farmers could be paid £200,000 a year simply to grow grass and prevent their land becoming scrubland. The current system pays some large-scale farmers millions of pounds to support intensive production. But the maximum payment available to a single farm would be cut to £200,000. The EU also proposes a flat-rate subsidy for each farm, based on payments made in previous years. This will be reduced by 3% a year for seven years. Farmers will be able to win back the lost cash by improving animal welfare, carrying out green farming and introducing schemes to encourage wild animals and birds. The need for reform has been fuelled by plans for enlargement (see Section 3 above). Announcing the plan, Franz Fischler said: 'In future, farmers will not be paid for over-production, but for responding to what people want - safe food, quality production, animal welfare and a healthy environment'.

Adapted from the *Daily Mail*, 11 July 2002.

Table (i)			
Losers Countries that pay more than they receive		**Winners** Countries that receive more than they pay	
Germany	-£6.2bn	Spain	+£3.37bn
Britain	-£2.5bn	Greece	+£2.91bn
Netherlands	-£1.1bn	Portugal	+£1.4bn
France	-£943m	Ireland	+£1.11bn
Sweden	-£784m	Italy	+475m
Austria	-£362m	Finland	+£144m
Belgium	-£218m	Denmark	+£112m
Luxembourg	-£43m		
All figures are for 2000			

Table (ii)	
France	£5.98bn
Germany	£3.76bn
Spain	£3.64bn
Italy	£3.35bn
Britain	£2.7bn
Greece	£1.73bn
Ireland	£1.1bn
Netherlands	£930m
Denmark	£869m
Austria	£678m
Belgium	£636m
Sweden	£532m
Finland	£485m
Portugal	£434m
Luxembourg	£13.7m
Total	**£26.8bn**

Figure 6.4 The cost of the CAP
Table (i) shows the amount that members of the EU pay or receive under the CAP. Table (ii) shows how much farmers in each member state received in 2000 under the CAP.

Product	Av UK price	Av NZ price
Butter (500g)	£1.73	66p
Beef, filet mignon (1kg)	£19.99	£7.35
Beef, minced (1kg)	£3.46	£2.64
Olive oil (1ltr)	£6.68	£3.25
Lamb, chops (1kg)	£9.22	£3.32
Lamb, leg (1kg)	£6.62	£2.73
Rice, white (1kg)	£1.97	53p
Margarine (500g)	£1.06	65p
Cheese, imported (500g)	£4.20	£3.95
Sugar, white (1kg)	60p	40p
Milk, pasteurised (1ltr)	51p	42p

Figure 6.5 A comparison of costs
This table shows how subsidised British prices compare to unsubsidised New Zealand prices. The figures are weighted to take into account differences in wages and cost of living in the two countries.

6 The Common Agricultural Policy (CAP) – (2)

Instead of tending his wheat, Polish farmer Ireneusz Filipowicz watches his television, waiting on word from bureaucrats 1,000 miles away in Brussels. It is they, not the weather, who decide what he will get paid. He is one of more than 9 million farmers in central Europe queuing for subsidies they hope will allow them to modernise and compete on an equal footing with western European farmers when they join the EU in 2004. It is a faint hope. Under proposals announced in July 2002, the newcomers will qualify for only 25% of what western European farmers will receive, with parity after a decade. In reality, Polish farmers argue, it will amount to a mere 12% because of the greater productivity of western European farms. 'I'm not asking for a silver-plated combine harvester', says Filipowicz who produces wheat, milk and pork, 'just the ability to survive and on as level a playing field as possible'. There have been improvements in recent years. A water supply was installed in Filipowicz's farm seven years ago and, for five years, he has had a radio telephone. But, the potholes in the road have grown. Rain pours through holes in the barn roof. The only visible sign of machinery is his wedding present, a 13-year-old tractor. Filipowicz argues that the onset of EU membership is a big problem. For the past two years, the prices of wheat and pork have fallen to all-time lows due to subsidised German grain being dumped on the Polish market. At the same time, Filipowicz, whose dairy production has increased by introducing vitamins and protein in feed, has been told that he will have to cut production by around a third in the next three years under nationwide milk quotas imposed by the EU. Despite an increase in production levels of c.50%, Filipowicz has seen the income from his farm decrease by the same amount. In what is increasingly typical in Poland's 1.8 million farms (on which 20% of the population are dependent for their income), Filipowicz's wife, Bozena, has taken a job as a cook to make ends meet. Filipowicz sits under a pear tree, surrounded by hand-made hayricks, organic vegetable patches and wild flowers. 'We hear on the radio that this is what western Europe is striving for', he says. 'It's more organic and environmentally friendly, but it's in danger of being annihilated'.

Adapted from the *Guardian*, 11 July 2002.

7 The Labour Party's stance on Europe

The Labour Party:
- promises no membership of the single currency without the consent of the British people in a referendum
- does not support a United States of Europe but believes that a Europe made up of nation states and offering a unique blend of intergovernmental cooperation where possible and integration where necessary can be a major force for the good for its own members and in the wider world.

Europe is a crucial market, accounting for more than half of the UK's trade. Key priorities are:
- to deliver more choice and lower prices through liberalisation of financial services and utilities
- to promote business development with a common EU patent and cuts in red tape
- to develop a common research effort in frontier technologies like bioscience
- to cut delays and fares by establishing an integrated Air Traffic Control system for Europe

- to develop effective labour market policy to tackle unemployment in dialogue with the social partners.

Under a Labour government, Britain will keep the veto on vital matters of national sovereignty, such as tax and border controls.

New countries joining the EU will give Britain a bigger market and Europe a bigger voice. Labour is pledged to do all it can to enable the first group of applicant countries to join in time to take part in the next European Parliamentary elections in 2004. The party believes that it is vital that the UK ratifies the Treaty of Nice which is essential to enlargement.

Labour supports a stronger role for national parliaments in European affairs, for example in a second chamber of the European Parliament, with a particular remit to oversee the division of competences.

Adapted from Labour 2001.
See also *British Politics in Focus*, Second Edition, pp.171-76.

8 The Conservative Party's stance on Europe

The guiding principle of Conservative policy towards the EU is to be in Europe, but not run by Europe. A Conservative government will insist on a Treaty 'flexibility' provision so that, outside the areas of the single market and core elements of an open, free-standing and competitive EU, countries need only participate in new legislative actions at a European level if they see this as in their national interest. At the same time, the Conservative Party is willing to support the principle of 'reinforced cooperation' in Europe, under which small groups of countries can become more closely integrated if they wish to do so, providing it does not damage Britain's national interest.

A Conservative government will keep the pound and maintain the UK's national veto on European legislation. It will not ratify the Nice Treaty but renegotiate it so that Britain does not lose its veto. A Conservative government will also amend domestic law to include 'reserved powers'.

This will prevent EU law from overriding the will of Parliament in areas which Parliament never intended to transfer to the EU. Should any future government wish to surrender any more of Parliament's rights and power to Brussels, they should be required to secure approval for such a transfer in a referendum.

The Conservative Party wants early enlargement of the European Union - the first wave, including Cyprus, should be admitted by 2004.

Conservatives have always supported stronger European defence cooperation, but always inside NATO. A Conservative government will not participate in a structure outside NATO, but will insist instead that any European initiative is under the NATO umbrella.

Adapted from Conservative 2001.
See also *British Politics in Focus*, Second Edition, pp.171-76.

9 The Liberal Democrats' stance on Europe

Liberal Democrat priorities in Europe are:
- enlargement of the EU to include the emerging democracies of central and eastern Europe
- reform of the EU's institutions to make them more open, democratic and effective
- reaching agreement on a constitutional settlement for Europe
- cooperation with European Liberal Democrat partners.

Liberal Democrats will work to:
- establish a constitution for the EU to define and limit its powers, ensuring that decisions are made at the most appropriate level
- set up a standing scrutiny committee in the European Parliament to ensure that EU proposals meet the criteria of subsidiarity and proportionality
- make the European Commission more democratically accountable
- make sure that European Union bodies are more open - the Council of Ministers should meet in public whenever it discusses legislation

- maintain the veto in areas of national interest to the UK
- improve Westminster's scrutiny of European legislation and the activities of UK ministers attending the Council of Ministers
- increase the transparency of the European Central Bank
- support a European Common Foreign and Security Policy that includes a significant defence capability consistent with the UK's membership of NATO and other international institutions
- hold meetings of the European Parliament only in Brussels
- push for the early enlargement of the EU
- remove unnecessary regulations and reduce administrative costs.

All EU policies should be analysed for their likely environmental impact, with results reported to the European Parliament.

Adapted from Liberal Democrat 2001.
See also *British Politics in Focus*, Second Edition, pp.171-76.

10 Globalisation – the GATS Treaty

In March 2001, a document marked 'confidential' was faxed to the journalist Greg Palast from the Secretariat of the World Trade Organisation (WTO). This document contained a plan to create an international agency with veto power over parliamentary and regulatory decisions. This shocked Palast. After all, for centuries Britain and many other countries have relied on elected Parliaments and politicians to set the rules and balance the interests of citizens and businesses. Now, however, that system is under threat. By signing the GATS Treaty (GATS stands for General Agreement on Trade and Services), states will be signing up to the 'Necessity Test'. Then Parliaments and regulatory bodies will be demoted, in effect, to advisory bodies. Final authority will rest with the GATS Disputes Panel to determine whether a law or regulation is 'more burdensome than necessary'. The GATS panel, not Parliament or Congress, will decide what is meant by 'necessary'. The Necessity Test had a trial run in North America where it was included in NAFTA, the region's free-trade agreement. The state of California had banned a gasoline additive MBTE, a chemical cocktail that was found to have contaminated water supplies. A Canadian producer of the 'M' chemical in MBTE filed a complaint saying that California's ban on the pollutant failed the Necessity Test. Instead of banning MBTE, the Canadians proposed, the Californians should require all petrol stations to dig up storage tanks and reseal them, and hire inspectors to make sure that it was done correctly. Despite the fact that the Canadian proposal would cost California a great deal and was impossible to police, it was judged to be the 'least trade restrictive' method for protecting California's water supply. If California doesn't take action, the US Treasury may have to pay $976 million to the pollutant's Canadian manufacturer. Under GATS, as proposed in the memo, national laws and regulations will be struck down if they are 'more burdensome than necessary' to business. This makes the GATS Treaty a means to wipe away restrictions on business and industry. Suppose in the future that the American

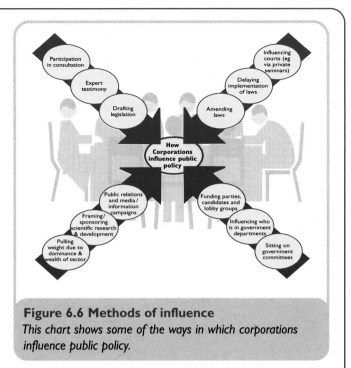

Figure 6.6 Methods of influence
This chart shows some of the ways in which corporations influence public policy.

company Wal-Mart wants to build a store in Britain on land in the greenbelt, the Necessity Test could lead the GATS Disputes Panel to judge that Wal-Mart should be allowed to build its store because Britain's planning regulations are 'more burdensome than necessary'. Even under the current weaker GATS, Japan was forced to tear up its planning rules to allow retailers to build their stores. Significantly, trade ministers have agreed that, before the GATS panel, a defence of 'safeguarding the public interest' should not be allowed. Instead, the 'efficiency principle' will be applied. This will allow GATS to make requirements which rulers know their democratic Parliaments could not accept.

Adapted from Palast 2002.
See also *British Politics in Focus*, Second Edition, pp.177-81.

11 Globalisation – the second Earth Summit

Corporations with a record of undermining UN initiatives - on climate change, toxic waste, tobacco and more - are now 'valued partners'. As Secretary General Kofi Annan put it: 'The UN and private companies are joining forces'. In January 1999, Annan announced the Global Corporate Compact, a partnership with the UN's old opponent, the International Chamber of Commerce (ICC). The ICC has announced it will use the Global Compact model in 'preparing the business contribution' for the second Earth Summit to be held in Johannesburg in the summer of 2002. This may suggest what to expect from the summit which, in the face of the growing anti-corporate movement, is seen by governments as a key moment to put a

Company	Country of origin	2001 revenue	Compared to country economies*
1. Wal-Mart	US	219,812	(approx size Sweden)
2. ExxonMobil	US	191,581	(larger than Turkey)
3. General Motors	US	177,260	(larger than Denmark)
4. Ford Motor	US	162,412	(larger than Poland)
5. DaimlerChrysler	Germany	149,608	(larger than Norway)
6. Royal Dutch/Shell Group	Netherlands/Britain	149,146	(larger than Norway)
7. BP	Britain	148,062	(larger than Norway)
8. Enron**	US	138,718	(larger than South Africa)
9. Mitsubishi	Japan	126,629	(larger than Finland)
10. General Electric	US	125,913	(larger than Greece)

* GDP, 2000 World Development Report. ** now declared bankrupt.

Figure 6.7 *This table shows the largest companies in the world by 2001 revenue (figures in $ millions).*

'human face' on globalisation. The summit is likely to promote the idea that partnership with the private sector is the best road to sustainability. Corporate initiatives sponsored by companies with terrible human rights records may be the shape of things to come.

There is a massive reality gap. The UN's green business partners are some of the very same corporations who have lobbied against UN environmental agreements. Crucially, the Johannesburg summit may be the clinching moment when international environmental agreements become subservient to World Trade Organisation (WTO) rules. While UN conventions have more focus on the environment and the South, WTO rules tend to favour Big Business. WTO rules have been repeatedly invoked by the ICC to undermine the environmental agreements that came out of the previous Earth summit in Rio on climate change, biodiversity, and the 1994 ban on trade in hazardous waste. The corporate vogue for self-regulation needs to be exposed as self-interest.

Adapted from Ainger 2002. See also *British Politics in Focus*, Second Edition, pp.177-81.

12 Britain's 'special relationship' with the USA

Tony Blair likes to see Britain as a bridge between Europe and the US, forging a new Euro-Atlantic unity in the post-Cold War world. The Labour Party manifesto at the 2001 general election declared: 'We reject the view of those who say we must choose between Europe and the USA. We shall remain the USA's firm ally and friend; but we are not going to turn our backs on Europe'. Such confirmations of Britain's 'special relationship' with the USA are supported by the evidence of the government's strong backing of the 'War on Terrorism' following the destruction of the World Trade Centre and the attack on the Pentagon on 11 September 2001.

Continuation of the special relationship does not, however, meet with universal support in Britain. Commentators such as Will Hutton (writing in the *Observer*) argue that it fails to take account of the significant shifts in US policy and ideology that have occurred since George W. Bush became President. Hutton argues that the ultra-conservative South is now the political centre of gravity in the United States and that American conservatives want no truck with the outside world unless wholly on their terms. The implication

is that Britain should review its relationship with the USA and, instead, work more closely with Europe on international matters.

Figure 6.8 The special relationship *This cartoon was first published in July 2002.*

Adapted from Labour 2001, the *Observer*, 6 May 2001 and Dunleavy et al. 2002. See also *British Politics in Focus*, Second Edition, pp.184-89.

13 The rapid reaction force

In June 1999, a meeting of the European Council in Cologne committed EU member states to a common policy on security and defence and to the creation of a permanent European military force. Later in the year, following a UK-French proposal for the establishment of a rapid reaction force, the European Council meeting in Helsinki agreed to the setting up of a permanent multinational corps of 50,000-60,000 troops by 2003. The idea was for this force to be able to mount an autonomous European mission if NATO declined to become involved in a

crisis. This arrangement was confirmed by the Nice summit in 2000 (see Section 1 above) where the decision was also made to transfer to the EU the crisis management functions previously within the remit of the Western European Union (WEU) which is part of NATO. As a result, the military aspects of the WEU were, effectively, incorporated into the EU.

Adapted from Blair 2002.
See also *British Politics in Focus*, Second Edition, pp.184-89.

References

Ainger (2002) Ainger, K., 'Earth summit for sale', *New Internationalist*, No.347, July 2002.

Blair (2002) Blair, A., 'Marching in time', *Talking Politics*, Vol.14.2, January 2002.

Conservative (2001) *Time for Common Sense*, Conservative Party manifesto, Conservative Party, 2001.

Dunleavy et al. (2002) Dunleavy, P., Gamble, A., Heffernan, R., Holliday, I. & Peele, G. (eds), *Developments in British Politics 6*, Palgrave, 2002.

Labour (2001) *Ambitions for Britain*, Labour Party manifesto, Labour Party, 2001.

Liberal Democrat (2001) *Liberal Democrat Manifesto: For a Liberal and*

Democratic Britain: Freedom, Justice, Honesty, Liberal Democrat manifesto, 2001.

McCormick (2002) McCormick, J., *Understanding the European Union* (2nd edn), Palgrave, 2002.

Palast (2002) Palast, G., 'For their eyes only', *New Internationalist*, No. 347, July 2002.

Talking Politics (2001) 'News briefing', *Talking Politics*, Vol.14.1, September 2001.

Talking Politics (2002) 'News briefing', *Talking Politics*, Vol.14.3, April 2002.

1 Apathy and the 2001 general election (a)

One of the key features of the 2001 general election was the low turnout. Just 59.4% of electors voted in June 2001, compared to 71.4% in 1997. Opinion poll evidence suggests that the fall in turnout was particularly acute among younger voters, with only 39% of 18- to 24-year-olds claiming to have voted. Also, turnout was lower among working-class voters than middle-class voters. The overall decline in turnout masked significant differences between different parts of the country. In Liverpool Riverside, the turnout was as low as 34.1% compared to the highest turnout of 72.3% in Winchester. The fall in the vote had been expected but not on such a scale. It followed low turnout in the European Elections in 1999 when only 24% of the electorate voted, in the Scottish Parliament and Welsh Assembly elections in 1999 and in many recent by-elections and council elections.

Figure 7.1 Apathy in the UK *This cartoon was drawn in response to reports that turnout in the 2001 general election was alarmingly low.*

MORI research

In 2001, the polling organisation MORI conducted a two-phase national opinion poll for the Electoral Commission. A first survey was conducted just after the date of the general election was announced and a second immediately after the general election was over, using the same panel of respondents. The findings of the poll were as follows:

- 21% said that they could not get to the polling station because it was too inconvenient
- 16% said that they were away on election day
- 15% said that they were not registered to vote
- 11% said that they did not receive a polling card/postal vote
- 10% said that they were not interested in politics.

The focus of these answers was on practical reasons for not voting rather than lack of interest or the failure of the political parties.

Those who did vote

When those who did vote were asked why they did so, 42% said that it was their civic duty. In addition, the poll revealed that there was a strong sense of the habit of voting among the older age groups. More than half of all those who said that they were not at all interested in politics still voted on election day. Further, the percentage of the population claiming to be interested in politics was actually higher than in 1997, leading MORI to the conclusion that declining turnout was not the result of declining interest in politics or elections but rather a failure of the campaign to connect with the electorate. Voting in 2001 may not, therefore, be an indicator of future trends. The respondents in the survey were positive about elections in general, but they were negative about the general election in June 2001 because the result was regarded as a foregone conclusion.

Opinion polls have to be treated with some caution as the answers are given in an artificial situation where the respondents may feel constrained to give acceptable answers. In addition, other research (see Section 2 below) contradicts some of the findings. Nevertheless the MORI poll does provide a useful account of the reasons for the low turnout.

Hansard Society

The Hansard Society conducted focus group research on non-voters following the general election in June 2001. The focus group was mainly made up of younger people, including some defined as political activists. This study suggests that the low turnout was not caused by apathy but because of a positive decision to abstain. The key findings were as follows:

- the decision not to vote was a conscious choice
- the respondents did not see a clear choice between the politicians
- younger voters were concerned that they did not know enough to make an informed choice
- respondents had already switched off from the political process before the election campaign began
- the media played a key role in creating or transmitting the images which gave the focus group their negative perceptions of politics.

Adapted from Electoral Commission 2001, MORI 2001 and Billinghurst 2001. Whitely et al. 2001, Curtice 2001.

See also *British Politics in Focus*, Second Edition, pp. 202-06.

2 Apathy and the 2001 general election (b)

The British Election Study 2001

The British Election Study 2001, a survey of 4,800 voters, found that the percentage not identifying with any party increased from 7% in 1997 to 10% in 2001. In addition, there was a reduction in leadership popularity. Whereas, in June 1997, 82% were satisfied with Tony Blair's performance as Prime Minister, only 49% were satisfied in December 2000. The other Party Leaders also remained unpopular. This suggests that there may have been growing disillusionment with politics which, in turn, led to a decline in turnout. The theory is that electors were unhappy with the policies pursued by New Labour but did not believe that the Conservatives would deliver on public services. As a result, they chose not to vote. The British Election Study concludes that the fall in turnout has resulted in a crisis of democratic politics in Britain.

Butler and Kavanagh's findings

In one of the main studies of the 2001 general election, Butler and Kavanagh describe some of the main features of the campaign as follows. First, the campaign was portrayed in the media as being boring. Second, the campaign was less energetic than that of 1997, with fewer people being leafleted or canvassed (14% compared to 24% in 1997). Third, only 66% of voters cared about the outcome. Fourth, voters' trust in politicians continued to fall. Fifth, there was a sense that there was little difference between the major parties. And sixth, those who had a strong or fairly strong attachment to a political party fell from 75% in 1997 to 70% in 2001.

Paul Whiteley's analysis

Figure 7.2 shows that the majority of advanced industrial democracies have experienced the same decline in turnout at elections as the UK. This suggests that we can rule out explanations that are specific to a single country or a few countries. Explanations such as political sleaze or the behaviour of MPs in the Commons may be attractive but they don't travel. A general explanation needs to identify factors which are widespread and growing in importance across the whole of the democratic world. One explanation is that the public is becoming increasingly alienated from politics and the political system. The problem with this is that surveys have shown

that there is not much evidence of growing dissatisfaction with democracy. Another explanation is that government is becoming remote and disconnected. But this does not work either. Switzerland has the most decentralised and participation-friendly institutions in the world but is at the top of the list of countries experiencing declining turnout. A better explanation is that people are becoming more rational and, because of this, they don't vote. This may sound bizarre, but political scientists have long recognised that if people behave rationally - ie if they only take action when the benefits outweigh the costs - then they will not vote. The logic is as follows. If your preferred party looks like winning an election, you will benefit even if you don't vote, by free-riding on the votes of others. On the other hand, if your preferred party looks like losing, your vote is not going to change that, so the rational thing to do is not to bother to vote. This assumes that voters are calculating and do not feel it a civic duty to vote. A globalising society in which market transactions drive out more traditional social relationships and in which the links between individuals are increasingly based on calculations has produced this state of affairs. The decline is not inevitable, however, as Scandinavian countries show. These countries are high in 'social capital' - citizens trust each other and feel a sense of civic duty. In Britain, there are also areas with high social capital. These tend to be areas with less crime and better levels of health and educational performance. Policies designed to build social capital will help to address the turnout crisis.

Adapted from BES 2001, Whiteley et al. 2001, Butler & Kavanagh 2002 and the *Guardian*, 1 May 2002.

See also *British Politics in Focus*, Second Edition, pp.202-06.

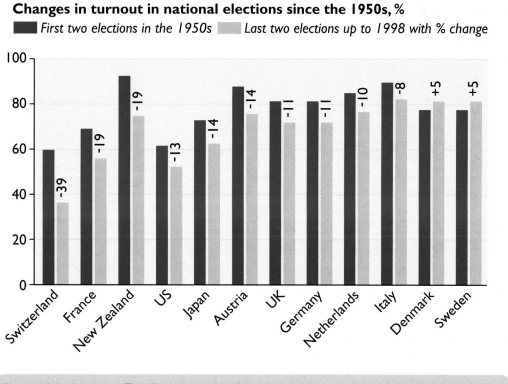

Changes in turnout in national elections since the 1950s, %

■ *First two elections in the 1950s* ■ *Last two elections up to 1998 with % change*

Switzerland -39, France -19, New Zealand -19, US -13, Japan -14, Austria -14, UK -11, Germany -11, Netherlands -10, Italy -8, Denmark +5, Sweden +5

Figure 7.2 Turnout *This chart shows the changes in turnout in national elections held in selected countries since the 1950s. The figures are in percentages.*

3 New election rules

Following the low turnout in many recent elections, the government has introduced electronic, telephone and internet voting in an attempt to persuade more people to vote. In January 2001, Robin Cook, the Leader of the House of Commons, described the traditional way of voting as 'astonishingly quaint'. Following the passage of the 2000 Representation of the People Act, local councils have run a number of pilot schemes (see Figure 7.3).

The 2000 Representation of the People Act

The 2000 Representation of the People Act allowed electronic voting and counting, early voting, mobile polling stations, all-postal voting and more postal voting. As Figure 7.3 shows, the results of the pilot schemes varied. However, in the councils where polling stations were closed down and replaced with all-postal voting, turnout did increase, in some cases substantially. Extended postal voting also attracted considerable interest. For example, in Milton Keynes the numbers of voters asking for postal votes rose from the usual 1,000 to 3,600. The 2000 Representation of the People Act made postal voting available on demand, with the result that any voter can now request a postal vote for a particular election or for an indefinite period. One result was that postal voting increased considerably in some parliamentary constituencies in the 2001 general election. For example, in Stevenage, some 25,000 of the 70,000 voters requested postal votes. More experiments were introduced in the 2002 local elections. There are, however, some concerns that these changes could lead to more electoral fraud as it is relatively easy to use another voter's signature. At least with voting in polling stations, the voter has to be there in person.

Compulsory voting

Compulsory voting for general and local elections has also been suggested as a solution to the problem of low voter turnout. Compulsory voting already exists, for at least some elections, in Australia, Luxembourg, Belgium, Singapore and Brazil. Where compulsory voting exists, penalties for non-voting include fines, withdrawal of certain government services or benefits and the 'naming and shaming' of those who do not vote. The arguments for and against compulsory voting are summarised in Box 7.1.

Council	Nature of pilot(s)	No. of wards	No. of polling stations/ dates/hours	1999 % turnout	2000 % turnout	Impact turnout
Amber Valley	Postal votes on request	2		Up to 41	33.5 (av.)	-
Blackburn	Early voting	all	2 29/4 9-5	30.0	30.9	=
Bolton	All-postal ballot	3		25.5 (av.)	37.7 (av.)	+
Bury	Electronic voting + counting	1	5 (voting machines)	21.5	20.7	=
Coventry	Early voting	all	1 26-29/4 shop hours	26.7	26.5	=
Doncaster	All-postal ballot	1		24.5	44.0	+
Eastleigh	Postal votes on request	12		34.3	33.5	=
Gateshead	All-postal ballot - papers mailed to all voters	2		25.2 (av.)	53.7 (av.)	+
Gloucester	Postal votes on request	3		19.9 (av.)	25.6 (av.)	+
Manchester	Early voting	all	6 29-30/4 11-4	21.4	20.5	=
Milton Keynes	Postal votes on request	all		32.3	27.3	-
Mole Valley	Extended voting hours	all	7-10	40.6	42.7	+
Plymouth	Early voting	all	1 28/4 8-7; 29/4 8-6	40 ('95)	31.9	-
Redditch	Early (earliest) voting	all	1 25-28/4 8-9; 29/4 8-6	25.7	25.3	=
St. Helens	Early voting; extended hours	6	2 28-29/4 7-10	16.4 (av.)	18.3 (av.)	+
Salford	Electronic voting + counting - programmed voting cards	1	(voting machines)	24.9	22.2	-
Stoke on Trent	Early voting	all	1 8/4 office hours	22.3	24.8	+
Stratford on Avon	Electronic voting + counting	all		40.1	39.1	-
Sunderland	Early voting Mobile voting	all 8	3 28/4-2/5 10-6	19.5 20.6 (av.)	21.2 23.1 (av.)	+ +
Watford	Early voting Weekend voting Mobile voting Freepost communications	all all	1 27-29/4 8-9 6-7/5 8-6 (NOT 4/5) (1 delivery per candidate)	35.5	27.0	-
Wigan	All-postal ballot	3		17.6 (av.)	26.0 (av.)	+
Windsor & M'head	Early voting/mobile voting	2	(1 day per ward)	40.6 (av.)	35.4	

Figure 7.3 Pilot voting schemes *This chart shows the types of pilot voting schemes that have been tried and their impact on turnout.*

Arguments for:	Arguments against:
● compulsory voting would solve the problem of low turnout	● compulsory voting will result in ill-considered judgements by those not interested in voting
● as non-voting is higher among the working class than the middle class, compulsory voting would ensure that the needs of all voters were considered	● the political process would become devalued
● the role of money in elections would be less significant	● it would be impractical to implement
● political literacy would increase	● it would favour established parties as it devalues new political activism
● compulsory voting would ensure that everybody did at least the minimum in terms of their public duty.	● voters have a right in a liberal democracy not to vote
	● it would not deal with the root causes of political disaffection.

Box 7.1 Arguments for and against compulsory voting

Adapted from the *Guardian*, 15 May 2000, 7 January 2001 and 4 June 2001, Game 2001 and Faulks 2001.

See also *British Politics in Focus*, Second Edition, pp.206-12.

4 'First order' and 'second order' elections

By-elections, the European election, the Scottish Parliament election, the Welsh Assembly election and the euro referendum can all be termed 'second order' elections. In contrast, 'first order' elections are national parliamentary or presidential elections. The elections are 'second order' in two senses. First, they are regarded as less important than 'first order' elections. Second, the elections are used by national parties as barometers of their standing rather than of worth in their own right. According to Rallings and Thrasher, 'second order' elections tend to have lower turnouts and the electorate may vote with 'their heart rather than their head' or make their vote a protest vote.

Adapted from Hix 2000 and Rallings & Thrasher 2000. See also *British Politics in Focus,* Second Edition, pp.206-12.

5 By-elections May 1997- September 2002

The 17 by-elections between the general elections in 1997 and 2001 were unusual in that the main opposition party - the Conservatives - failed to gain a single seat while Labour managed to hold all the seats it was defending. The normal assumption is that governments lose by-elections as their popularity wanes. A second significant characteristic was the low turnout (the level fell back to that of by-elections in the 1970s). Typical were the by-elections in November 2000 in West Bromwich East, Glasgow Anniesland and Preston, where Labour won each seat but on a turnout of 28%, 38% and 29% respectively. In the first by-election held after the 2001 general election, the same pattern continued. Labour held Ipswich with a turnout of 40% (down by nearly 17% from that in the general election five months earlier). Labour's majority was reduced from 8,081 to 4,087 - see Figure 7.4.

Adapted from Butler & Kavanagh 2000 and the *Guardian*, 23 November 2001.

IPSWICH							Labour hold
No. voting & % turnout		27,405	40.16%	**Nov. 2001**	38,873	57.0%	**June 2001**
Mole, C	Lab	**11,881**	**43.35**	**-7.98**	**19,952**	**51.33**	**Lab**
West, C	Con	7,794	28.44	-2.10	11,871	30.54	Con
Munt, T	LD	6,146	22.43	+7.24	5,904	15.19	LD
Cooper, D	CPA	581	2.12	-	-	-	-
Wright, J	UK Ind	276	1.01	-0.60	624	1.61	UK Ind
Slade, T	Green	255	0.93	-	-	-	-
Ramirez, J	LCA	236	0.86	-	-	-	-
Leech, P	Soc All	152	0.55	-0.23	305	0.78	Soc All
Winskill, N	Eng Ind	84	0.31	-	-	-	-
		Lab majority 4,087 (14.91%)			**Lab majority 8,081 (20.79%)**		

Figure 7.4 The Ipswich by-election *This table shows the result of the Ipswich by-election held on 22 November 2001 compared to the general election held in June 2001. The by-election took place because of the death of the sitting Labour MP Jamie Cann.*

6 The 1999 European election

The 1999 elections to the European Parliament produced one of the Labour Party's worst nationwide election performances in living memory. Its 28% of the vote was marginally worse than the percentage it won in the 1983 general election and it was down 16.4% on the percentage won in the 1997 general election. The Conservatives emerged as chief victors, but their result marked only a limited revival. At 35.8%, the Conservative vote represented an increase of only 4.4% on their worst result in modern times at the 1997 general election. The Liberal Democrats won 12.7% of the vote and the minor parties fared well, with the UK Independence Party securing 7% of the vote and the Greens 6.3%.

The European elections were the first in which a system of proportional representation (PR) was used for a nationwide election, bringing the UK into line with other EU member states. The 'Closed List' system chosen by the government was, however, controversial. Under PR, it was inevitable that the Labour Party would not repeat its 1994 European election total of 62 seats. In fact, it won 29 seats (the same as it would have won under a first-past-the-post system). The Conservatives won 36 (up from 18 in 1994, but they would have won 50 seats under the old system). The Liberal Democrats won ten seats (up from two). SNP and Plaid Cymru both won two seats, as in 1994. The Greens also won two seats (their first ever) and the UK Independence Party three seats (their first ever), but this did not fully reward their combined 13% of the vote. The turnout was the lowest in Europe at 24%. This may have been due to the negative publicity about the closed lists and the large size of the constituencies. In addition, the Conservatives' anti-European stance and the abstention of Labour voters have been cited as causes of the low turnout.

Adapted from Hopkins & Lynch 1999 and Hix 2000.

7 Elections to the Welsh Assembly in 1999

The elections to the Welsh Assembly in May 1999 redrew the Welsh political map. The electoral system used was the Additional Member system, with 40 members elected from Wales' existing Westminster constituencies and an additional 20 elected from regional lists. The aim was to ensure that parties which won fewer constituency seats than their votes entitled them to would, nevertheless, win their fair share of seats in the Assembly. The chief beneficiary was the Conservative Party which won no seats in Wales in the 1997 general election, despite winning 20% of the vote. It was anticipated that Labour would win an overall majority. This expectation, however, was confounded as Labour lost seats, leaving it the largest party but with no overall majority - see Figure 7.5. Despite the fact that these were the first Assembly elections, only 46.6% of the electors voted.

Adapted from Griffiths 2000.

Party	Constituencies % vote	Seats	Regional lists % vote	Seats	Total seats Seats	% seats
Labour	37.6	27	35.5	1	28	47.7
Plaid Cymru	28.4	9	30.6	8	17	28.3
Conservatives	15.8	1	6.5	8	9	15.0
Liberal Democrats	13.5	3	12.5	3	6	10.0
Others	4.7	0	5.1	0	0	0
Totals		40		20	60	

Figure 7.5 The election to the Welsh Assembly *This table shows the results of the election to the Welsh Assembly held in May 1999.*

8 Elections to the Scottish Parliament in 1999

On 6 May 1999, using the Additional Member system, Scottish voters returned 129 MSPs, but no party majority. Labour won the most seats with 56 (nine short of an overall majority) while the SNP formed the largest opposition party with 35 seats. The Conservatives failed to win any of the constituency seats, but won 18 of the top-up seats. Despite being the main party with the smallest number of seats at 17, the Liberal Democrats became part of the government through coalition. Three other MSPs were also elected - Robin Harper (Scottish Green Party), Tommy Sheridan (Scottish Socialist Party) and Dennis Canavan (the Labour MP rejected by Labour's selection committee and forced to stand as an independent). For many, the low turnout rate of 58.7% suggested that the hoped-for increased level of political engagement was still out of reach.

Adapted from Henderson & Sloat 1999.

Party	Constituencies % vote	Constituencies Seats won	Regional lists % vote	Regional lists Seats won	Total seats Seats won	Total seats % seats
Labour	38.8	53	33.6	3	56	43.4
Scottish National Party	28.7	7	27.3	28	35	27.1
Liberal Democrats	14.2	12	12.4	5	17	13.2
Conservatives	15.5	0	15.4	18	18	14.0
Scottish Green Party	0.0	0	3.6	1	1	0.8
Scottish Socialist Party	1.1	0	2.0	1	1	0.8
Member for Falkirk West	0.8	1	1.2	0	1	0.8
Others	0.9	0	4.5	0	0	0
Totals		73		56	129	

Figure 7.6 The election to the Scotish Parliament, 1999 *This table shows the results of the election to the Scottish Parliament held in May 1999.*

9 Local elections, May 2002

The 2002 local elections will be remembered as the year in which the British National Party got three councillors elected (in Burnley) and people voted for a monkey as Mayor of Hartlepool (the new Mayor, Stuart Drummond, worked as the mascot for the local football team and spent much of the campaign dressed in a monkey suit). But, in some ways, the more remarkable feature of the results was that they were not used by those who could not be bothered to vote as a stick to beat an unpopular government over the head. In the 1980s and 1990s, every May saw the slaughter of Tory councillors as voters vented their anger on the government. Not any more. Turnout was low - though all parties breathed a sigh of relief that it didn't fall to a record low. In fact, the 5% national increase to 35% marked a reversal of a long-term decline. Some 40 councils out of 174 being contested changed hands. Not all of them can be explained by national voting trends. For example, the Liberal Democrats seized the Labour citadel of Norwich, but lost their own stronghold of Richmond. Labour's strategists in particular will breathe a sigh of relief that after five years in power they have had to endure only modest losses of around 300 seats and a net loss of eight councils on the back of a 33% share of the vote. Labour's share was down c.7% on the figure won in 1998 when the seats were last contested, a modest reversal. For the Conservatives the results were not spectacular, but continued the modest local government revival.

Adapted from the *Guardian*, 4 May 2002.

Party	Councils Gain	Councils Lose	Councils Control	Councillors Gain	Councillors Lose	Councillors Total	Balance
Labour	4	12	63	103	442	2402	-339
Conservatives	15	6	42	357	119	2006	+238
Liberal Democrats	6	4	15	227	183	1262	+44
Independent	0	0	0	27	106	136	-79
Others	2	0	2	31	29	101	+2
No overall control	13	18	52	-	-	-	-

Figure 7.7 Local elections, 2002 *This table shows the results of the local elections held in May 2002. In addition to electing local councillors, seven towns elected mayors for the first time. In Hartlepool, the Supplementary Vote system was used to elect the mayor.*

10 Labour and the 2001 general election campaign

Labour targeted three groups of voters - (1) voters who had voted Labour in 1997 for the first time (2) other Labour voters whose support was lukewarm and (3) Labour voters who lived in low turnout areas. In addition, Labour focused on 148 seats, nearly all of them gains in 1997. Labour Party members were encouraged to concentrate their activities in these constituencies. The Labour Party's campaign focused mainly on two general themes, namely 'prudent' economic management and stability, and improved public services. Indeed, the two were often linked, with continued economic growth to provide the basis of increasing investment in education and health, without raising income tax. Three other features of Labour's campaign are worth noting. First, Labour gave little attention to the twin issues of the European Union and Britain's possible membership of the euro. Second, there were no significant attacks on the Liberal Democrats at national level. And third, the party issued a late warning about the danger of complacency or apathy. In view of the depressingly low turnout, it seems that the fears of the Labour leadership in this respect were entirely justified.

Adapted from Dorey 2002. See also *British Politics in Focus*, Second Edition, pp.212-17.

11 The Conservatives' and Liberal Democrats' election campaign

Commentators agree that the Conservatives fought a poor campaign. They focused heavily on three issues - (1) tax-and-spend (2) asylum seekers and (3) saving the pound from the euro. The problem was that Labour had a good reputation for economic competence and so it was difficult to make headway with the first issue, while the other two were low on voters' list of priorities. A further problem was tension within the Conservative Party over Europe. The leadership ruled out Britain's membership of the euro for the next Parliament, but some candidates publicly declared they were opposed to Britain ever joining the euro. The Liberal Democrats sought to depict the Conservatives as extremist and intolerant (particularly towards asylum seekers and the EU), while New Labour was attacked as being too timid on higher taxation and constitutional reform and as worryingly centralist and authoritarian on other issues. The Liberal Democrats claimed to be the only party genuinely committed to freedom and fairness, as well as to decentralisation. Most commentators agree that the party's campaign enhanced the reputation of the new Leader, Charles Kennedy.

Figure 7.8 The 2001 election campaign
This cartoon was produced in March 2001 as speculation grew that a general election would be called in May. In fact, it was delayed to June because of the foot-and-mouth crisis.

Adapted from Butler & Kavanagh 2002, the *Times*, 7 June 2001 and Dorey 2002. See also *British Politics in Focus*, Second Edition, pp.212-17.

12 The internet and the campaign

All the parties used modern technology in the election campaign. Telephone canvassing became much more widespread, replacing door-to-door canvassing. E-mails and text messages were sent by the major parties and websites were developed for the campaign. A survey conducted for the Hansard Society showed that:

● one-third of the electorate had e-mail or internet access during the 2001 election campaign (compared to 5% in 1997)

● 8% of those with access used the internet for some election-related activity

● 17% of 18 to 24-year-olds with access claimed that it was a 'very or fairly important' influence.

Coleman argues that 2001 was for the internet what 1959 had been for television. Both were elections in which a new medium found its way on to the political stage and was tested.

Adapted from Coleman 2001 and the *Guardian*, 30 July 2001.
See also *British Politics in Focus*, Second Edition, pp.212-17.

References

Billinghurst (2001) Billinghurst, A., 'General election 2001', *Sociology Review*, Vol.11.2, November 2001.
BES (2001) *British Election Study 2001*, ESRC, University of Essex, 2001.
Broughton (2000) Broughton, D., 'Political participation in Britain', *Politics Review*, Vol.9.4, April 2000.
Butler & Kavanagh (2002) Butler, D. & Kavanagh, D., *The British General Election of 2001*, Palgrave, 2002.
Coleman (2001) Coleman, S., 'Online campaigning' in *Norris (2001)*.
Curtice (2001) Curtice, J., 'General election - repeat or revolution', *Politics Review*, Vol.11.1, September 2001.
Dunleavy et al. (2000) Dunleavy, P., Gamble, A., Holliday, I., & Peele. G. (eds), *Developments in British Politics*, Vol.6, Macmillan, 2000.
Electoral Commission (2001) Electoral Commission, *Election 2001: The Official Results*, Politicos, 2001.
Faulks (2001) Faulks, K., 'Should voting be compulsory?' *Politics Review*, Vol.10.3, February 2001.
Game (2001) Game C., 'The changing ways we vote' in *Lancaster (2001)*.
Griffiths (2000) Griffiths, D., 'The Welsh Assembly', *Talking Politics*, Vol.12.2, Winter 2000.
Hansard Society (2001) *None of the Above: Non-Voters and the 2001 General Election 2001*, Hansard Society 2001.
Henderson & Sloat (1999) Henderson, A. & Sloat, A., 'New politics in Scotland? A profile of MSPs: part 1', *Talking Politics*, Vol.12.1, Summer 1999.
Hix (2000) Hix, S., 'Britain, the EU and the euro' in *Dunleavy et al. (2000)*.
Hopkins & Lynch (1999) Hopkins, S. & Lynch, P., 'The 1999 European elections', *Politics Review*, Vol.9.2, November 1999.
Labour (2001) *Ambitions for Britain*, Labour Party manifesto, Labour Party, 2001.
Lancaster (2001) Lancaster, S. (ed.), *Developments in Politics*, Vol.12, Causeway Press, 2001.
McNaughton (2001) McNaughton, N., 'Populist Movements', *Talking Politics* Vol.14.1, September 2001.
MORI (2001) *Survey of Attitudes During The 2001 General Election*, MORI Research Institute, 4 July 2001.
Norris (2001) Norris, P., *Britain Votes 2001*, Oxford University Press, 2001.
Rallings & Thrasher (2000) Rallings, C. & Thrasher, M., 'Assessing the significance of the elections in 1999', *Talking Politics*, Vol.12.2, Winter 2000.
Seyd (2001) Seyd, P., 'The Labour campaign' in *Norris (2001)*.
Whitely (2001) Whitely, P., Clarke, H., Sanders, D. & Stewart, M., 'Turnout' in *Norris (2001)*.

1 Funding of political parties and election campaigns

The Political Parties, Elections and Referendums Act (based on the recommendations of the Neill Committee) became law in November 2000, but it did not actually come into effect until February 2001.

Donations to political parties

In accordance with the recommendations of the Neill Committee, the Act decreed that:

- donations to political parties of more than £5,000 at national level, and more than £1,000 at local level, must be made public
- donations must be declared on a quarterly basis outside a general election campaign, but weekly during an election campaign
- donations can no longer be provided via 'blind trusts' (where a donor sets up a trust fund to finance a party while remaining anonymous)
- donations by companies must be approved by a ballot of shareholders and such ballots are to be held at least every four years
- donations from foreign sources are prohibited.

Figure 8.1 shows the most important sources of donations and funding for the Conservative and Labour parties during the first quarter of 2002.

(i) Donations and funding for the Conservative Party, January–March 2002.

Amount	Date	Source	Category of donor
£913,999	27 March	House of Commons (Opposition funding)	Public
£520,000	26 March	IIR Ltd	Company
£120,500	4 March	Sir Stanley Kalms	Individual
£110,000	3 March	Leonard Steinburg	Individual
£100,000	9 January	Philip Brown	Individual
£ 80,000	19 February	Arthur Brassington	Individual
£ 50,000	19 March	John Madejski	Individual
£ 17,250	31 March	Lord (Michael) Ashcroft	Individual

(ii) Donations and funding for the Labour Party, January–March 2002.

Amount	Date	Source	Category of donor
£ 2,000,000	13 January	Lord Sainsbury	Individual
£ 225,125	23 March	TGWU	Trade union
£ 200,000	24 February	Sir Ronald Cohen	Individual
£ 163,849	3 March	USDAW	Trade union
£ 120,125	16 February	UCW	Trade union
£ 76,119	23 February	MSF	Trade union
£ 50,000	8 February	Dr Paul Drayson	Individual
£ 37,250	17 February	GPMU	Trade union

Figure 8.1 Donations and the two main parties

The Liberal Democrats receive much lower sums than the two main parties, the lion's share emanating from Liberal clubs, associations, constituency parties and individual members. The largest donation to the Liberal Democrats during the first three months of 2002 was just under £25,000, from an individual, while the Richmond-upon-Thames Liberal Democrats' Council Group donated £11,220.

Expenditure during election campaigns

With regard to expenditure during election campaigns, the Political Parties, Elections and Referendums Act stipulated:

- a limit equivalent to £30,000 per constituency contested in a general election, so that if a party was fielding candidates in all 641 seats in Britain (ie excluding the 18 Northern Ireland seats), it would be entitled to spend a maximum of £19.23 million
- a limit of £45,000 per MEP (or candidate) in a region for European Parliament elections
- a limit of £12,000 for each constituency contested, and £80,000 for each region contested (linked to the regional 'top-up' used in these elections) for Scottish Parliament elections
- a limit of £10,000 per constituency, and £40,000 for each region for elections to the National Assembly for Wales.

To address the question of precisely when an election campaign begins (a party could spend money on advertising or mail-shots prior to the formal dissolving of Parliament, for example) the Act decreed that the spending limit would apply to the 365 days preceding polling day. However, because the Act did not come into effect until early 2001, a limit of just over £16 million was set for the June 2001 general election.

In order to ensure compliance with these and other electoral regulations, the Political Parties, Elections and Referendums Act set up an Electoral Commission.

Whereas in the 12 months preceding the 1997 election, the Conservative Party spent a total £28.3 million, during the corresponding period for the 2001 election, it spent £12.8 million. The Labour Party's overall expenditure in the 1997 and 2001 election campaigns was £25.7 million and £11.1 million respectively, while that of the Liberal Democrats was £3.5 million in 1997 and £1.4 million in 2001.

State funding of political parties?

The issue of how far political parties should be reliant on wealthy patrons or corporate backing for their income, and the potential for a 'conflict of interests', has revived the debate about whether a system of state funding should be introduced in Britain. Although the issue is not new, it has risen up the agenda following the allegations of sleaze which have been made against both the Conservatives and Labour. In the spring of 2002, for example, the issue of state funding was raised when it became known that the Labour leadership had accepted £100,000 from Richard Desmond, the owner of the *Daily Express* and a number of pornographic magazines.

Although the Conservative Party remains opposed to state funding, in the summer of 2002 a number of prominent Labour politicians came out in support for such a reform. The Liberal Democrats also support state funding. As if to imbue the issue with added relevance, it was announced in June 2002 that Britain's largest rail union, the Rail, Maritime and Transport Union, was slashing its donations to the Labour Party and withdrawing its funding from a number of senior Labour politicians, including John Prescott and Robin Cook, in protest at the Blair government's employment and transport policies.

Adapted from Fisher 2001 and the *Guardian*, 17 April, 13 June and 25 June 2002.

See also *British Politics in Focus*, Second Edition, pp.240-43.

2 The Conservative leadership election

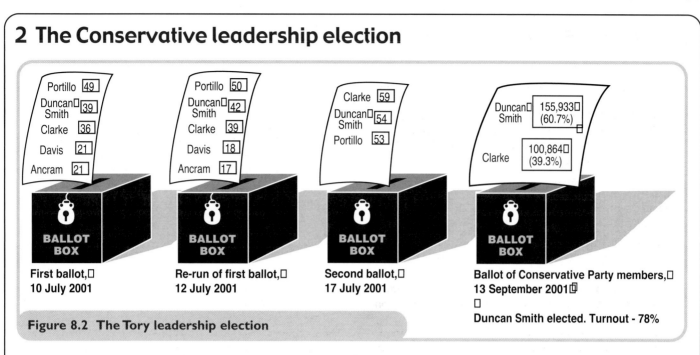

	Portillo 49			Portillo 50			Clarke 59			Duncan Smith	155,933 (60.7%)
	Duncan Smith 39			Duncan Smith 42			Duncan Smith 54			Clarke	100,864 (39.3%)
	Clarke 36			Clarke 39			Portillo 53				
	Davis 21			Davis 18							
	Ancram 21			Ancram 17							

BALLOT BOX	BALLOT BOX	BALLOT BOX	BALLOT BOX
First ballot, 10 July 2001	Re-run of first ballot, 12 July 2001	Second ballot, 17 July 2001	Ballot of Conservative Party members, 13 September 2001
			Duncan Smith elected. Turnout - 78%

Figure 8.2 The Tory leadership election

The 2001 Conservative leadership contest was the first in the party's history in which the mass membership was granted the final say as to which of two remaining candidates would become Leader. Previously, the Conservative Parliamentary Party had jealously guarded its autonomy from the extra-parliamentary party. Although MPs could, and sometimes were encouraged to, take soundings as to opinions in their constituency parties, the final decision remained with individual MPs. This all changed following William Hague's internal reforms of the Conservative Party.

First, though, a series of ballots had to be held to determine which two MPs would be presented to the mass membership for the final decision. The rules stipulated that, when more than three candidates presented themselves, a series of ballots would be held. The candidate polling fewest votes in each ballot would be eliminated from the contest so that, eventually, only two were left.

In the first ballot on 10 July 2001, two candidates tied for last place. This meant holding a re-run two days later. This time, Michael Ancram came last, albeit by just one vote. Following the re-run, David Davis announced that he was withdrawing from the contest. This ensured that the second ballot would be between three contenders - Ken Clarke, Michael Portillo and Iain Duncan Smith.

The result of the second ballot placed Michael Portillo, previously the frontrunner, last, his tally of 53 votes just one fewer than that obtained by Iain Duncan Smith. The winner was Ken Clarke. As a result, the final ballot, involving Conservative Party members on the basis of 'one member, one vote', was between a pro-European on the left of the party, and a strong Eurosceptic from the Thatcherite right.

The most notable feature of the campaign preceding the ballot was the lack of detailed or specific policy commitments and, instead, the often personal, acrimonious character of the contest. Animosities were not confined to the candidates. Other senior Conservatives used the leadership campaign to perpetuate existing enmities or settle old scores. The most notable of these attacks came from John Major who declared his support for Clarke and launched an attack against Margaret Thatcher. By encouraging anti-Maastricht rebels such as Iain Duncan Smith, he claimed, Thatcher had undermined his government in 1992-97. Major's allegations provoked a robust response from Norman

Tebbit who simultaneously lambasted both Major and Clarke.

When the result of the third and final ballot was announced on 13 September (a day later than originally planned, due to the terrorist attacks in New York and Washington two days previously), Iain Duncan Smith was the clear victor (see Figure 8.2).

While many on the right of the party jubilantly viewed Duncan Smith's victory as a clear endorsement of continued Thatcherism and Euroscepticism, some of Clarke's supporters were at pains to point out that, with almost 40% of grass-roots members voting for the former Chancellor, there remained a sizeable element within the Conservative Party nationally which still supported 'One Nation' Conservatism and which was also less hostile to Europe. Such an assessment, however, assumes that those Conservatives who voted for Clarke actually supported his brand of Conservatism and his pro-European views. This may not have been the case. Some may have voted for him primarily on the grounds that he was more likely to prove a vote-winner among the British electorate. In other words, some at least are likely to have shared the stance of the *Daily Mail* which supported Clarke in spite of, not because of, his pro-European stance.

Adapted from Lynch & Garnett 2002.

See also *British Politics in Focus*, Second Edition, pp.261-63.

Figure 8.3 Iain Duncan Smith
Iain Duncan Smith's victory was seen as a victory for continued Thatcherism and Euroscepticism.

3 The Liberal Democrats' election of Charles Kennedy

Paddy Ashdown's announcement, in January 1999, that he intended to resign as Leader of the Liberal Democrats that summer was unexpected not least because, under his leadership, the party had won a post-war record of 46 seats in the 1997 general election and it had secured representation on the Cabinet Committee on Constitutional Affairs. But, for some Liberal Democrats, the closer ties which Ashdown had cultivated with New Labour and the Blair government were a source of anxiety, particularly as the government seemed increasingly unlikely to deliver on its manifesto pledge to hold a referendum on electoral reform for Westminster. While this discontent had not erupted into an open challenge to Ashdown leadership, it may well have been a factor in Ashdown's decision to stand down. Ashdown himself, however, cited both pressure from his family and a desire to seek new political challenges.

There were no immediate 'heirs-apparent' to succeed Ashdown. As a result, there was speculation about the leadership ambitions of many Liberal Democrat MPs during the spring of 1999, with the names of about a quarter of the parliamentary party mentioned as possible contenders at various stages. When candidates formally announced their candidacy at the end of June, however, there were just five contenders - Jackie Ballard, Malcolm Bruce, Simon Hughes, Charles Kennedy and David Rendel. A sixth, Don Foster, withdrew from the contest at the last minute.

Despite a reputation for being a 'lightweight' (because he had appeared on light-hearted or satirical TV programmes such as *Have I Got News For You*), Charles Kennedy quickly emerged as the front-runner. He campaigned on a broad range of issues, such as increased public expenditure, joining the single European currency, pensions reform, and greater

Candidate	1st Round	2nd Round	3rd Round	4th Round
Charles Kennedy	22,724	+895=23,619	+1,545=25,164	+3,261=28,425
Simon Hughes	16,233	+1,145=17,378	+1,982=19,360	+2,473=21,833
Malcom Bruce	4,643	+598=5,241	+827=6,068	N/A
Jackie Ballard	3,978	+627=4,605	N/A	N/A
David Rendel	3,428	N/A	N/A	N/A

Figure 8.4 *Result of the Liberal Democrats' 1999 leadership contest.*

emphases on environmentalism and social justice. With regard to the relationship between the Liberal Democrats and the Blair government (a key issue for many Liberal Democrats), Kennedy merely made it clear that he supported the principle of cooperation and believed that it might even be extended to other policy areas, such as welfare reform.

The result of the Liberal Democrats' leadership contest was announced on 9 August 1999, the party's MPs, peers and ordinary members having voted using the Single Transferable Vote method of election (favoured by many Liberal Democrats for general elections). As Figure 8.4 illustrates, Charles Kennedy finally emerged victorious at the fourth stage, having attracted the support of 56.6% of the votes cast, compared to the 43.4% won by Hughes. The turnout, however, was a rather modest 62%, with barely 51,000 of the Liberal Democrats' 83,000 members voting. This was rather ironic for a party which places such a high emphasis on grass-roots political activity and the extension of democracy through greater decentralisation.

Adapted from Alderman & Carter 2000.

See also *British Politics in Focus*, Second Edition, pp.268-69.

4 Policy-making in the Labour Party

Question: *If you had to choose between one of the three methods for forming Labour party policy, which of the following would you favour?*

Members:	All	Very active	Inactive
Policy formed by the party leadership and endorsed by a postal vote of members	37%	15%	42%
Policy formed by annual conference	25%	35%	22%
Policy formed at regional and national policy forums	39%	50%	36%

Figure 8.5 Labour Party policy-making

Figure 8.5 shows the results of a survey conducted in 1999. Interestingly, only about a quarter of Labour Party members want the annual conference to make policy. More than a third opt for the plebiscitary model in which members vote on proposals made by the leadership. The favourite choice, however, was participation - making policy in the policy forums. About 11% of respondents had attended a policy forum. This translates into c.35,000 members. By large margins they found them interesting, friendly, efficiently-run and easy to understand. But only 32% thought the forums influential (36% not). More generally, 53% of those attending forums agreed that the party leadership did not pay a lot of attention to ordinary members. Labour's modernisation strategy meant transforming itself into an electable, participatory party. The survey shows that, in the minds of many members, the party is becoming a plebiscitary party. But only 15% of very active members want a plebiscitary party (compared to 42% of the inactive). As a result, moves in the direction of excluding activists will demotivate them.

Adapted from the *Guardian*, 11 October 1999.

See also *British Politics in Focus*, Second Edition, pp.247-50.

5 Labour Party membership

Organisation	2002	2001	2000	Earlier
Labour	280,000	×	311,000	400,465 (1996)
Lib Dems	76,023	74,176	71,641	98,611 (1996)
Conservatives	330,000	×	318,000	350,000-400,000
Greens	5,000	4,000	×	3,500 (1996)
SNP	*Figures are confidential*			
Plaid Cymru	11,000	×	×	*no previous figures*
TUC	×	69 unions 6.7m members	76 unions 6.8m members	73 unions (1996) 6.7m members
Amnesty International	×	154,611	136,348	125,362 (1998)
Greenpeace	×	193,500	176,000	194,309 (1998)
Friends of the Earth	×	110,248	105,185	94,528 (1996)
CND *(approx figures)*	×	27-32,000	25-30,000	*no previous figures*
Stonewall	×	6,000	5,000	*no previous figures*
RSPB	1.19m	1.11m	1.4m	925,000 (1996)
RSPCA	×	49,760	54,000	29,504 (1996)
National Trust	2.8m	2.7m	×	2.29m (1996)

Figure 8.6 Party membership in recent years
This table shows the membership of political parties in recent years, compared to that of selected pressure groups.

In January 2002, Labour's General Secretary, David Triesman, admitted that disengagement of young people from party politics was threatening the lifeblood of democracy. Triesman said that Labour Party membership had fallen by 10% since January 2001, down to 280,000. The Tories claim a higher membership - over 300,000. The Liberal Democrats admit falling from a peak of 100,000 to 71,000 in 2000, but they rose to 74,000 in January 2001 and 76,000 in January 2002. The Labour Party's all-time low was in 1991 (261,000 members). At the time of the 1997 general election, it had 401,000 members. The drop in numbers in 2002, Triesman claimed, was, in part, the result of an administrative change - the party was terminating any membership more than five months in subscription arrears. This led to a drop of 13,000 members at a stroke. But Triesman acknowledged that there was a move away from political organisations, especially by younger voters. Labour's average membership age was creeping up to between 40 and 45, he said. In a move that will be welcomed by party activists, Triesman said that, after an era of central control, Labour had to take more risks by opening up debate inside the party. He acknowledged that Labour's policy forum, set up as an alternative to party conference policy-making, lacked credibility. 'Forum members put up an idea and then there was absolutely no way of tracking what had happened to the idea', he said. He was considering publishing how many manifesto ideas in 2001 came from individuals within the forum and he argued that more minority positions should go from forums to the party conference so there could be public debate and division. Triesman and Party Chair, Charles Clarke, have an uphill task. They need to be seen to be loosening Millbank reins since disillusionment with 'control freak' politics is deep inside the party itself, while outside the drift away from traditional politics continues.

Adapted from the *Guardian*, 29 January 2002.

See also *British Politics in Focus*, Second Edition, pp.247-50.

6 Labour Party activism

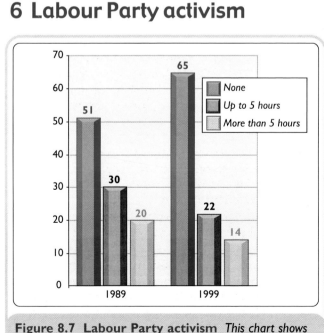

Figure 8.7 Labour Party activism *This chart shows the time that Labour Party members devote to party activities in an average month. The figures are percentages.*

Figure 8.7 shows that there has been a long-term decline in activism in the Labour Party. If the trends in activism are projected to 2002, then currently around 70% of a shrinking membership do no work at all for the Labour Party in the average month, compared to 50% in 1989. Members are important because they provide three key resources in elections. First, they provide 'clean' money - donations untainted by the idea the donor is seeking influence. Second, they provide 'ambassadors in the community' - people who promote the party among friends and relatives. And third, they provide the foot soldiers in local campaigns. Tightened restrictions on campaign spending mean that campaigns crucially depend on volunteers. Research shows that such campaigning has an important and growing influence on voting behaviour. So why has there been a reduction in activism? Some of the causes derive from social changes which cannot be influenced by the party leadership - such as the growth of leisure activities and long working hours. But, in one respect, the party leadership is responsible. Party organisation is now more centrally controlled and the policy-making structures are increasingly seen by members as weak and ineffective. These structures make it difficult for the leadership to be held to account, so members feel marginalised.

Adapted from the *Guardian*, 18 June 2002.
See also *British Politics in Focus*, Second Edition, pp.247-50.

7 Minor parties and the 2001 general election

Party	Votes	% Share	Av vote %	Candidates	Lost Deposits
UK Independence	390,575	1.5	2.1	428	422
Green	166,487	0.6	2.8	145	135
Scottish Socialist	72,279	0.3	3.3	72	62
Socialist Alliance	60,496	0.2	1.8	98	95
Socialist Labour	57,536	0.2	1.4	114	113
British National	47,129	0.2	3.9	33	28
Liberal	10,920	0.0	3.2	9	8
Pro-Life Alliance	9,453	0.0	0.7	37	37
Independent	127,590	0.5	2.2	139	128

Figure 8.8 Minor parties in 2001 *This table shows the performance of minor parties in the 2001 general election.*

In the general election of June 2001, a relatively high proportion of the vote was won by parties other than the Conservatives, Labour or Liberal Democrats. The most significant performances were those of the nationalist parties in Scotland and Wales. In Wales, Plaid Cymru advanced to its highest share of the vote yet in a UK general election. Its 14.3% of the vote was nearly 3% higher than its previous best of 11.5% in 1970. In contrast, the SNP's share of the vote dropped an unexpected 2% to 20.1%. Neither party, however, came anywhere close to its performance in the first devolution election (when Plaid Cymru won 28.4% and the SNP 28.7%). This suggests that devolved elections are a more favourable forum for nationalist parties.

UK Independence Party

Of the remaining smaller parties, by far the biggest challenge was posed by the UK Independence Party (UKIP) which, following the demise of the Referendum Party, became the sole vehicle for the anti-European cause. Even so, it failed to make the impact the Referendum Party made in 1997. On average in those seats fought by UKIP in 2001 and by either the UKIP or Referendum Party in 1997, the share of the vote was down 1.6%, with the heaviest falls in those seats where the anti-European vote was highest in 1997. The party tended to do better in seats with an older population and in seats where a low proportion of people had degrees, away from most urban constituencies and in the southern half of England, outside London.

Socialist parties

The most successful of the small parties was the Scottish Socialist Party which fought all 72 seats in Scotland, following the election of its Leader, Tommy Sheridan, to the Scottish Parliament in 1999. It won 3.1% of the vote in Scotland, the biggest percentage of the vote for a minor party since the nationalist parties broke through in the 1970s. South of the border, the far left made less of an impact. Even so, candidates from the Socialist Alliance and Socialist Labour Party in combination secured an average vote of 2% in England, up from 1.7% in 1997 - despite doubling the number of seats they fought. As a result, more votes were cast for far left candidates across Britain as a whole than at any election since 1945. Far left candidates did best in working-class, urban constituencies.

Figure 8.9 Dr Richard Taylor *One of the major surprises of the 2001 general election was Dr Richard Taylor's victory in Wyre Forest. Taylor stood as an indepedent, campaigning against the closure of a local hospital. He won a landslide, beating the sitting Labour MP by nearly 18,000 votes.*

The Green Party

The Greens recorded their best ever performance in a UK election with an average vote of 2.8% in the 145 seats they contested. In seats fought in both 1997 and 2001, their share of the vote increased by an average of 1.6%. The party's share of the vote rose less the higher the level of car ownership in a constituency, suggesting the party's vote was shaped by its environmentalist message.

The British National Party

The far right British National Party (BNP) was the only party not represented in Parliament to win over 10% of the vote in a constituency (it achieved this in both Oldham constituencies and Burnley). This can be explained, in part at least, by the high level of racial tension in Oldham at the time of the election. Across Britain as a whole, the party's share of the vote rose by just 0.3% on average in the 13 seats the party fought in both 1997 and 2001.

Adapted from Curtice & Steed 2002.
See also *British Politics in Focus*, Second Edition, pp.270-76.

8 Political parties in Northern Ireland

Following the 'Yes' vote in the 1998 referendum on the Good Friday Agreement, elections were held for the new 108-member Assembly, using the Single Transferable Vote system. The results are shown in Figure 8.10, Table (i). The vote showed a marked division within the unionist community, with the hard-line DUP receiving only 3% less of the vote than the UUP, while on the nationalist side, Sinn Fein's share of the vote was only 4% less than that of the SDLP.

While the fundamental divide between the unionist and nationalist/republican blocs dominated voting behaviour in 2001 (see Table (ii) in Figure 8.10), there was a struggle within each bloc for supremacy. Within the unionist bloc, Ian Paisley's DUP continued in its aim to replace David Trimble's UUP as the voice of unionism (the DUP won three seats from the UUP). Within the nationalist/republican bloc, Sinn Fein continued in its aim to replace the SDLP as the voice of nationalism/republicanism (Sinn Fein won two new seats). The election confirmed the growing scepticism of unionists about the Good Friday Agreement and showed the increasing strength of Sinn Fein at the expense of the SDLP, making this a 'watershed' election.

(i) Result of 1998 election to the Northern Ireland Assembly

Unionists				Nationalists				Others	
UUP		DUP		SDLP		SF			
%	seats	%	seats	%	seats	%	seats	%	seats
21	28	18	20	22	24	18	18	20	18

(ii) Northern Ireland results in the 2001 election (1997 result in brackets)

Party	Seats	Share of votes	Change from 1997
Ulster Unionist Party	6 (10)	26.8%	-5.9%
Democratic Unionist Party	5 (2)	22.5%	+8.9%
SDLP	3 (3)	21.7%	-3.1%
Sinn Fein	4 (2)	21.0%	+5.6%
Other	0 (1)	8.0%	-5.5%

Figure 8.10 Result of elections in Northern Ireland, 1998 and 2001

Adapted from Mitchell et al. 2001 and Hopkins 2001.
See also *British Politics in Focus*, Second Edition, pp.273-74.

9 Britain's 'party system' in the 21st century

The traditional view is that there have been two main eras of party politics since 1945. The first was from 1945 to 1970 and consisted of two dominant and quite closely competitive parties, each commanding 40% or more of the vote with relatively small swings at each election. The largest swing in support for one of the main parties was the 6% fall in the Conservative vote between 1959 and 1964. The second era began in 1974 with the break up of the two-party system and the rise of the Liberals, nationalists and independent Ulster Unionists. The combined share of support for Labour and the Conservatives fell from 89.4% in 1970 (a peak of 96.8% in 1951) to 75% in February 1974 and has not subsequently gone over the 80.6% reached in 1979. While Conservative support partially recovered after 1974, Labour's did not. Party support was fluid in 1974-83, but from 1983 up to and including 1992, the British party system seemed to have settled down into a position of Conservative dominance on a minority vote, and Labour weakness. The general election of 1997 seems to have marked a turning point, perhaps the beginning of a new, third era. First, there is the apparent long-term decline in the Conservative vote. Labour's second landslide in a row in 2001 suggests that 1997 was no blip. Second, although Labour and the Conservatives remain the two dominant parties in the House of Commons, the Liberal Democrats have made important gains and may even be able to challenge the Conservatives for the position of main opposition party at the next general election. Third, the election of independents Martin Bell in 1997 and Richard Taylor in 2001 suggests that the local context can make all the difference. Fourth, there is much greater diversity away from Westminster. Longer-term trends in voting behaviour - particularly party dealignment and the rise of issue voting - combined with more recent initiatives (such as devolution, and the use of alternative electoral systems which enshrine an element of proportionality), have produced multi-party systems and coalition governments in Scotland and Wales. And fifth, in local council elections, there has been a growth in success for third parties (such as the BNP's victories in Burnley in the local elections of 2002), while the establishment of the Greater London Authority has provided a platform for the Green Party. In general, 'majoritarian two-partyism' no longer seems a particularly convincing description of the UK as a whole.

Adapted from Webb 2000 and Baston 2001.
See also *British Politics in Focus*, Second Edition, pp.276-80.

References

Alderman & Carter (2000) Alderman, K. & Carter, N., 'The Liberal Democrat leadership election of 1999', *Parliamentary Affairs*, Vol.53.2, April 2000.
Baston (2001) Baston, L., 'The party system' in *Seldon (2001)*.
Butler & Kavanagh (2002) Butler, D. & Kavanagh, D., *The British General Election of 2001*, Palgrave, 2002.
Curtis & Steed (2002) Curtis, J. & Steed, M., 'An analysis of the results' in *Butler & Kavanagh (2002)*.
Fisher (2001) Fisher, J., 'Campaign finance: elections under new rules' in *Norris (2001)*.
Hopkins (2001) Hopkins, S., 'General election 2001: Northern Ireland, a place apart', *Politics Review*, Vol.11.2, November 2001.

Lynch & Garnett (2002) Lynch, P. & Garnett, M., 'Conservatives' convictions: 2001 Tory leadership election', *Politics Review*, Vol.11.3, February 2002.
Mitchell et al. (2001) Mitchell, P., O'Leary, B. & Evans, G., 'Northern Ireland: flanking extremists bite the moderates and emerge in their clothes' in *Norris (2001)*.
Norris (2001) Norris, P. (ed.), *Britain Votes 2001*, Oxford University Press, 2001.
Seldon (2001) Seldon, A. (ed.), *The Blair Effect: the Blair Government 1997-2001*, Little, Brown and Company, 2001.
Webb (2000) Webb, P., *The Modern British Party System*, Sage, 2000.

1 Class and voting

Figure 9.1 shows that, in 2001, the Conservative Party lost ground among the middle classes (the A, B and C1s) while Labour increased its middle-class support. Taking the figures for the A, B and C1s together, only two percentage points now separate Labour from the Conservatives in terms of their respective middle-class support. Dorey argues that the Labour gains among middle-class voters vindicate the Labour government's explicit strategy of targeting Middle England.

By targeting Middle England, however, Labour lost some support from working-class voters (the C2, D and Es). Its lead over the Conservatives within the working class overall fell from 31% to 21%. Compared to 1997, Labour's share of the D and E vote (the semi-skilled and unskilled working class) decreased from 57% to 50%, votes being lost in almost equal measure to the Conservatives and the Liberal Democrats. This loss of support for Labour among the Ds and Es did not, however, translate into a great loss of seats. It merely reduced the size of Labour's majorities in some of its safe seats.

Overall, though, there is still a relatively clear relationship between class and voting behaviour in British elections, with

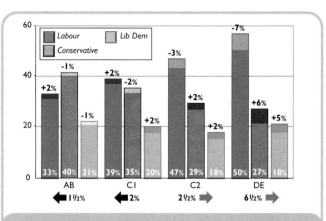

Figure 9.1 Class and voting (a) *This chart shows how voting according to class differed in 1997 and 2001. Each column shows the percentage voting for one of the three main parties in 2001 and the rise or fall in the percentage compared to 1997.*

Labour still more popular among working-class voters and the Conservatives (just) with middle-class voters. But the statistical relationship appears to be weakening and is probably weaker now than at any time in post-war British politics (see Figure 9.2). Curtice argues, however, that this does not necessarily endorse the class dealignment thesis. He argues that voters are changing their behaviour not because their motivations have altered but rather because the choices on offer from the parties have changed.

Adapted from Kellner 2001b, Curtice 2001 and Dorey 2002. See also *British Politics in Focus*, Second Edition, pp.282-87.

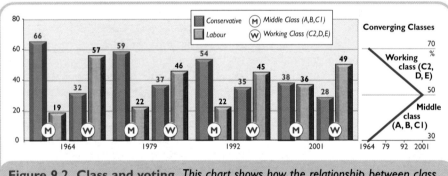

Figure 9.2 Class and voting *This chart shows how the relationship between class and voting for the two main parties has changed between 1964 and 2001.*

2 Gender and voting

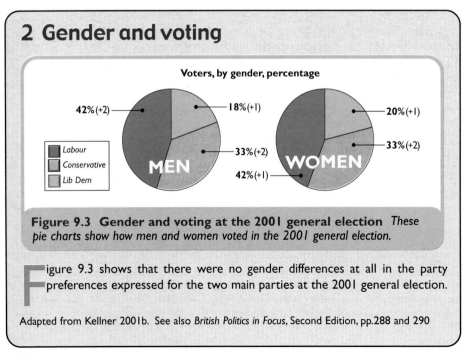

Figure 9.3 Gender and voting at the 2001 general election *These pie charts show how men and women voted in the 2001 general election.*

Figure 9.3 shows that there were no gender differences at all in the party preferences expressed for the two main parties at the 2001 general election.

Adapted from Kellner 2001b. See also *British Politics in Focus*, Second Edition, pp.288 and 290

3 Electoral volatility

Electoral volatility (other than a switch between voting and non-voting, which is discussed below - see Section II below) was not a significant factor in the 2001 election, The net change in votes was the smallest for any election after a full Parliament for almost 50 years and the net turnover of seats was the lowest for 100 years. The Pedersen index of volatility, ie the sum of the net percentage change since the previous election was 5.0, the lowest since 1955.

Adapted from Crewe 2002. See also *British Politics in Focus*, Second Edition, pp.294-96.

4 Age and voting

In 2001, the thesis that younger electors tend to vote Labour and older voters tend to vote Conservative held true. Figure 9.4 shows that 47% of voters aged 18-34 chose Labour, while 29% chose the Conservatives. Conversely, only in the 65+ age group did support for the Conservative Party exceed that for Labour. Support for the Liberal Democrats was fairly evenly distributed over all age groups.

It used to be thought that as people got older they became more inclined to vote Conservative. This assumption, however, was challenged by Butler and Stokes in 1969, when they put forward their 'generational cohorts' theory. They suggested that many of the Conservative-voting elderly in the 1960s would have acquired their political views and values from their parents in the early part of the 20th century when the Labour Party had not fully established itself as a credible party of government and before the marked decline in the Liberal Party had set in. Since many of the parents of those who were elderly in 1969 were Conservatives and would have transmitted their Conservative views to their children, this would explain why many of the elderly in the 1960s were Conservatives. It was not that they had become Conservative when they grew older. They had always been Conservatives.

Evidence in support of this theory can be found by examining voting behaviour over the last two decades. Figure 9.5 shows that more than half of all voters aged 65+ voted Conservative in 1983, giving the Conservatives a 25% lead over Labour among this section of the population. In 2001, however, 42% voted Conservative, compared to 37% voting Labour. In other words, during the last five general

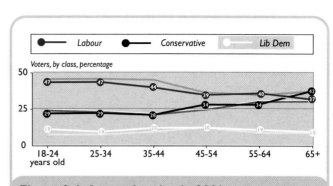

Figure 9.4 Age and voting in 2001
This graph shows the way in which different age groups voted in the 2001 general election.

elections, the Conservatives' support among voters in the 65+ age group has fallen by 11%. It is also worth noting that among the 55-64 age group in the 2001 general election, 40% voted Labour compared to 34% voting Conservative. This suggests that the Conservatives' advantage among the elderly is, quite literally, dying out.

Adapted from Kellner 2001b and Dorey 2002.

See also *British Politics in Focus*, Second Edition, pp.288 and 290.

How people aged 65+ voted, 1983-2001 (%)					
	1983	**1987**	**1992**	**1997**	**2001**
Conservative	53	50	49	44	42
Labour	28	27	36	34	37
Lib/Lib Dems	19	23	14	16	18

Figure 9.5 How people aged 65+ voted, 1983-2001 in percentages
This table shows how people aged over 65 voted in elections between 1983 and 2001.

5 Leadership and voting

During his first term, Tony Blair was, on the one hand, described as weak and indecisive but, on the other, criticised for being arrogant and autocratic. Nevertheless, he remained the most popular Party Leader by a wide margin - see Figure 9.6.

A poll published a few days before the 2001 election showed that, when asked 'who do you think would make the

Best Leader	1992	1997	2001	Change 1992-2001
Conservative	40	21	13	- 27
Labour	30	34	47	+17
Liberal Democrats	9	8	5	- 4

Figure 9.6 Who is the best Party Leader?
This table shows which of the Leaders of the three main parties were chosen as 'the best' between 1992 and 2001.

best Prime Minister?', 54% chose Blair and only 18% opted for William Hague, the Leader of the Conservative Party. Hague fared slightly better in another poll which asked people to rate how well he was doing his job. But, while 25% chose 'good' or 'excellent', this was still a long way behind Blair's 56%.

While William Hague lacked credibility with the electorate, most commentators agree that Charles Kennedy, the Liberal Democrat Leader, had a good election campaign. This helped to boost his personal popularity during the run up to polling day.

It is not possible, however, to determine the precise effect that leadership and perceptions of leadership have on the outcomes of elections. This is because it is difficult to separate voters' attitudes towards Party Leaders from a whole range of other possible variables.

Adapted from the *Observer*, 3 June 2001, Butler & Kavanagh 2002 and Dorey 2002.

See also *British Politics in Focus*, Second Edition, pp.300-03.

6 Issues and voting

	Issue	Voters citing issue as important in deciding how to vote		Issue	Voters citing issue as important in deciding how to vote
1.	The NHS	89%	7.	Taxation	64%
2.	Law and order/crime	82%	8.	Public transport	64%
3.	Education	81%	9.	Asylum/immigration	52%
4.	The economy	74%	10.	Membership of the EU	43%
5.	Employment	70%	11.	Joining the euro	40%
6.	Pensions	65%			

Figure 9.7 Issue saliency in the 2001 election
This table shows the percentage of voters citing particular issues as important in deciding how to vote.

Figure 9.7, which shows which issues voters judged as 'salient' (ie important) in 2001, is quite similar to the results of the same sort of exercise carried out at the time of the 1997 election. This may have been one reason why the election outcomes in 1997 and 2001 were very much the same in terms of the extent of Labour's victory.

Figure 9.7 shows that the National Health Service and Education, traditionally seen as 'Labour issues', rated very high in terms of voter saliency in 2001. Other issues which at pre-1997 elections had been high on the list of voter concerns (law and order, the economy and taxation) still featured at the 2001 election. But, more significantly, they were not now seen as 'Conservative issues'. For example, voters were concerned about crime and social disorder, but they no longer assumed that only the Conservatives had the answers.

While Labour seemed to benefit from voters' issue priorities at the 2001 election, the Conservatives did not. Two of the main policy areas on which the Tories concentrated in their campaign (Europe and asylum seekers) were low on voters' saliency list. Dorey argues that, to some extent, the Tories were constrained in their selection of campaign issues because Labour had already stolen what had at one time been seen as Conservative vote-winners (eg privatisation, tight control of public expenditure and low rates of income tax).

On the other hand, by promising a referendum on the euro some time after the election, Labour managed successfully to sidestep the one issue which could have caused it some difficulty - Britain's possible adoption of the European single currency. Although the official Conservative policy on the euro was supported by 70% of the public, voters did not regard it as a salient issue for the 2001 general election. Besides, if an issue is to cause large numbers of voters to switch between political parties it has to satisfy other tests. Voters have to see clear differences between the parties, for example. Yet extraordinarily, ICM found that, at the end of the campaign and despite heavy media coverage of the euro issue, a majority of Conservative voters still did not recognise the official Conservative line.

Issue voting and issue saliency relate to voter perceptions of competence. Dorey's analysis of relevant polling questions reveals that Labour fared measurably better than the Conservatives in 2001 on both prospective (likely future performance) and retrospective (past performance) voter evaluations over a range of issues.

Nonetheless, it is difficult to disentangle exact links between particular issues and voting behaviour. In any case, voters rarely decide their vote on a single issue, even a salient one. Exceptionally, this can occur at a local level but, in general, a problem with the issue voting model (even if combined with 'perceptions of competence') is that voting is not simply an instrumental act (what's good for me?). It is also often in part expressive (how do I feel about voting for this party?).

Adapted from Butler & Kavanagh 2002 and Dorey 2002.

See also *British Politics in Focus*, Second Edition, pp.296-303.

7 The Wyre Forest constituency at the 2001 general election

In Wyre Forest, a retired consultant, Richard Taylor, stood in the 2001 general election as the Kidderminster Hospital and Health Concern candidate, his main concern being to highlight local anxiety and anger over the closure of Kidderminster Hospital's Accident and Emergency Unit. Such was the local concern that Taylor transformed a Labour majority of 6,946 into a majority of 17,630, having polled more than 28,000 votes. For an independent candidate to poll so many votes and defeat the sitting MP is nothing short of phenomenal. His success confirmed opinion poll evidence concerning issue saliency and the priority which voters ascribed to the NHS.

Adapted from Dorey 2002.

8 The press support for the main parties

Figure 9.8 shows that, as in 1997, the Labour Party had the support of a significant part of the press at the time of the 2001 general election. Indeed, in 2001, there was a record level of support for Labour from the national dailies and Sundays including, for the first time, the *Times* and *Daily Express*.

What the data in Figure 9.8 does not show, however, is the quality of press support for Labour - namely, the fact that much of it was lukewarm or qualified. There was a noticeable increase in negative stories about Labour compared to 1997, and press coverage in the early stages of the 2001 campaign was not favourable to the party. In other words, by 2001, Labour had disarmed and contained the press but not converted it. It should also be noted that press support for Labour in 2001 may have been a reflection of the fact that the outcome of the election was seen as a foregone conclusion. The increasingly consumer-oriented press did not want to be seen to be on the losing side.

If many of the newspapers offered less than wholehearted support for Labour, the picture for the Conservatives was worse. Only two of the national dailies, supported the Conservatives - the *Daily Telegraph* and the *Daily Mail*. And, not only did the *Mail* noticeably limit its front-page coverage of the election campaign, it could not bring itself to endorse William Hague as a possible future Prime Minister.

Adapted from MacArthur 2001 and Scammel & Harrop 2002 .

See also *British Politics in Focus*, Second Edition, pp.304-08.

Newspaper	Circulation (000s)		Preferred winner	
	2001	1997	2001	1997
Dailies				
Sun	3,288	3,935	Lab	Lab
Daily Mail	2,337	2,127	Con	Con
Mirror	2,056	2,390	Lab	Lab
Daily Telegraph	989	1,126	Con	Con
Express	929	1,208	Lab	Con
Times	667	772	Lab	Eurosceptic
Daily Star	585	660	Lab	Lab
Guardian	362	402	Lab	Lab
Independent	197	256	Not Con	Lab
Financial Times	176	304	Lab	Lab
Sundays				
News of the World	3,675	4,365	Lab	Lab
Mail on Sunday	2,238	2,112	Con	Con
Sunday Mirror	1,761	2,238	Lab	Lab
Sunday People	1,277	1,978	Lab	Lab
Sunday Times	1,206	1,310	Lab	Con
Sunday Express	870	1,159	Lab	Con
Sunday Telegraph	767	909	Con	Con
Observer	408	454	Lab	Lab
Independent on Sunday	211	276	Lab	Lab
Sunday Business	53	-	Lab	-

Figure 9.8 The press and the 2001 general election

9 To what extent did the press set the agenda in the 2001 campaign?

One argument is that the press did not set the agenda at all. Rather, journalists realised that people were, in general, uninterested and uninspired and they reflected this in the way in which they covered the election. Certainly, the *Daily Mail* was not the only paper to keep its election coverage off the front page. Scammell and Harrop conclude that the 2001 election received the most subdued press coverage for 30 years.

A second argument is that the press attempted to set the agenda, but with little success. Figure 9.9 presents a statistical breakdown of front-page lead stories and editorials during the 2001 election campaign. A comparison with Figure 9.7 above (on issue saliency) reveals little similarity between what the press and the public each saw as the most important issues. Whereas health matters topped the table in terms of issue saliency, they received little in the way of front-page press coverage. Conversely, the EU was the top front-page lead story and, by a long way, the single topic receiving most editorial consideration, but it rated very low in terms of public concern.

Adapted from MacArthur 2001 and Scammel & Harrop 2002.

See also *British Politics in Focus*, Second Edition, pp.304-08.

Topic	Front-page lead stories		Editorials	
	Number	%	Number	%
European Union	21	18	33	12
Party strategies/prospects	16	14	18	7
Prescott (punch)	16	14	11	4
Opinion polls	11	9	3	1
Taxation/public spending	7	6	14	5
Public services	6	5	12	4
Asylum/race	5	4	21	8
Exhortation to vote/advice on voting	4	3	17	6
Health	3	2	18	7
Party Leaders	3	2	15	6
Manifestos	2	2	14	5
Thatcher	-	-	6	2
Northern Ireland	-	-	6	2
Tactical voting/strong opposition needed	-	-	5	2
Constitutional reforms	-	-	5	2
Other	24	20	73	27
Total	118	99	271	100

Figure 9.9 Press reporting in the 2001 election campaign *This table shows the issues that the press focused on during the 2001 election campaign.*

10 The press and voting behaviour

Given that, from the outset, there was not much doubt about the outcome of the 2001 general election in terms of the eventual winner, there is little evidence that the press had much direct or short-term influence on the voting behaviour of its readers. Looking at the influence of the press in the longer term, however, political scientists are still divided about the extent to which newspapers reinforce people's outlooks or determine the way in which they vote. In recent years, perhaps more significant than the way in which the press influences the behaviour of voters is the way in which it affects the positions taken by the leadership of the main parties. Certainly, there is evidence to suggest that the Labour leadership repositioned itself, in part at least, to win the support of sections of the press.

Adapted from MacArthur 2001 and Scammel & Harrop 2002. See also *British Politics in Focus*, Second Edition, pp.304-08.

11 Turnout

The most striking feature of the 2001 general election was the dramatic fall in turnout. At 59.4% for the UK as a whole, the figure was 12% lower than that in 1997, which itself was the lowest turnout for 62 years. Box 9.1 provides some key statistics.

Box 9.1 Key statistics

- 59.4% was the lowest recorded turnout since 1918 (when the situation was complicated by end of war confusion and by a trebling of the electorate following an extension of the franchise)
- Lowest turnout: 34.1% - Liverpool Riverside
- Highest turnout in UK: 80.5% - Ulster Mid
- Highest turnout in Great Britain: 72.3% - Winchester
- Number of constituencies where turnout was under 50%: 68 (none in 1997)

- Fall in turnout, from 1997, was fairly uniform across every region in UK (except for Northern Ireland) at between 11.6% and 13.1% (in Northern Ireland turnout increased by 0.6%)
- A far higher proportion of the electorate abstained (41%) than voted for the winning party (25%)
- Turnout was twice as high among older voters (65 and over) than among younger voters (18-24): 79% to 38%.

12 Reasons for low turnout

In their analysis of the results of the 2001 general election, Curtice and Steed examine three possible reasons for decreasing turnout.

1. Long-term changes such as a decline in party identification

Decline in party identification has produced an electorate that is less motivated, more disillusioned and less trustful of politics and politicians. Young people and the less well educated are particularly likely not to vote. Significantly, turnout fell least in those constituencies with a relatively old age profile and a relatively well-educated population. The variations, however, are not great and there is some doubt whether a lack of trust can account for the significant fall in turnout. Allegations of sleaze and perceptions of dishonesty and insincerity may well have led to politicians being held in lower regard than ever before. But these allegations and perceptions have been around for some time. On their own, they cannot account for the steep fall in turnout in 2001.

2. Shorter-term changes

Shorter-term changes such as the obvious large lead for Labour in the opinion polls and a perceived lack of difference between the parties may have played a part. An ICM poll carried out shortly before the 2001 election found that 57% of the electorate agreed (39% disagreed) with the statement: 'It won't make much difference to my daily life who wins the coming election'.

The increased turnout in Northern Ireland may be significant in this regard. Here, the election was seen to matter (for many unionist voters it was seen as a referendum on the future of the Good Friday Agreement) and there were clear differences between the parties.

On its own, however, the perceived absence of significant differences between the main parties cannot satisfactorily account for the drastic fall in turnout. Turnout was considerably higher at the height of the 'post-war consensus' period during which there was thought to be little difference between the Conservatives and Labour. There is also little evidence to support the argument that turnout was low because the result of the election was a foregone conclusion

Cohen points out that there were elections in the 1950s and 1980s when the outcome was not in doubt but at which voters turned out in much higher numbers than in 2001.

3. Dissatisfaction among Labour supporters

According to this argument, many Labour supporters, especially in the older industrial 'heartlands', were alienated by New Labour's willingness to appeal to the middle classes and its courting of Big Business. If this were the case, then the drop in turnout would be greatest in those constituencies where the Labour vote had previously been highest. There is some evidence to support this thesis. Voters were particularly likely to stay at home in Labour's safer seats. Of course, precisely because the drop in turnout was higher in Labour safe seats, this abstention did not translate into a corresponding loss of seats for Labour.

It should also be pointed out, however, that turnout in safe seats is normally lower than in marginals. But the argument looks strong when the evidence for the 2001 election shows that 96 of the 100 lowest turnout constituencies were safe Labour seats.

It should also be noted that the UK is not alone in experiencing a fall in the rates of turnout at elections (see Chapter 7, Section 2 above). Similar trends are occurring elsewhere and some commentators have linked this to broader cultural changes in an increasingly individualistic and post-modern world.

Adapted from Cohen 2001, Kellner 2001a, Curtice 2001, Butler & Kavanagh 2002, Curtice & Steed 2002, Bartle 2002 and Dorey 2002.

See also *British Politics in Focus*, Second Edition, pp.313-18.

13 Tactical voting

Tactical voting occurs when voters, rather than choosing their preferred party, vote instead for another party in order to prevent the party they least like from winning the seat. Anti-Conservative tactical voting was important at the 1997 general election, benefiting both the Labour Party and the Liberal Democrats. There was also evidence of tactical voting at the 2001 election and, once again, it was more often than not used against Conservative candidates. There had been speculation in advance of polling day that tactical voting would substantially increase, but, in the event, this did not happen.

There is evidence that tactical voting (Labour supporters voting Liberal Democrat) probably helped the Liberal Democrats to defeat Conservative candidates in Ludlow, North Norfolk and Teignbridge. There were also other seats - notably Kingston & Surbiton - where narrow Liberal Democrat wins in 1997 were converted into substantial majorities for the party, strongly suggesting tactical voting. In most other Conservative/Liberal Democrat marginals, however, Labour voters do not appear to have voted tactically in significant numbers. Tactical voting was, however, thought to be significant in helping Labour to win some crucial marginal seats.

The 'vote swap' campaign

The musician Billy Bragg achieved a certain amount of national publicity for his 'vote swap' campaign. Bragg claimed that the object of his campaign was wider than just tactical voting, describing it as 'spontaneous electoral reform' and as a way of encouraging proportional representation 'by the back door'.

Bragg launched a website from Dorset in which he urged Labour and Liberal Democrat supporters to 'swap' votes, the idea being that Liberal Democrats would agree to vote Labour in Dorset South, in return for Labour supporters switching to the Liberal Democrats in Mid-Dorset & North Poole, Dorset North and Dorset West. In these constituencies, the success of tactical voting appears to be mixed, with the Liberal Democrats winning Mid-Dorset & North Poole, Labour winning Dorset South, and the Conservatives retaining both Dorset North and Dorset West. Certainly, Labour's victory in Dorset South seems attributable to tactical voting since, against the national trend,

the Liberal Democrats' vote fell by more than 3,000 there. In Mid-Dorset & North Poole, however, the evidence of tactical voting appears less convincing. While the Liberal Democrats did capture the seat from the Conservatives, they did so with fewer votes than they had polled in 1997, suggesting perhaps that their victory owed more to a slump in the Conservative vote than a surge in Liberal Democrat support caused by Labour 'switchers'.

Adapted from Denver 2001, Norris 2001, Ferguson 2001, Butler & Kavanagh 2002, Curtice & Steed 2002 and Dorey 2002.

See also *British Politics in Focus*, Second Edition, pp.313-18.

Figure 9.10 Billy Bragg
During the 2001 general election campaign, the singer and political campaigner Billy Bragg set up a 'vote swap' campaign in the hope of increasing tactical voting in several constituencies in Dorset.

References

Austin & Hames (2001) Austin, T. & Hames, T. (2001) *The Times Guide to the House of Commons June 2001*, Times Books, 2001.
Bartle (2002) Bartle, J., 'Why Labour won - again' in *King (2002)*.
Butler & Kavanagh (2002) Butler, D. & Kavanagh, D., *The British General Election of 2001*, Palgrave, 2002.
Cohen (2001) Cohen, N., 'Democracy is dead. Now what?', *New Statesman*, 11 June 2001.
Crewe (2002) Crewe, I., 'A new political hegemony?' in *King (2002)*.
Curtice (2001) Curtice, J., 'General election 2001: repeat or revolution?', *Politics Review*, Vol.11.1, September 2001.
Curtice & Steed (2002) Curtice, J. & Steed, M., 'An analysis of the results' in *Butler & Kavanagh (2002)*.
Denver (2001) Denver, D., 'The Liberal Democrat campaign' in *Norris (2001)*.
Dorey (2002) Dorey, P., 'A languid landslide: the 2001 general election' in *Lancaster (2002)*.

Ferguson (2001) Ferguson, E., 'King Billy assumes tactical mantle', *The Observer*, 3 June 2001.
Kellner (2001a) Kellner, P., 'Voters signal a political earthquake', *The Observer*, 3 June 2001.
Kellner (2001b) Kellner P., 'It was always mission impossible for Hague', *The Observer* (Election 2001 Supplement), 10 June 2001.
King (2002) King, A. (ed.), *Britain At The Polls 2001*, Chatham House, 2002.
Lancaster (2002) Lancaster, S. (ed.), *Developments in Politics*, Vol.13, Causeway Press, 2002.
MacArthur (2001) MacArthur, B., 'Fleet Street avalanche to back the landslide' in *Austin & Hames (2001)*.
Norris (2001) Norris, P. (ed.), *Britain Votes 2001*, Oxford University Press, 2001.
Scammell & Harrop (2002) Scammell, M. & Harrop, M., 'The press disarmed' in *Butler & Kavanagh (2002)*.

10 Pressure groups

1 New concepts

In recent years, there has been a number of new developments in the analysis of pressure group activity. These can be summarised as follows.

Policy communities

One new concept is that of a 'policy community'. The idea is that policy-making in Britain takes place within a series of vertical compartments or segments, organised around a government department and its client group, and generally closed off to the general public. An example of a policy community is the British Medical Association (which represents doctors) and the Department of Health. These policy communities are sometimes called 'iron triangles' to acknowledge the close and effective nature of the links between pressure groups, civil servants and ministers. These communities are generally stable, integrated and based on a general consensus. The argument is that the insider pressure groups involved in these policy communities generally have a great deal of influence.

Policy network

By way of contrast, another concept is that of 'policy network'. A policy network is a larger grouping and less integrated. There is likely to be greater conflict between the pressure groups in the policy network and the executive. An example can be found in the dealings of the newly formed Ministry of Agriculture, Fisheries and Food. This government department is different from the old Ministry of Agriculture (with its traditional policy community relationship with the National Farmers' Union). A policy network has been set up involving other groups with an interest in agriculture, such as the supermarkets and groups representing consumers. Here, the argument is that the pressure groups involved in the policy network have less influence than those in a policy community.

A multi-level polity?

Recently, the view has developed that policy-making cannot be explained in terms of policy communities and policy networks. This is because there has been a trend towards a 'multi-level polity'. Powers have been transferred to the European level and even to the new devolved assemblies in Scotland, Wales and Northern Ireland.

Pressure groups and collective consumption

Traditionally, much pressure group activity has taken place around the politics of production, involving the trade unions and the employers' organisations. Recently, however, the politics of production has been replaced by 'the politics of collective consumption' which is concerned with the outcomes of production rather than what happens within the process itself. Typically, there is a focus on environmental issues, food quality and safety, and animal welfare. Membership of pressure groups concerned with these issues has grown significantly. This focus on consumption is based on a belief that the UK has achieved a level of material well-being and politics has become post-modern. The theory maintains that we have moved to a new kind of society where there is fragmentation and a huge range of different interests and identities. Supporters of post-modernism argue that there is likely to be a proliferation of different kinds of pressure groups functioning in a range of different ways.

New social movements

Some of the pressure groups that have developed in recent years have been described as 'new social movements'. These are characterised by:

- informal modes of operation and a lack of leaders or charismatic leaders
- broad objectives
- new methods of activity, including direct action
- a claim to represent people outside established political institutions
- an anti-politics, anti-Establishment, anti-government stance
- an attempt to lead private lives in line with beliefs
- a commitment to changing values.

Members of new social movements do not acknowledge the routines of party politics, seeing political parties as largely irrelevant in their bid to push their particular concerns to the forefront of political debate. While traditional pressure groups are seen as formal, organised bodies attempting to influence those in power, new social movements want to challenge the whole political system and replace it with their preferred alternative.

Figure 10.1 New social movements
This cartoon caricatures members of new social movements.

Adapted from Watts 1999, Simpson 1999, Gamble 2000 and Grant 2002. See also *British Politics in Focus*, Second Edition, pp.324-29.

2 New Labour and the CBI (an insider group)

The dominant influences in the contemporary policy process in the UK are Big Business and the numerous lobbyists and organisations which represent it. This is inevitable where there is a free-market economy, as there is bound to be a structural bias in support of Big Business. However, New Labour has gone further by involving Big Business in numerous task forces, seeking the views of the business world at every opportunity (while taking little notice of the trade unions) and working to promote the UK's flexible labour market. Even when policies are advanced which appear to be in contradiction to business interests, they are so tailored as to be acceptable. Examples are the national minimum wage which was set at a rate that businesses could accept, and the very limited guarantees given to workers transferred to the private sector under privatisation.

In return for this pro-business stance, the CBI has adopted a classic insider stance, with the Director General emphasising in a message to members that it does not intend to adopt a confrontational strategy against Labour's employment agenda. The extent of the change in the relationship between New Labour and the CBI could be seen in the annual dinner just before the 2001 general election. Six Labour ministers, including the Chancellor, attended but not one Conservative frontbench spokesperson. The Chancellor, Gordon Brown, confirmed Labour's commitment to the enterprise agenda in an interview with the *Financial Times* in March 2002, saying that the wealth-creating agenda, support for public-private partnerships and the encouragement of small businesses were all central to everything the Labour government does.

Adapted from Grant 1999, the *Financial Times*, 28 March 2002 and Gamble 2000 and 2002.

See also *British Politics in Focus*, Second Edition, pp.329-33 and 337-47.

Figure 10.2 New Labour and business
The Chancellor, Gordon Brown, speaking at the CBI annual dinner in 2001.

3 New Labour and the Barbed Wire Britain Network (an outsider group)

New Labour is determined to take a strong stance on asylum seekers. As the Home Secretary, David Blunkett, put it: 'trust and confidence in the asylum system is vital for our social cohesion'. Given this stance, it is hardly surprising that a newly formed national pressure group - Barbed Wire Britain Network to End Refugee and Migrant Detention - is treated as an outsider group by the government. The group is small and lacks expertise. Furthermore, given the radical nature of the group's main demands (the ending of detention of asylum seekers in detention centres and prisons), it is not surprising that the group uses outsider group tactics, including:

● demonstrations at the main detention centres
● local public protest meetings
● visiting detainees
● the printing of publications
● the launch of a campaigning website
● national events to draw attention to the problem.

The protest group has also supported hunger strikes and roof top protests undertaken by the detainees themselves. Despite the campaign by the pressure group, the Home Secretary has announced plans to increase the numbers held in detention centres and prisons from the 1,500 held in 2002 to 4,000 in 2003.

Adapted from HMSO 2002 and www.barbedwirebritain.org.uk.
See also *British Politics in Focus*, Second Edition, pp.329-33 and 337-47.

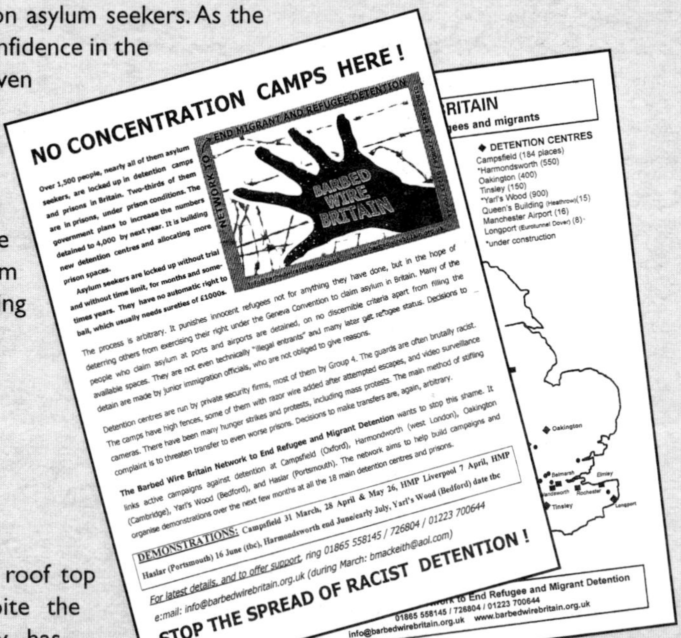

Figure 10.3 The Barbed Wire Britain Network to End Refugee and Migrant Detention
This leaflet was produced by Al Cane/Barbed Wire Britain Network to End Refugee and Migrant Detention.

4 Fox hunting

The issue of fox hunting has caused difficulties for the Labour government since 1997. Attempts made to resolve the problem through legislation before the 2001 general election generated enormous pressure group activity, but failed through lack of time. In May 2001, Labour's election manifesto promised a free vote on the issue early in the life of the next Parliament and, in June 2001, a commitment was made, in the Queen's Speech, to introduce an appropriate Bill. This was passed in the Commons in March 2002 with a clear majority in favour of a ban on hunting. The vote in the House of Lords the following day produced a strong majority in favour of allowing hunting under licence.

Anti-hunting groups

The League Against Cruel Sports is one of the main groups campaigning against cruel sports, including hunting with dogs. It provides educational information, undertakes undercover investigations, monitors hunts as well as mounting political campaigning. The League claims that its political campaigners:

- have been instrumental in drafting bills for Parliament
- have arranged for sympathetic MPs to ask parliamentary questions and make appropriate speeches
- have been in the forefront of the campaign to ban hunting with dogs.

Other anti-hunting groups have also tried to influence the government's thinking on hunting. The Political Animal Lobby, formerly linked to the International Fund for Animal Welfare, gave nearly £50,000 to the Labour Party before the 2001 general election in the hope that a Bill would be introduced in Parliament to end hunting with dogs.

The Countryside Alliance

Formed from a number of different but linked pressure groups, the Countryside Alliance has been the foremost critic of the intended ban on fox hunting. At its height in 1998, c.250,000 supporters marched through London to protest about the neglect of the countryside and the proposed ban on hunting. The Countryside Alliance has both an individual and trade membership. It is also able to draw financial support from very wealthy individuals, including the Duke of Westminster. In addition, the movement has many supporters in the House of Lords and in the Conservative Party.

Since 1998, the Alliance has had some difficulty in maintaining momentum and its leadership has changed. The ban on hunting in Scotland, introduced in early 2002, gave the campaign a revived focus as did the votes in the House of Commons and Lords in March 2002. The campaigners, though, decided not to organise a large-scale protest when the votes took place in Parliament, citing the terrorist attacks in the USA on 11 September 2001 and the need to develop the support and sympathy of the general public. Instead, a 'virtual march' was organised through the internet and a delegation met with politicians, presenting them with a pair of walking boots to signal the willingness of the organisation to return to the streets.

The Countryside Alliance has been described as a 'populist movement'. Populist movements explode quite suddenly onto the political scene. They are concerned with a single issue which captures the public imagination. They blur the distinction between a cause and an interest group and have a new kind of status which is neither insider nor outsider.

Outcome of the vote to ban hunting

Following the two contradictory votes in Parliament in March 2002, the government announced that there would be a six-month period of consultation. The Countryside Alliance was delighted with the vote in the House of Lords and welcomed the period of consultation. However, it also threatened to resist strongly if further attempts were made to produce legislation banning hunting. Groups opposed to hunting were afraid that the period of consultation and the threat of further action from the Countryside Alliance would result in the government backtracking.

Figure 10.4 Anti-hunt literature
This leaflet was produced by the League Against Cruel Sports.

Adapted from the *Guardian*, 14 October 1999, the *Independent*, 8 August 2001, www.league.uk.com, www.countryside-alliance.org, McNaughton 2001 and the *Guardian*, 1 April 2002.

See also *British Politics in Focus*, Second Edition, pp.329-33 and 337-47.

5 The Institute for Public Policy Research (IPPR)

The IPPR describes itself as one of the UK's leading independent think tanks. Based in London, it employs 50 staff. At the beginning of 2002, it was headed by Matthew Taylor, a past Assistant General Secretary of the Labour Party. It is registered as an independent charity and claims to have influenced Labour government thinking in a number of key areas, not least in the field of public-private partnerships.

There has, however, been growing criticism of the IPPR as it has come to rely increasingly on private-sector sponsorship of its work. The report into private-public partnerships was sponsored by leading firms with an involvement in the private finance initiative including Nomura, Norwich Union, KPMG and Serco. These firms stood to gain commercially from the policies promoted by the report. Professor Alyson Pollock claimed that, far from being dispassionate observers, those working on the report represented a striking coalition between Big Business and government, including a long list of corporate Chairs, advisers on earlier privatisations and government officials. Another piece of IPPR research (on the subject of providing social housing tenants with a financial stake in the value of their homes) was sponsored by the building society Nationwide. Defending private sponsorship, Matthew Taylor asked: 'How else do people think our projects get funded? If they were funded by a trade union we would be attacked, if they were funded by the government we should be attacked. Should independent think tanks just close down?' Against this, the *Guardian*, in an editorial, claimed that the intellectual integrity of the IPPR was in jeopardy. This claim appeared to have substance when an *Observer* reporter, posing as a potential American donor to the IPPR who wanted to have contact with government ministers, was offered the opportunity to meet ministers and the chance to influence government policy. The IPPR now receives £1.5 million a year from private sector donors.

Gamble takes a positive view of the future role of think tanks and their ideas in shaping the policy agenda. He predicts that new areas will develop as a result of devolution and the growing role of the European Union. Others are more critical. An article in the *Guardian*, for example, claimed that in order to be heard, think tanks are forced to make ever more overblown and ludicrous claims.

Adapted from Gamble 2000, the *Guardian*, 4 April, 26 June and 8 August 2001, the *Observer*, 30 June 2002, www.politics.guardian.co.uk/thinktanks and www.ippr.org. See also *British Politics in Focus*, Second Edition, pp.333-37.

6 Repeal of Section 28 of the Local Government Act 1988

Figure 10.5 Section 28 *This photo shows a supporter of Brian Souter's referendum trying to persuade William Hague, then Leader of the Conservative Party, to support the campaign against the repeal of Section 28.*

According to Section 28 of the Local Government Act 1988, a local authority shall not:

- intentionally promote homosexuality or publish material with the intention of promoting homosexuality

- promote the teaching in any maintained school of the acceptability of homosexuality as a pretend family relationship.

Following the Labour victory in 1997, pressure groups which supported gay rights (for example Stonewall and Outrage!) campaigned for the repeal of Section 28, and the government declared publicly its support for change. The Local Government Minister, Hilary Armstrong, described Section 28 as 'an outdated and discriminatory piece of legislation which is a barrier to creating a more tolerant and supportive society'. In 1999, Estelle Morris, then a junior minister, declared that 'the government has long made clear its opposition to Section 28 and intends to repeal it when the legislative opportunity arises'. The 1999 Queen's Speech announced a proposed Local Government Bill which included proposals for repeal of Section 28.

This Bill was passed by the Commons, and then went to the Lords. There followed a 'ping pong' between the two Houses. In the end, a majority of 42 voted against repeal. This led the government to abandon the abolition of Section 28 as there was a danger that the whole Bill might be lost.

In Scotland, a similar measure was considered. There, a private referendum was organised by Brain Souter, a well-known Scottish businessman. Although 80% voted in the referendum to retain Section 28, only one third of the electorate voted. The Scottish Executive maintained its position and the Scottish Parliament voted to repeal the clause (known in Scotland as Clause 2a), by 99 votes to 17.

Following the vote in the Lords, another round of pressure group activity began, with Stonewall pressing to ensure that Labour made an election pledge to repeal Section 28. Labour's 2001 election manifesto stated that: 'The repeal of Section 28 of the 1988 Local Government Act was grossly misrepresented as an attempt to use teaching to promote particular life styles. We will ensure that such teaching continued to be prohibited...while removing discrimination on grounds of sexual orientation'.

Adapted from Pugsley 2000, www.outrage.org.uk and Labour Party 2001.

See also *British Politics in Focus*, Second Edition, pp.337-47.

7 Lobbying and sleaze

In early 2002 the United States energy giant, Enron, collapsed. In the publicity surrounding the collapse, it became clear that the company had donated £38,000 to the Labour Party and that Enron's Chief Executive had met a number of key government ministers, including Peter Mandelson and Tony Blair's senior energy adviser, Geoff Norris. The company wanted the ban on the building of gas-fired power stations to be lifted and to be able to buy Wessex Water without interference. In both cases, the objective was achieved.

A storm then developed over a donation of £125,000 to the Labour Party, made by an Asian businessman, Lakshmi Mittal. This steel tycoon wanted to buy Sidex, a Romanian steel company, and was helped to do so by a letter signed by Tony Blair and sent to the Romanian Prime Minister. Critics argued that Blair must have been aware of the £125,000 donation to the Labour Party when he wrote the letter. It also emerged that the Lakshmi Mittal Group was not a British company and it was operating against the interests of the steel industry in Wales. The Conservatives called for an inquiry. Blair, however, remained unapologetic, claiming that he was merely following Foreign Office advice in signing a letter which advanced British interests.

Then, in May 2002, it was revealed that the millionaire publisher of OK magazine and a range of soft core porn titles, Richard Desmond, had given a £100,000 donation to the Labour Party in February 2000. The donation was made within days of a decision by the then Trade and Industry Secretary, Stephen Byers, to allow Desmond to buy Express Newspapers. Byers claimed that the two events were not linked and that it was the Director General of Fair Trading who decided that the takeover should not be referred to the Competition Commission. The Conservatives, however, argued that Byers had the legal right to intervene and that he had been swayed by the donation. Another controversial

Figure 10.6 New Labour and sleaze *This cartoon comments on the Labour government's involvement in a series of allegations of sleaze.*

aspect of the donation was that it had been made just before a deadline which would have required it to have been made public before the next general election.

The Labour Party then announced the creation of an internal ethics committee to vet future donations and promised that, in future, all donors to the Labour Party would have to agree to a statement that they were not giving money for commercial advantages or advantages for themselves or others.

Despite these allegations, Andrew Rawnsley claimed, New Labour has a teflon coating ensuring that nothing, including allegations of sleaze, sticks. The main reason for this, he argues, is continued economic prosperity.

Adapted from the *Guardian*, 11 February and 13 May 2002 and the *Observer*, 3 February, 3 March and 12 May 2002.

See also *British Politics in Focus*, Second Edition, pp.347-52.

8 The government and the trade unions

Trade unions have opposed the government's support for privatisation and the private finance initiative (PFI) for the following reasons. First, they believe that members' jobs will be lost. Second, they are concerned that pay and conditions will deteriorate as workers are transferred to the private sector. Third, there is concern that public services will be cut as money will need to be used to pay back the money borrowed from the private sector.

Three major unions with members in the public sector - the TGWU, UNISON and the GMB - have all campaigned publicly against the proposals, for example by taking out newspaper advertisements. In addition, the leaders of these unions have made speeches at Labour Party conferences and proposed motions opposing the changes. There has also been a withdrawal of funding from the Labour Party. In the case of the GMB, this has amounted to a reduction in money paid to the Labour Party of £500,000 each year for four years.

The influence of the unions has declined for the following reasons. First, the Labour Party has found new sources of income. Second, union membership has declined and the ability to block change by industrial action has been reduced by legal restrictions. Third, unions' voting strength has been reduced within the Labour Party and there are divisions between the unions on the issues. Fourth, Tony Blair and those who support his views on the public services have considerable support within the party and a huge parliamentary majority.

Adapted from Monbiot 2000, the *Guardian*, 3 January and 26 March 2002. See also *British Politics in Focus*, Second Edition, pp.347-52.

9 Anti-capitalists and the European Union (EU)

Figure 10.7 An anti-capitalist demonstration *This photograph shows one of the anti-capitalist protestors in Barcelona in March 2002.*

In March 2002, leaders of the 15 members of the EU met in Barcelona to discuss the economic reforms which would have to be undertaken before the EU could allow new members from Eastern Europe to join.

The British Prime Minister, Tony Blair, favoured liberalisation of markets and the reduction in protection for workers' rights. In this, he was joined by the Italian Prime Minister, Silvio Berlusconi, and the Spanish Prime Minister, Jose Maria Aznar. The *Guardian* noted that, across Europe, the three had become known as 'the BAB axis', committed to deregulation, in contrast to the more cautious approach of France and Germany.

The protest began before the summit when over 100,000 trade unionists marched to demonstrate against cuts in services and against privatisation. Their slogans included the demand for 'a Europe with full employment and social rights'. During the weekend, the city was alive with numerous events representing a wide range of different concerns. On the Sunday, there was a huge demonstration of up to 500,000 people, mainly from Barcelona itself, marching behind a banner with the slogan 'Against Capitalism in Europe and War'. The Spanish Minister of the Interior had decided to avoid the demonstration by attending the local Barcelona versus Real Madrid football match, only to find that demonstrators with slogans on their backs had handcuffed themselves to the goal posts as part of the protest.

The effectiveness of the anti-capitalist movement has to be questioned. In part, the movement is not effective because there are so many different views within it. In part, it is not effective because the loose organisational structures mean the lack of a coherent strategy. In addition, the strength of capitalism within the European Union is considerable and has the full backing of state forces.

Adapted from Lloyd 2001, the *Guardian*, 16 March 2002 and Grant 2002.

See also *British Politics in Focus*, Second Edition, pp.352-55.

References

Dunleavy et al. (2000) Dunleavy, P., Gamble, A., Holliday, I., & Peele. G. (eds), *Developments in British Politics*, Vol.6, Macmillan, 2000.
Gamble (2000) Gamble, A., 'Policy agenda in a multi-level polity' in *Dunleavy (2000)*.
Grant (1999) Grant, W., 'Insider and outsider pressure groups', *Politics Review*, Vol.9.1 September 1999.
Grant (2002) Grant, W., 'Pressure groups' in *Lancaster (2002)*.
Held (1996) Held, D., *Models of Democracy* (2nd edn), Polity, 1996.
HMSO (2002) HMSO, *Secure Borders, Safe Haven: Integration with Diversity in Modern Britain*, cm 5387, 2002.
Labour (2001) *Ambitions for Britain*, Labour Party manifesto, Labour Party, 2001.
Lancaster (2002) Lancaster, S., *Developments in Politics*, Vol.13, Causeway Press 2002.

Lloyd (2001) Lloyd. J., *The Protestant Ethic: how the Anti Globalisation Movement Challenges Social Democracy*, Demos, 2001.
McNaughton (2001) McNaughton, N., 'Populist movements - a new development in the politics of pressure', *Talking Politics*, Vol.4.1, September 2001.
Monbiot (2000) Monbiot, G., *The Captive State*, Macmillan, 2000.
Pugsley (2000) Pugsley, R., 'Section 28: pressure groups and the House of Lords', *Politics Review*, Vol.10.2, 2000.
Simpson (1999) Simpson, D., *Pressure Groups*, Hodder and Stoughton, 1999.
Watts (1999) Watts, D., *The Environment and British Politics*, Hodder and Stoughton, 1999.

1 Councillors

The National Census of Local Authority Councillors in 2001, covering nearly all of the 410 town and county halls in England and Wales, found that local government was run by white, male, greying councillors nearly half of whom were retired or not in the labour market. The survey was based on replies from 374 of the 410 local authorities in England and Wales and from 12,013 of the 21,268 councillors in office after the May 2001 local elections. The key findings are shown in Figure 11.1.

Adapted from I&DEA 2002,
See also *British Politics in Focus*, Second Edition, pp.357-361.

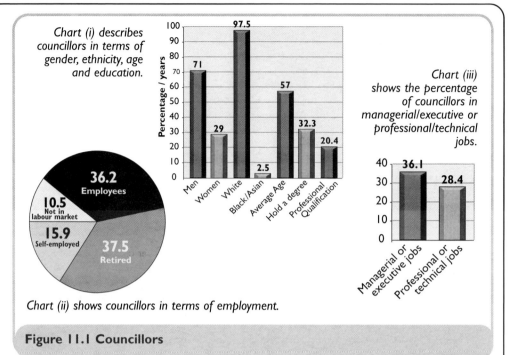

Chart (i) describes councillors in terms of gender, ethnicity, age and education.

Chart (iii) shows the percentage of councillors in managerial/executive or professional/technical jobs.

Chart (ii) shows councillors in terms of employment.

Figure 11.1 Councillors

2 The selection of parliamentary candidates 1999–2002

The Labour Party

The emphasis, after 1997, was to convert the party to a culture of government by means of a more professional candidate screening process and the creation of a new National Parliamentary Panel - a list of approved eligible candidates. The aim was to remove the need for the NEC to refuse endorsement of certain candidates, as had happened with left-winger Liz Davies who was barred from standing in 1995. Candidates for the panel were required to attend training weekends, to submit CVs to a standardised format and to be interviewed by a panel including at least one MP. Supporters claimed the result would mean more professional candidates and more women. Critics argued that the result was identikit, middle-class, on-message New Labourites. Screening for the National Panel began in spring 1999. The panel was published at the end of 1999 and seat selections began early in 2000. Access to the panel was also available to candidates chosen separately by affiliated bodies such as unions and the Cooperative Party. Of the 681 names on the panel, 103 were nominated by unions. Labour made two further changes at constituency level. First, all bodies nominating candidates must nominate at least one man and one woman and all shortlists must have equal numbers of men and women. And second, the percentage of nominations a sitting MP required to avoid going through a contested reselection was reduced from 66% to 50%.

In the run-up to the general election in 2001, the party leadership persuaded a number of sitting Labour MPs to retire (promising peerages as a reward) and imposed favoured candidates in their place. One favoured candidate was Shaun Woodward who defected from the Conservative Party in 1999. He was placed on the shortlist for the St Helens South seat (despite the fact that he had no connections with the constituency). An NEC panel excluded two of the four candidates put forward by the CLP, including Marie Rimmer the local Council Leader and a party member for 30 years. The panel refused to explain why it did this. As a result, there was no local candidate on the shortlist. Woodward was then chosen by 81 votes to 71, defeating Barbara Keeley (a councillor from Trafford in Manchester). The NEC also intervened in the Ogmore by-election in January 2002. Mark Seddon, an activist, NEC member and editor of the *Tribune* newspaper, was excluded from the shortlist following a meeting of the NEC selection panel. He was criticised by the Party Chair, Charles Clarke, for a lacklustre performance in the selection meeting and lack of local connections. Critics, however, argued that his crime had been to oppose the national party line on key issues. A local, loyal candidate was then chosen to fight the seat.

The Conservative Party

The Conservatives revamped their national candidates' list and required more rigorous tests of would-be candidates. This reduced the national panel from over 1,000 to 600. Additional tests were introduced to check for listening skills and the ability to cope with TV interviewing. However, despite earlier Conservative rhetoric about the need to include candidates from a wider set of backgrounds, there was little innovation in the procedures before the 2001 general election. In the selection meetings in the constituencies, there was some evidence that pro-Europe MPs, like Ian Taylor, were threatened by deselection. Intervention by Central Office ensured that Taylor kept the nomination.

The Liberal Democrats

The Liberal Democrats have introduced no new procedures for selection of their parliamentary candidates in recent years. The party conference in 2001 rejected a proposal to introduce all-women shortlists to ensure greater numbers of female candidates.

Adapted from Kelly 1999, the *Guardian*, 23 January and 14 May 2001 and 17 January 2002, Cowley 2001, Criddle 2001.
See also *British Politics in Focus*, Second Edition, pp.362-67.

3 The selection of women

In total, women only made up 18% of all MPs after the 2001 general election. To discover why this percentage was so low, The Equal Opportunities Commission undertook a survey of 408 would-be and actual candidates. More than eight out of ten female Conservative candidates, six out of ten Labour candidates and one third of Liberal Democrat candidates believed that their party's selection committees were biased in favour of men. When asked to consider the most important reasons for the low number of women in parliament, 50% of all candidates cited family commitments or childcare issues. Other reasons included:

- the hours of work in Parliament
- women not putting themselves forward for selection
- the culture of the House of Commons
- sex discrimination within parties or the attitudes of the parties.

Since the 2001 general election, both Labour and the Conservatives have changed their approach. Labour has reduced its target of having women as half the party's MPs. While this figure remains an aspiration, the target has been reduced to 35%. In February 2002, the Sex Discrimination (Election Candidates) Bill finally received Royal Assent, allowing parties to discriminate positively in favour of women. This Act amends the 1975 Sex Discrimination Act, permitting measures such as all-women shortlists when selecting candidates. On 10 July 2002, the *Guardian* reported that Labour's NEC had drawn up plans to impose all-women shortlists on at least half of vacant winnable seats for the next election. Sitting MPs were asked to provide early warning of their intention to retire. Any seat where an MP announced retirement plans after 23 December 2002 would automatically have an all-women shortlist imposed on it.

In response to criticism about the low number of Conservative female MPs, Conservative Central Office is planning to impose shortlists of candidates in the most

(i)	Total	Lab	Con	Lib Dem
1997	360	155 (24%)	66 (10%)	139 (21%)
2001	381	148 (23%)	93 (15%)	140 (22%)

(ii)	1997	By-elections	2001 A	B	New total
Lab	101	-1	-9	+4	95
Con	13	+1	-1	+1	14
Lib Dem	3	+1	-2	+3	5
SNP	2	-	-2	+1	1
Speaker	1	-1	-	-	-
SF	-	-	-	+1	1
UUP	-	-	-	+1	1
DUP	-	-	-	+1	1
Total	**120**	**-**	**-14**	**+12**	**118**

A Number of sitting women MPs who did not stand in 2001 or were defeated

B Number of new women MPs elected in June 2001

Figure 11.2 Women candidates and MPs 1997-2001
Table (i) shows women candidates and Table (ii) shows women MPs 1997-2001.

winnable seats before the next general election. The shortlists of 15 to 20 names would consist of a high number of women and ethnic minority candidates. It is likely that these proposals will be resisted by Conservative local associations which traditionally jealously guard their independence. In addition, these proposals provide no guarantees that the local associations will actually choose women candidates.

The Liberal Democrats rejected all-women shortlists for women at their conference in September 2001. Instead, they have opted for a 40% target for female candidates in winnable seats and in those where a Liberal Democrat MP is retiring. In other words, they will not take advantage of the change in the law to allow women-only shortlists.

Adapted from Lovenduski 2001, the *Guardian*, 17 October and 27 September 2001, 24 January, 23 February and 10 July 2002, Butler & Kavanagh 2002, EOC, 2002.
See also *British Politics in Focus*, Second Edition, pp.369-72.

4 Black and Asian candidates

Figure 11.3 shows that there was an increase in the number of black and Asian candidates in the 2001 general election. Most of the new candidates were selected in unwinnable seats, however. Only two new Asian MPs were elected, making a total of 12 black and Asian MPs in the Commons. All 12 were Labour MPs. The number elected amounted to 2% of the Parliamentary Labour Party, ensuring that black and Asian people remained under-represented in the House of Commons. The number of black and Asian MPs would have to triple to make it representative of the black and Asian population in the country as a whole.

Despite low numbers of black and Asian MPs, Saggar has suggested that, in seats where there is a significant ethnic minority population, black and Asian candidates are potential vote winners. For example, in Keith Vaz's seat in Leicester, all the main parties selected Asian candidates in order to win the sizeable ethnic minority vote. Some evidence for the view that selectorates tend to see black and Asian candidates as vote

	Total	Lab	Con	Lib Dem
1997	42	13	10	19
2001	66	22	16	28

Figure 11.3 Black and Asian candidates
This chart shows the number of black and Asian candidates in the general elections held in 1997 and 2001.

losers comes from the contrast between Labour's National Parliamentary Panel, where 78 of the 681 names were black or Asian (some 11% of the total), compared to the numbers of black and Asian candidates actually selected. Despite the small number of black and Asian MPs, the major parties have taken no significant measures to effect change.

Adapted from Saggar 2001 and Butler & Kavanagh 2002.
See also *British Politics in Focus*, Second Edition, pp.372-75.

5 Composition of the House of Commons

(i) Occupation	Lab	Con	Lib Dem
Professions:	**179**	**64**	**27**
Lawyer	31	31	6
Civil servant/local government	30	2	3
Teaching (all levels)	98	7	12
Other professions	20	24	6
Business	**33**	**60**	**14**
Manual worker	**51**	**1**	**0**
Miscellaneous:	**149**	**41**	**10**
White collar	73	2	1
Politics	44	18	4
Publisher/journalist	32	14	4
Other	0	7	1

(ii)	Lab	Con	Lib Dem
State school	48	3	4
State school & degree	296	57	30
Public school	2	6	1
Public school & degree	66	100	17
Total	**412**	**166**	**52**
Oxford or Cambridge	65	79	14
Other universities	210	59	22
All universities	**275**	**138**	**36**
%	67	83	70
Eton	2	14	2
Other public schools	66	92	16
All public schools	**68**	**106**	**18**
%	17	64	35

Figure 11.4 Occupational and educational background of MPs
These tables show the occupational and educational background of MPs elected in June 2001.

Following the 2001 general election, the Labour Party can be described as a party of public sector professionals (teachers and administrators), political 'staffers', union officials, journalists, and lawyers. Working-class MPs now amount to only 12% of the total. Of the 38 new Labour MPs elected in 2001, most had been councillors and about half had some kind of political position either as policy adviser or working for a trade union. This confirms the trend towards the 'professional politician'. Most Labour MPs attended state schools and most went to university. A total of 95 female MPs were elected for Labour, a reduction of six on the 1997 total. This amounts to 23% of the Parliamentary Labour Party. The median age of Labour MPs was 50. Only four were under 30.

Conservative MPs came mainly from the ranks of the private sector professions, banking and business. The legal profession provided the largest number, while 16 had a background as a party 'staffer'. This again supports the thesis of the rise of the professional politician. Only one Conservative MP had a working-class background. Two-thirds of Conservative MPs had attended private schools and 83% attended university, with Oxford and Cambridge predominating. Only 14 women were elected as Conservative MPs, some 8% of their total number. The median age of Conservative MPs was 48.

Just over half the 52 Liberal Democrat MPs came from the professions while only a single MP had a working-class background. Under half of Liberal Democrat MPs went to private schools and over half went to university. Just five women were elected as Liberal Democrats, 10% of the total. The median age of Liberal Democrat MPs was 47.

Adapted from Brierley 2001 and Butler & Kavanagh 2002. See also *British Politics in Focus*, Second Edition, pp.375-82.

6 Peers' interests

The first compulsory Register of Interests of members of the House of Lords was published in May 2002. It reveals that companies and peers have an enduring relationship. One in three Lords is a director of a company and 80 hold some sort of consultancy with firms (see Figure 11.5). The busiest Tories are Lord Parkinson and Lord Fraser of Carmyllie who each hold 11 boardroom seats. Canadian Conrad Black, owner of the *Daily Telegraph*, who won a legal battle to get his peerage, comes next with ten directorships. Nearly 40% (57) of Labour peers are directors of companies, the ratio taking into account the members of government who have to resign all directorships. The busiest Labour Lord is Viscount Chandos who holds a stunning 17 boardroom seats. And 20% of Liberal Democrat peers are directors of companies. Lord Razzall tops the list for the party - and the Lords - with 21 directorships. Nearly one in four - 20% - of crossbenchers and peers from minority parties have directorships. Lord Powell of Bayswater, the former Private Secretary to Margaret

Thatcher, is busiest with 13 directorships. Some of the most valuable companies in the UK clearly find it advantageous to have a link with the Lords - 28 of the top 100 FTSE companies have a peer on their board.

Party	No. of peers	Directorships	No. of peers	Consultancies
Conservative	102	315	30	47
Labour	57	152	13	22
Lib Dem	14	49	13	16
Cross-benchers & minor parties	45	107	23	45
Total	**218**	**623**	**79**	**130**

Figure 11.5 Lords with directorships and consultancies

Adapted from *Labour Research*, May 2002.
See also *British Politics in Focus*, Second Edition, pp.383-86.

7 Keith Vaz and MPs' interests

The Parliamentary Commissioner for Standards has a responsibility to keep the Register of Members' Interests, advise MPs on their conduct and to investigate complaints against MPs. Elizabeth Filkin, who replaced Sir Gordon Downey as the Parliamentary Commissioner in 1999, developed a reputation as a tenacious investigator who followed through all allegations in a serious manner. She undertook some 30 inquiries out of more than 300 complaints against MPs. These cases involved Labour Cabinet ministers (Peter Mandelson who failed to declare loans and Geoffrey Robinson who misled Parliament over undeclared financial interests) and past Conservative Leaders. William Hague and John Major were both criticised for failing to give full information in the Register of Members' Interests.

Keith Vaz, the Europe Minister in the 1997-2001 Labour government, was accused of a number of misdemeanours. These included:

- misuse of Foreign Office premises
- lobbying on behalf of the Hinduja brothers (suspects in an illegal arms deal)
- intimidation of Labour Party members
- undeclared cash payments
- misuse of donations made to his local Labour Party.

The task of Elizabeth Filkin was to establish whether these allegations were true and whether Keith Vaz had broken parliamentary rules. A long inquiry was carried out during which time Downing Street continued to offer full support to the embattled minister. For example, in February 2001, Alastair Campbell the Prime Minister's spokesperson, said: 'The Prime Minster's view is that Keith Vaz yesterday put out a detailed rebuttal of all the various stories that have appeared. The fact that the papers keep repeating them doesn't make them any truer'.

The investigation was hampered by the decision of Keith Vaz and other witnesses to refuse to answer questions on eight of the matters under investigation. The Standards and Privileges Committee of the House of Commons reported in March 2001, finding that Vaz had broken the MPs' code of conduct by not declaring a financial interest with a City lawyer when he recommended him for an honour. In addition, he had broken Commons' rules by failing to disclose a property in the MPs' Register. After a further review, in February 2002, the committee decided to suspend Vaz for one month from the House of Commons, upholding three of the allegations against him. These failings would normally only have merited an apology to MPs. The suspension, however, was imposed because of Vaz's intimidation of a witness in the cases against him. By this time Vaz had been quietly dropped from ministerial office on the grounds of ill health, becoming a backbencher.

The Parliamentary Commissioner for Standards reports to the Standards and Privileges Committee of the House of Commons. This body consists of MPs in proportion to their party's strength in the House of Commons. Unlike the Commissioner, the committee has the powers to press for evidence and demand that witnesses give evidence. Elizabeth Filkin, however, stated publicly that the committee was reluctant to use its powers. In addition, she claimed that she had been undermined by a whispering campaign against her by MPs. A poll showed that more than two-thirds of MPs gave their backing to Filkin and believed that MPs were wrong not to renew her contract.

The previous Commissioner, Sir Gordon Downey, commented that: 'MPs need to watch their system of self-regulation rather carefully if public trust is not to be forfeited'.

In 2002, Philip Mawer, retiring General Secretary of the Church of England and a former civil servant, became the new

Figure 11.6 Keith Vaz *This photograph shows Keith Vaz apologising to MPs for his conduct prior to being suspended from the Commons for a month.*

Commissioner. He began working just one day a week and was seen by many as an insider figure who would not challenge the Establishment (see also Chapter 14, Section 6).

Figures are percentages		1985	1994	2001
Most MPs make a lot of money by using public office improperly	Agree	46	64	50
	Disagree	31	22	39
	Don't know	23	14	11
Most MPs have a high personal moral code	Agree	42	28	46
	Disagree	35	59	46
	Don't know	23	15	8
Most MPs will tell lies if they feel the truth will hurt them politicallty	Agree	79	87	79
	Disagree	12	8	15
	Don't know	9	5	6
Most MPs care more about special interests than they care about people like you	Agree	67	77	65
	Disagree	19	12	26
	Don't know	14	11	8

Do you think an MP should or should not accept?

	1994 Right	1994 Not right	2001 Right	2001 Not right
Payment for asking questions in parliament	2	95	4	94
A free holiday abroad	6	92	8	90
Money or gifts in connection with parliamentary duties	7	89	9	88
Payment for giving advice about parliamentary matters	9	85	13	83
Free tickets to Wimbledon or other major sports events	25	69	23	74
Free lunch at restaurant	48	47	26	71
Bottles of wine or whisky at Christmas	51	45	48	48

Recently MPs decided not to renew the contract of Elizabeth Filkin, the parliamentary standards watchdog who has the responsibility to investigate the conduct of MPs. From what you have seen or heard do you think they were right or wrong to dismiss her?	Right	9
	Wrong	68
	Don't know	22

Figure 11.7 Standards of MPs *This table shows the result of a poll carried out in December 2001.*

Adapted from the *Guardian*, 6 February, 15 March and 27 June 2001 and 9 February 2002.
See also *British Politics in Focus*, Second Edition, pp.383-86.

8 Members of the European Parliament (MEPs)

Elections to the 626 seat European Parliament take place every five years. In 1999, the UK was divided into 87 seats. Of the 84 seats in mainland Britain, 24% of those elected were women, a figure significantly behind most other European countries. The Liberal Democrats achieved 50% female MEP representation through 'zipping', a device which alternates men and women on the lists of candidates for whom the electors cast their votes. The Labour Party did not adopt any special measures to help secure greater female representation, with the consequence that only 34% of Labour MEPs were women. The party did use the candidate selection process, though, to rid itself of troublesome existing MEPs. By placing them well down party lists, the party ensured they were not re-elected.

The Conservatives won the largest number of seats, but only 8% of their MEPs were female. This was not surprising as there were only two regions where a female name featured at the top of a list and none where there was more than one woman in the top four. Northern Ireland elected three male MEPs.

Analysis of the websites of the MEPs suggests that their backgrounds were largely middle class, with the professions and business figuring significantly. Quite a number were ex-Westminster politicians including the Liberal Democrat Emma Nicholson (who defected from the Conservative Party while she was an MP). Others, like the Green Party's Caroline Lucas, had a background in local government as councillors. Black and Asian people were under-represented, despite the attempts by the Labour Party to place some black and Asian candidates high up the party lists.

Figure 11.8 Caroline Lucas
Caroline Lucas was one of the two members of the Green Party to be elected as MEP in 1999.

Davies claims that: 'membership of the European Parliament is not seen as a way of making a political career in the UK; it is not an alternative to Westminster, and is seen by critics as a "resting place" for second rate politicians'.
Adapted from Davies 1988 and Longmate 2000. See also *British Politics in Focus*, Second Edition, pp.391-95.

9 Pay and allowances for Members of the European Parliament (MEPs)

The salary of MEPs is identical to that of the members of the national parliaments of their respective member states. This means that British MEPs received a salary of £51,800 from April 2002. MPs who are also MEPs receive a duality rate of a further third of their MP's salary. The allowances for MEPs include:
- a general expenditure allowance amounting to 3,546 euros per month for office management costs
- a flat rate travel allowance for official meetings based on

distances travelled
- a further travel allowance for world travel in performance of their duties
- a flat rate subsistence allowance of 251 euros a day for attending official meetings
- a secretarial allowance of 12,052 euros a month.

Adapted from European Parliament 2002.
See also *British Politics in Focus*, Second Edition, pp.391-95.

10 Quangocrats

When the Labour Party came to office in 1997, the new government promised to open up the appointments system, especially as both women and ethnic minorities were under-represented. In June 1998, the government published *Quangos: Opening up Public Appointments* which committed the government to achieving the equal representation of men and women in public appointment and a pro-rata representation of ethnic minorities. Recent research, however, suggests that little progress has been made.

The Institute for Public Policy Research investigated ten 'cultural gatekeeper bodies' - organisations that control standards across the media - including:
- BBC governors
- the Independent Television Commission (ITC)
- OFTEL
- the Radio Authority.

The members of the boards of these organisations, who have an important policy-making role, are appointed by the government. Other bodies considered in the research (for example, the Advertising Standards Authority, the British Board

of Film Classification and the Press Complaints Commission) elect their own boards. The study found that:
- the average age of board members was 56, a figure that rose to 63 for the Chairs of organisations
- 65% of board members were men
- more than 25% were educated at Oxford or Cambridge.

Typical examples include:
- Gavyn Davies the 52-year-old, Cambridge-educated Chair of the BBC
- Sir Robin Biggam, the 64-year-old chartered accountant who runs the ITC
- Lord Borrie the 71-year-old, Oxford-educated, Chair of the Advertising Standards Authority.

The IPPR concluded that the situation had actually deteriorated since Labour came to power and that 'the great and the good' continued to be appointed rather than a set of different faces.

Adapted from Flinders & Cole 1999, the *Observer*, 14 April 2002 and IPPR 2002. See also *British Politics in Focus*, Second Edition, pp.396-99.

11 The Scottish Parliament

The first election for the Scottish Parliament in 1999 produced a high percentage of female candidates:

- 45% for the Labour Party
- 30% for the SNP
- 29% for the Liberal Democrats
- 18% for the Conservatives.

The high figure for the Labour Party was achieved, in part, by the policy of 'twinning' - pairing constituencies together, with each pair required to select a male and female candidate. This meant that Labour women obtained nearly half the Labour seats in the Parliament. In contrast, special measures were not taken by the other main parties. After the election, women accounted for 40% of the total number of members elected to the Scottish Parliament (MSPs).

Only seven black and Asian candidates were chosen to fight the election by the four largest parties and these candidates were placed in seats that were difficult to win, or low down on the regional lists. The consequence was that no black or Asian candidates were elected to the Scottish Parliament. The median age of the candidates was in the mid-40s and just under half of the MSPs elected had previously stood as candidates in local, national or European elections. Sixteen of those elected as MSPs were already Members of the House of Commons.

Adapted from Henderson & Sloat 1999 and Longmate 2000.
See also *British Politics in Focus*, Second Edition, pp.392-93.

12 MSPs' pay

In March 2002, MSPs were warned that they risked allegations of hypocrisy after they voted themselves a pay rise of 13.5% while urging wage restraint on public sector workers. The pay rise meant MSPs' salaries rose to nearly £49,000 per year. Some backbench MSPs warned that such a large pay increase would alienate voters since public service workers had only been a offered a few percent above inflation, but the majority said that they voted for the pay rise because it was recommended by an independent body. The Senior Salaries Review Body recommended the pay rise to narrow the gap between MSPs and their counterparts at Westminster who earned £51,800 a year in 2002. MSPs are now the best paid politicians in any devolved assembly in Europe. Under the new pay structure, the First Minister, Jack McConnell, saw his salary rise to £118,000 and Cabinet ministers earned almost £85,000 per year. This was the last time MSPs could vote on their pay. Under new arrangements, their salaries will be pegged at 87.5% of the level of their colleagues at Westminster.

Adapted from the Guardian, 22 March 2002.
See also *British Politics in Focus*, Second Edition, pp.392-93.

13 The Welsh Assembly

The election for the Welsh Assembly in 1999 resulted in high female representation with 24 women being elected to the 60 seats. Two measures helped achieve this. First, Labour introduced 'twinning' for paired constituencies to increase female representation. Second, 'zipping' was used for the list element of the election by both Plaid Cmyru and the Liberal Democrats. Zipping involves alternating male and female names on the list of candidates for a party. Zipping meant that 35% of Plaid Cmyru, and 50% of Liberal Democrat Members of the Welsh Assembly were female. In contrast, the Conservative Party, which did not introduce any positive action measures, failed to achieve any female representation in the Welsh Assembly.

Adapted from Bradbury 1999 and Longmate 2000.
See also *British Politics in Focus*, Second Edition, pp.392-93.

14 Northern Ireland Assembly

In Northern Ireland, elections were held using the STV system of voting. No special measures were adopted by the mainstream parties, with the result that only 13% of the new Assembly members were women. One novelty was the breakthrough made by the Women's Coalition. It won two seats in the Assembly.

Adapted from Bradbury 1999 and Longmate 2000.
See also *British Politics in Focus*, Second Edition, pp.392-93.

References

Bradbury (1999) Bradbury, J., 'Labour's bloody nose', Politics Review, Vol.9.2, November 1999.
Brierley (2001) Brierley, N., 'Rise of the professional politician', New Statesman, 18 June 2001.
Butler & Kavanagh (2002) Butler, D. & Kavanagh, D., The British General Election of 2001, Palgrave, 2002.
Cowley (2001) Cowley, P., 'The House of Commons' in Norris (2001).
Criddle (2002) Criddle. B., 'MPs and Candidates' in Butler & Kavanagh (2002).
Davies (1998) Davies, A., British Politics and Europe, Hodder and Stoughton, 1998.
EOC (2002) Equal Opportunities Commission, Man Enough for the Job? A Study of Parliamentary Candidates, EOC, 2002.
European Parliament (2002) European Parliament, Fact Sheet on the Expenses and Allowances of Members of the European Parliament DG III, Information and Public Relations Rapid Response Unit, 2002.
Flinders & Cole (1999) Flinders, M. & Cole, M., 'Opening or closing Pandora's Box? New Labour and the quango state', Talking Politics, Vol. 12.1, summer 1999.

Henderson & Sloat (1999) Henderson, A. & Sloat, A., 'New politics in Scotland? A profile of MSPs: Part 1', Talking Politics, Vol.12.1, summer 1999.
I&DEA (2002) National Census of Local Authority Councillors in England and Wales, 2001.
IPPR (2002) IPPR, Not the Great and the Good. Just the Good, www.ippr.org.uk, 21 April 2002.
Kelly (1999) Kelly, R., 'Selecting party candidates - developments since 1997', Politics Review, Vol. 12.1, summer 1999.
Labour Research (2000) Labour Research, 'Which Lords are leaping?', Labour Research, Vol.91.7, July 2002.
Lancaster (2000) Lancaster, S. (ed.), Developments in Politics, Vol.11, Causeway Press 2000.
Longmate (2000) Longmate, J., 'Women and politics' in Lancaster (2000).
Lovenduski (2001) Lovenduski, J., 'Women and politics: minority representation or critical mass?' in Norris (2001).
Norris (2001) Norris, P., Britain Votes 2001, Oxford University Press, 2001.
Saggar (2001) Saggar, S., 'The race card again' in Norris (2001).

1 President Blair?

Some commentators have complained that Tony Blair is becoming presidential. In support of this theory, they point to the way in which Blair organises his office in Ten Downing Street, his elevation above his colleagues, the way in which he attempts to appeal to the public across the political spectrum and his high media profile. They argue that the media's increasing tendency to focus on personalities and the increase in summitry contributes to the distancing of the Prime Minister from his colleagues.

Accusations of Blair-inspired 'control freakery' (in relation to the media, Parliament, the Labour Party and backbench MPs) are common. Following the events in the United States on 11 September 2001, Blair's globe-trotting activities in support of the anti-terrorist coalition provoked claims that he appeared more presidential than George Bush himself. Within the UK, despite the Prime Minister's protestations of the desirability of dispersing power away from the centre, there is evidence of the further concentration of power. Labour's reform programme is full of contradictions. It wishes to decentralise and disaggregate power while retaining, or increasing, central control.

Constraints

One of the traditional constraints on the exercise of prime ministerial power has been from the party. Blair was rarely troubled with this during his first term as Prime Minister. His huge Commons majority and the capturing of the Labour Party by New Labour ensured an extraordinarily easy ride. There are signs, however, that this may not continue throughout Blair's second term of office. Many Labour backbench MPs who were new and raw in 1997 are now more experienced and less ready to be used as 'lobby fodder'. There is also evidence that some members of the Cabinet are more prepared to flex their muscles over crucial issues such as levels and sources of public spending, UK support for elements of US foreign policy and the single European currency.

Some political scientists argue that the constraints on the Prime Minister are increasing in potency due, in part, to the way in which 'governance' has changed since 1980. The structure of government is now, these political scientists argue, fragmented into a maze of institutions and organisations. The 'Westminster model' fails to capture the complex reality of the British system. It implies that in a unitary state there is only one centre of power. In practice there are many centres and diverse links between many agencies of government at local, regional, national and supranational levels. In turn, each level has a diverse range of horizontal relationships with other government agencies, privatised utilities, private companies, voluntary organisations and community groups. There is a complex architecture to systems of government which governance seeks to emphasise and focus attention on. The centre has come to have less and less control over a much smaller public sector.

Figure 12.1 President Blair *This cartoon suggests that there is little to distinguish Tony Blair from George Bush.*

It now involves itself more in the overall direction, rather than the details, of policy.

According to political scientists such as Richard Rose, this trend is exacerbated by the effects of globalisation. The British state has become less autonomous and more dependent on supranational and transnational bodies such as the European Union, the G7, the World Trade Organisation and the International Monetary Fund. Internationally, there is the additional constraint of growing United States hegemony. Taken together with constitutional changes within the UK - notably the devolution of power to Scotland, Wales and Northern Ireland - these developments reduce the capacity of the centre to control. Rose argues that they also mean that modern British Prime Ministers are forced to become more involved in management and overall coordination rather than concentrating on the development of policy. Blair has to manage complex relations, cajole public and private agencies and reinvent the machinery of the state in order to deliver. The public still expects results but the machine is increasingly incapable of providing quick responses. This fundamentally challenges the notion that Britain is a unitary state with a strong executive.

Adapted from Rose 2001, Kavanagh 2001, Richards & Smith 2001, Thain 2002, Pierre & Stoker 2002 and *Talking Politics* 2002.

See also *British Politics in Focus*, Second Edition, pp.404-07.

2 The core executive

Because of the developments described in Section 1 above, an increasing number of political scientists have become doubtful of the relevance of the debate about whether Tony Blair has become too presidential or too powerful. Instead of arguing that power is held by one person or a small group of individuals, they claim that the crucial focus for analysis is the 'core executive'. As Thain puts it: 'Whatever the appearance of a "one-man show", the reality is that there is an identifiable core executive in the UK, made up of a number of key political actors, departments, agencies, civil servants and advisers. Power is shared.' Even resource-rich actors, such as the Prime Minister, are dependent on other actors to achieve their goals. Therefore, government works through building alliances rather than command.

According to some commentators, the trend away from government and towards governance has produced problems in ensuring the delivery of public services and effecting policy changes. Thain, for example, claims that: 'The first term of Tony Blair's administration is a case study in the enormous difficulty of steering the core executive when the state has been hollowed out'. It is, therefore, not surprising that, as Prime Minister, Blair is continuing to attempt to shore up control from the centre. That explains the attempts to reinforce the Prime Minister's position, the attempts to coordinate the executive's internal operations and the attempts to manage relationships with the wider world (including the media). In some ways what Blair has done is to retreat still further than any of his predecessors into the executive domain in order to project from a position of strength on to the wider Labour Party and country as a whole. Blair's core executive is more substantial and more integrated than any of its predecessors.

Adapted from Foley 2000, Thain 2002, Holliday 2002 and Smith 2002. See also *British Politics in Focus*, Second Edition, pp.404-07 & 428-30.

3 Blair's style of government

Media charges that Tony Blair was 'Napoleonic' in style were always a bit rich. But the 'dirigiste' (top-down) nature of the Blair regime was established early on. His is not a collegial style. Cabinet meetings are brief and none too frequent. There were 87 a year under Attlee, 60 a year under Heath but only 40 a year under Major. Blair, who calls even fewer, follows a trend in his preference for dealing with colleagues on a one-to-one basis. The idea that the Blair years have seen a harmful shift in the way we are governed is quickly scotched (the exception being the devolution of power). There is not much of a template for the powers of the Prime Minister. No law sets rules or requirements. The rough and ready code that governs the conduct of ministers applies to the Prime Minister, but there is nobody to judge whether it has been broken - except perhaps the Cabinet Secretary. As Asquith observed, the job of Prime Minister is what a person makes of it. Tony Blair's tenure comes from his personal dominance of his party and from his Commons majority. It is constrained by the power of his Chancellor, Gordon Brown. None of Napoleon's generals got anywhere close to the 'bi-stellar' relationship between Number Ten and Number Eleven. Devolution of power makes the Blair administration different from that of his predecessors. The scale of recent constitutional innovations, human rights and all, has been camouflaged by the Prime Minister's aversion to talking about it in the round. All Prime Ministers have dignitaries to see and appointments to make. Figure 12.2 shows the changing pattern of business from the 1940s to 1960s. We can surmise that Blair spends time on presentation, meeting columnists and entertaining newspaper editors. Predecessors such as Attlee would have found the media life of Tony Blair

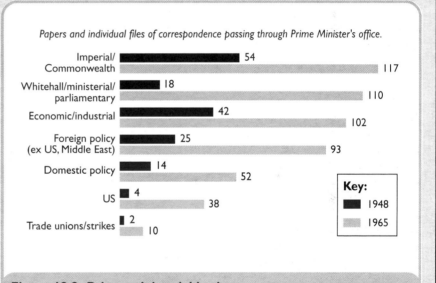

Papers and individual files of correspondence passing through Prime Minister's office.

Figure 12.2 Prime ministerial business
This chart shows the changing pattern of business from the 1940s to the 1960s. Information after 1969 has not been released because of the Thirty Year Rule.

incredible. But Blair is in tune with his predecessors in terms of his attitude to war. Actually, he is the first premier since 1945 to have presided over two conflicts in the space of six months. The Cabinet was consulted over Kosovo before Nato's air strikes and regularly informed after that. Then and during the Gulf emergencies a version of the traditional War Cabinet met, comprising the Foreign Secretary, Defence Secretary, Attorney General and Chief Press Officer. There are also precedents for the close involvement of personal advisers. In the ultra private business of government (for example, consuming the products of intelligence agencies), Blair has broken no mould. Nothing of the usual way of doing prime ministerial business has been thrown away since 1997.

Adapted from the *Guardian*, 9 October 2000.

See also *British Politics in Focus*, Second Edition, pp.408-12.

4 Blair and Brown

Tony Blair's relationship with Gordon Brown is crucial and is closer than that between any other Prime Minister and Chancellor in recent years. Unusually, Blair has not sought independent economic advice and has accepted Brown's superiority in economic policy. In a departure from previous prime-ministerial practice, he has allowed Brown to chair the key Economic Affairs Committee of the Cabinet. Brown has taken on the role of overlord over a wide range of domestic policies, especially welfare reform, which has gone beyond the usual Treasury interest in all aspects of spending.

The Chancellor has had a leading role in the design of the New Deal welfare-to-work programme and changes to pensions policy. He has gained influence over large parts of domestic policy through the imposition by the Treasury of public spending agreements, in which departments have to account for the conduct of their affairs before money is released.

There are many accounts of the stormy relationship between Blair and Brown. In particular, Brown is said to harbour intense resentment over the way he was elbowed out of the running to succeed John Smith as Leader of the Labour Party. Whatever the truth of the personal friction, there is no evidence of the slightest disagreement

Figure 12.3 *Tony Blair and Gordon Brown.*

about how to handle the economy, something which most commentators agree to have been the success story of the first Blair government.

Adapted from Thomas 2002.

See also *British Politics in Focus*, Second Edition, pp.409-12.

5 Political advisers

Tony Blair prefers working informally with small teams of people. He likes to appoint people he trusts to work on specific projects. These individuals are often recruited from outside of the ranks of the Labour Party to advise on particular policy areas - for example, John Birt (the former Director-General of the BBC) was chosen by Blair to advise on future transport policy. Blair is accused of relying on his personal advisers in preference to his Cabinet ministers as well as devaluing the policy advice of senior civil servants.

The increased reliance on political advisers is not confined to the Prime Minister. Most ministers make use of them (individually or in the form of think tanks).

Nonetheless, a minister surrounded by political advisers risks provoking jealousy and resentment among Cabinet colleagues. Previous Prime Ministers have found that this can backfire on them.

The widespread use of political advisers, and the blurring of the distinction between adviser and the traditionally 'neutral' civil servant (who now often work alongside one another) has become a source of tension in Blair's government. This came to a head with the crisis over the Transport Secretary's special adviser, Jo Moore, and the civil servant heading the DTLGR's communications office, Martin Sixsmith - both leaving their posts following the press exposure of disputes within their department.

Adapted from Kavanagh 2001 and Thain 2002. See also *British Politics in Focus*, Second Edition, pp.414-15.

6 The Cabinet Committee on Constitutional Affairs

The Cabinet Consultative Committee on Constitutional Affairs was set up soon after the 1997 general election. The committee was chaired by Blair, but contained an equal number of Labour ministers and leading Liberal Democrats. This committee was seen as part of 'the Project' devised by Blair and Paddy Ashdown, Leader of the Liberal Democrats, in 1994. The two men hoped to realign the progressive forces in British politics and to bring the Liberal Democrats into government alongside New Labour.

In 1999, however, Ashdown resigned as Leader of the Liberal Democrats. He was replaced by Charles Kennedy. In September 2001, Kennedy, announced that his party would

no longer participate in the joint Cabinet committee. In the last two years of its existence, the joint Cabinet committee met only twice. Charles Kennedy recognised that it was merely a way of making the Liberal Democrats feel that they were being consulted, without actually giving them any real power. Ending the relationship with Labour also fitted more easily with Kennedy's wish to see the Liberal Democrats become the main opposition party, not the junior party to Labour in some future coalition arrangement.

Adapted from Rathbone 2002.

See also *British Politics in Focus*, Second Edition, pp.423-24.

7 The Prime Minister's Office

Under Tony Blair, the Prime Minister's Office has taken on a greater policy and coordinating role. Number Ten has become the 'powerhouse' of government, keeping a tight reign on its activities in order to drive policy forward and to coordinate the work of government generally. Since 1997, there has been:

- a considerable increase in the number of political appointments
- a considerable increase in the number of people employed to work in Number Ten (by 2002, there was double the number working there under John Major and three times as many as in 1962)
- a growing tendency of staff working for Number Ten to intervene in the policy-process of individual departments
- pressure on ministers to consult and inform Number Ten before launching policy initiatives
- the increased politicisation of the Downing Street Policy Unit.

Significant changes were made after the 2001 general election. The aim was to enhance the ability of Number Ten to monitor the work of government across the board, possibly threatening the role of the Treasury and increasing the tension between the Prime Minister's and Chancellor's supporters. The most significant change was the merging of the Prime Minister's Private Office and the Policy Unit. This became one of three new units headed by key allies of Tony Blair:

- Alastair Campbell, until then the Prime Minister's official spokesperson, was asked to head a new Communications

Figure 12.4 Number Ten *Since 1997, Number Ten has become the 'powerhouse' of government. This photo provides a glimpse inside.*

and Strategy Unit
- Anji Hunter, formerly the Prime Minister's Personal Assistant, was asked to head a new Government Relations Unit to oversee relations with ministers and the devolved assemblies, as well as with the Labour Party and others (when Hunter left, Sally Morgan took over)
- Jeremy Heywood, a civil servant, was asked to head the merged Private Office and Policy Unit - Heywood works alongside Jonathan Powell (Blair's Chief of Staff who retains overall management of the Prime Minister's Office).

Adapted from Smith 2002 and Thomas 2002.
See also *British Politics in Focus*, Second Edition, pp.412-16.

8 Should there be a Prime Minister's department?

No hard-and-fast boundary can be drawn around the Prime Minister's Office. Externally it has long been amorphous and permeable. Its shape and size vary, depending on time, activity and political circumstances. It can incorporate aides in a variety of Whitehall offices to work for the Prime Minister, or transfer to new or existing institutions roles once undertaken within Number Ten. Its porous boundaries enable staff appointed to other ministries or offices to liaise so closely and so frequently with Number Ten that it becomes a quibble whether they work for the Prime Minister, the Chief Whip, the Cabinet or the Treasury. Setting up a Prime Minister's Department would freeze current structural arrangements, and persistence would be needed by Prime Ministers intent on changing practices to suit their styles of working. It might become less efficient and versatile, exposing some ambiguous relationships that help facilitate the process of governance.

A formal Prime Minister's department would also be likely to interfere with the increasingly integrated nature of the relationships between the Prime Minister's Office and the Cabinet Office which itself underwent major reforms following a report by Sir Richard Wilson, the Cabinet Secretary in 1998. The two offices now work closely together and are overseen by the Chief of Staff. The result is that there are increasingly close links between the various secretariats in the Cabinet Office and officials in Number Ten, especially the Policy Unit. Regular meetings led by the Cabinet Secretary include a small group of Permanent Secretaries from the most important departments plus aides from Number Ten. Although these changes mean a transformation at the heart of the British state, they should be seen as the continuation of trends that were set in motion some time ago, rather than any revolutionary break with the past.

Adapted from Thain 2002 and Thomas 2002.
See also *British Politics in Focus*, Second Edition, pp.414-15.

9 Cabinet committees

Even early in Blair's first term, there were indications that less use was being made of the system of Cabinet committees. This trend seems to have continued, with Cabinet committees being downgraded in importance. Although they still feature in the formal organisational structure of government (see Figure 12.5), their use is patchy.

Cabinet committees (February 2002)	
Economic & Domestic - committees 11	
sub-committees & working groups 19	
Domestic Affairs	(DPM, 21)
Economic Affairs	(CE, 19)
Public Services & Public Expenditure	(CE, 9)
Legislative Programme	(LC, 15)
Environment Dep	(PM, 20)
Civil Contingencies - committees 1	
Civil Contingencies	(HS 2+*)
Central - committees 2	
sub-committees & working groups 3	
Constitutional Reform Policy	(LdC, 12)
JCC (Consultative with Lib Democrats)	(PM, 2+*)
Overseas & Defence - committees 3	
sub-committees & working groups 3	
Defence & Overseas Policy	(PM, 7)
Northern Ireland	(PM, 7)
Intelligence Services	(PM, 7)
Europe - committees 2	
European Issues	(FS, 23)

Membership varies according to issue.

Figure 12.5 Cabinet committees *This table shows the Cabinet committees in existence in February 2002.*

Blair is not unusual in using the creation of a committee, or the amendment of a committee's membership or terms of reference, as a means of signalling a change in the priorities of his administration. He creates sub-committees or working groups as a means of developing policy in new emergent areas of activity (for example the sub-committees on biotechnology and E-democracy). The committee structure is also used to ensure balance between factions of the Cabinet and to protect the Prime Minister from the growing power of Gordon Brown's Treasury. The Chairs of the key committees have remained the same throughout the Blair premiership, although personnel in some of those offices of state have varied. The Deputy Prime Minister chairs the core Domestic Affairs Committee, the Lord Chancellor remains in charge of Constitutional Reform, and the Prime Minister chairs all the overseas and defence committees.

Where is the portion of business that would once have been transacted in Cabinet committee now being handled? The answer is complex. Some strategic thinking takes place in ad hoc meetings of senior ministers convened by Blair. Further policy planning is done in meetings involving the Prime Minister, his closest officials and advisers, and a senior minister and their advisers, or between the Prime Minister and a senior minister alone. The most important of the latter are Blair-Brown meetings which happen several times a week. Blair-Prescott, on the domestic front, and Blair-Irvine are other important bilaterals. Peter Mandelson also remains a significant figure in the Prime Minister's entourage. On a quarterly basis, Blair meets with key ministers and officials to check progress on the government's programme. More detailed cross-departmental policy development takes place in the welter of units, task forces, reviews and groups created by this government.

Adapted from Thomas 2002, Thain 2002 and Holliday 2002.
See also *British Politics in Focus*, Second Edition, pp.422-25.

10 The decline of Cabinet government

According to Dennis Kavanagh, it is difficult to think of any other Prime Minister who has shown so little regard for the Cabinet as Blair. Colin Thain talks about 'a lack of drive, energy and debate within the Cabinet' and asks whether this heralds the terminal decline of this institution of government. He also notes that Blair regards the formal Cabinet (that meets weekly on a Thursday) as essentially a reporting body. Blair uses the Cabinet in a very different way from the earlier Labour Prime Minister, Harold Wilson, for whom it was a policy and political debating forum.

Allegations about a decline in Cabinet government are not new. Blair's apparent preference for making decisions in one-to-one meetings with ministers or in small groups can be seen as part of a longer-term trend away from collective government. This trend seems to have intensified under Blair. Certainly, since 1997 Cabinet meetings have been brief, generally under an hour, with Blair trying to focus on strategic issues. A joke became popular among ministers. Why does the tea trolley serve only half the Cabinet? Because the meetings are over before it can reach the other side.

Even so, it should not be concluded that the Cabinet has become defunct. Thain argues that it remains at the head of

Figure 12.6 Is Cabinet government dead?
This photo shows Tony Blair sitting alone in the Cabinet room.

a complex web of Cabinet committees and sub-committees and of various groups of ministers, officials and advisers of varying degrees of formality and permanence. And it is in these groups and committees, as well as in bilateral meetings, that the big policy debates under Blair are conducted.

Adapted from Rawnsley 2000, Kavanagh 2001 and Thain 2002.
See also *British Politics in Focus*, Second Edition, pp.427-30.

11 The Cabinet Office

The shake-up of the Cabinet Office in July 1998 had important consequences. In the view of a number of commentators, the reforms made the Cabinet Office an executive office (similar to that in the White House). In particular, the Social Exclusion Unit, created in December 1997, and the Performance and Innovation Unit, set up in 1998, seek to deal with issues which cut across departmental boundaries. Although these units are staffed by civil servants, members of the Policy Unit are closely involved in the projects. The Prime Minister's Office and Cabinet Office are now closely integrated by the Chief of Staff who seeks to pull the work together. There are increasingly close links between the various secretariats in the Cabinet Office and officials in Number Ten, especially the Policy Unit. Regular meetings led by the Cabinet Secretary include a small group of permanent secretaries from the most important departments plus aides from Number Ten.

Adapted from Thomas 2002. See also *British Politics in Focus*, Second Edition, pp.425-26.

12 The Cabinet enforcer

In July 1998, as part of a re-organisation of the Cabinet Office, a Cabinet minister was appointed as its political head with strategic responsibility to drive Tony Blair's agenda in Whitehall. This post was dubbed 'Cabinet enforcer' and its first holder was Jack Cunningham. As Minister for the Cabinet Office, Cunningham was expected to attend weekly planning meetings with the Prime Minister, the Prime Minister's Chief of Staff and the Cabinet Secretary. He also chaired the daily strategy meetings about the presentation of policy to prevent 'inter-departmental muddles that cause bad publicity'.

After a little over a year in the job, Cunningham was replaced by Mo Mowlam. For Mowlam, following a period as Secretary of State for Northern Ireland, the move was seen by many as a demotion. Mowlam eventually decided to leave government - and Westminster politics - and her duties were for a while taken on by the Deputy Prime Minister, John Prescott. Following the 2001 general election, however, the post of Cabinet enforcer (Minister for the Cabinet Office) was handed to Gus MacDonald. MacDonald was not in the Cabinet (which might indicate that the job has been somewhat downgraded since its initial conception) but, as far as his 'enforcing' role is concerned, he does report direct to the Prime Minister. Based in the Office of Deputy Prime Minister and Cabinet Office, MacDonald's duties were described by John Prescott as follows: '[MacDonald] has day-to-day responsibility for the work of the Delivery Unit, which supports the Prime Minister on matters to do with the delivery of public services. He will [also] work closely with me as appropriate on related cross-cutting issues covered by the Cabinet committees under my chairmanship'.

Figure 12.7 The Cabinet enforcer
Gus MacDonald was appointed as Cabinet enforcer after the 2001 general election.

Adapted from McSmith 1999 and material on the Cabinet Office website.
See also *British Politics in Focus*, Second Edition, pp.425-27.

References

Cabinet Office website: http://www.cabinet-office.gov.uk
Dunleavy et al. (2000) Dunleavy, P., Gamble, A., Holliday, I. & Peele. G. (eds), *Developments in British Politics*, Vol.6, Macmillan, 2000.
ESRC (2002) ESRC Whitehall Programme, *The Changing Nature of Central Government in Britain*: www.ncl.ac.uk/politics/resources/whitehall/index.html.
Foley (2000) Foley, M., *The British Presidency: Tony Blair and the Politics of Public Leadership*, Manchester University Press, 2000.
Holliday (2002) Holliday, I., 'Executives and administrations' in *Dunleavy et al. (2002)*.
Kavanagh (2001) Kavanagh, D., 'Tony Blair as Prime Minister', *Politics Review*, Vol.11.1, September 2001.
Lancaster (2002) Lancaster, S. (ed.), *Developments in Politics*, Vol 13, Causeway Press, 2002.
Ludlam & Smith (2001) Ludlam, S. & Smith, M.J. (eds), *New Labour in Government*, Palgrave, 2001.
McSmith (1999) McSmith, A., 'So what exactly does Jack the Enforcer do?', *The Observer*, 28 February 1999.

Pierre & Stoker (2002) Pierre, J. & Stoker, G., 'Towards multi-level governance' in *Dunleavy et al. (2002)*.
Rathbone (2002) Rathbone, M., 'Labour and the Liberal Democrats', *Talking Politics*, Vol.14.3, April 2002.
Rawnsley (2000) Rawnsley, A., *Servants of the People: The Inside Story of New Labour*, Hamish Hamilton, 2000.
Richards & Smith (2001) Richards, D. & Smith, M.J., 'New Labour, the constitution and reforming the state' in *Ludlam & Smith (2001)*.
Rose (2001) Rose, R., *The Prime Minister in a Shrinking World*, Polity Press, 2001.
Smith (2002) Smith, M. 'The "core executive" in Britain?' in *ESRC (2002)*.
Talking Politics (2002) 'News briefing', *Talking Politics*, Vol.14.2, January 2002.
Thain (2002) Thain, C., 'The core executive under Blair: the first term' in *Lancaster (2002)*.
Thomas (2002) Thomas, G., 'The Prime Minister and the Cabinet', *Politics Review*, Vol.11.4, April 2002.

1 Ministers on the way up

Tessa Jowell

Born September 17 1947, London. Married with two children, three step-children.

Education St Margaret's, Aberdeen; University of Aberdeen; University of Edinburgh; Goldsmith's College, London.

Career history
Childcare officer, London Borough of Lambeth, 1969-71; psychiatric social worker, Maudsley hospital, 1972-74; Assistant Director, Mind, 1974-86; Senior Visiting Research Fellow, Policy Studies Institute 1987-90; Director of the Joseph Rowntree Foundation's Community Care Programme, 1990-92.

Political career
Councillor, London Borough of Camden (1971-86); Chair, Social Services Committee of the Association of Metropolitan Authorities (1978-86); Governor of National Institute of Social Work (1985-97) and member of Mental Health Act Commission (1986-90); MP for Dulwich and West Norwood since 1992; Opposition Spokeswoman: Health 1994-95; Women, 1995-96, 1996-97. Minister for Public Health, 1997-99; Employment Minister, 1999-2001; Privy Counsellor October 1998; Secretary of State for Culture, Media and Sport since June 2001.

High
Proud of her part in bringing in the New Deal, putting long-term unemployed into work.

Low
Acting like a state broadcaster when the TV show *Brass Eye* tackled paedophilia. Jowell said the programme was in bad taste, though she had not seen it. She spoke to the Head of Channel 4 and challenged the Independent Television Commission over why it failed to react to complaints.

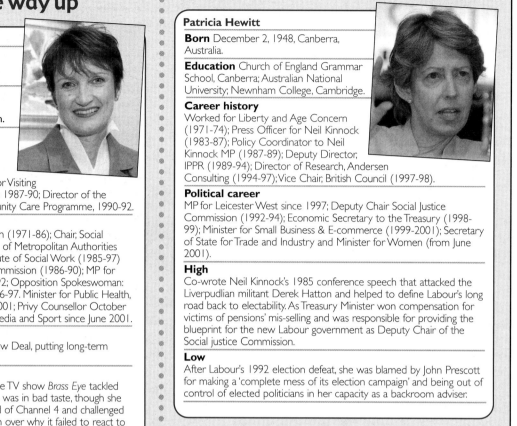

Patricia Hewitt

Born December 2, 1948, Canberra, Australia.

Education Church of England Grammar School, Canberra; Australian National University; Newnham College, Cambridge.

Career history
Worked for Liberty and Age Concern (1971-74); Press Officer for Neil Kinnock (1983-87); Policy Coordinator to Neil Kinnock MP (1987-89); Deputy Director, IPPR (1989-94); Director of Research, Andersen Consulting (1994-97); Vice Chair, British Council (1997-98).

Political career
MP for Leicester West since 1997; Deputy Chair Social Justice Commission (1992-94); Economic Secretary to the Treasury (1998-99); Minister for Small Business & E-commerce (1999-2001); Secretary of State for Trade and Industry and Minister for Women (from June 2001).

High
Co-wrote Neil Kinnock's 1985 conference speech that attacked the Liverpudlian militant Derek Hatton and helped to define Labour's long road back to electability. As Treasury Minister won compensation for victims of pensions' mis-selling and was responsible for providing the blueprint for the new Labour government as Deputy Chair of the Social justice Commission.

Low
After Labour's 1992 election defeat, she was blamed by John Prescott for making a 'complete mess of its election campaign' and being out of control of elected politicians in her capacity as a backroom adviser.

Adapted from the *Guardian* 11 March and 15 April 2002.
See also *British Politics in Focus*, Second Edition, pp.433-36.

2 The restructuring of government departments, 2001

Following the 2001 general election, Tony Blair appointed a new Cabinet and took the opportunity to restructure government departments. One of the major changes was the division of the DETR - Department of Environment, Transport and the Regions (created in 1997 and run by the Deputy Prime Minister, John Prescott). In 2001, the environment function was taken away from the DETR and a new department created - the Department of Transport, Local Government and the Regions (DTLR). This new department has been described as: 'a loose and baggy monster responsible for the Queen Elizabeth Conference Centre, home helps for the elderly, the fire service college, coastguards, and driving licences as well as rail, road, air and sea transport, councils, the English regions, elections and a lot more'. The fact that transport was the first mentioned item in the department's title was an indication that this would be a priority for the Labour government during its second term. As a department, the DTLR has a high budget of £56 billion a year but £37 billion is given directly to local councils. The department employs some 16,700 staff but only 20% of them work at the department's headquarters in London.

The environment function of the DETR was given to a second newly formed department - the Department for the Environment, Food and Rural Affairs (DEFRA). This new department marked the end of the old Ministry of Agriculture, Fisheries and Food, signalling a growth in the importance of the environment and a decline in the relative importance of farming. It also signalled the displeasure felt by the government about the handling of the foot-and-mouth crisis by the old ministry.

A third new department was the Department for Education and Skills (DfES). This department had previously been the Department for Education and Employment and marked the emphasis the government placed on training.

The final change was the creation of the Department for Work and Pensions (DWP). Previously this had been the Department for Social Security. The new department has the responsibility for 'pensions, the Child Support Agency and the new Working Age Agency which has merged employment services with benefits agencies'. There is a very large staff of 125,000 and a budget of £100 billion but most of the staff are involved in paying benefits and the budget is largely determined by entitlements of the claimants. All the other departments, within the Cabinet, remained largely unchanged.

Adapted from the *Times*, 9 June 2001, the *Guardian*, 26 February 2002 and Thain 2002.
See also *British Politics in Focus*, Second Edition, pp.433-36.

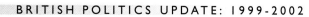

3 Reshuffle in 2002

Only a year after forming his new government following the 2001 general election, Tony Blair was forced to reshuffle his government following the resignation of Stephen Byers on 28 May 2002.

Resignation of Stephen Byers

Stephen Byers, the Transport Secretary, had been under pressure for many months, following a series of mishaps in his department. These included:

- the furore that arose when it was discovered that Jo Moore, Byers' spin doctor, had sent an e-mail on 11 September 2001 suggesting it was a good day to bury bad news
- criticism from the City over Byers' decision to force Railtrack into administration
- criticism that Byers had played a part in allowing Richard Desmond, who owned pornographic magazines, to take over the *Express* newspaper
- a series of claims that Byers lied to parliament.

Stephen Byers said in his resignation speech: 'What is clear to me...is that I have become a distraction from what the government is achieving; that the debate we need to have about key policy issues is being distorted by my involvement; that by remaining in office I damage the government'. Critics noted that he announced his resignation when the Commons was in recess so there could be no debate on the issues and that he failed to apologise for his actions. While the resignation could be seen as the minister taking individual responsibility for his actions, the resignation could also be seen as an attempt to head off criticism of the collective actions of the government and Tony Blair.

Changes in personnel

The changes in personnel in the reshuffle of May 2002 were extensive. Eight junior ministers were sacked from the government, 25 were reshuffled and seven new junior ministers were appointed. At Cabinet level, the following changes took place:

- Alistair Darling, who had been Secretary of State for Work and Pensions, became Secretary of State for Transport
- Andrew Smith, who had been Chief Secretary to the Treasury, became Secretary of State for Work and Pensions
- Paul Boateng, who was Financial Secretary of State to the Treasury, became Chief Secretary to the Treasury (see Figure 13.1).

Several MPs elected for the first time in 2001 were promoted to ministerial level, including David Milliband who became the new Schools Minister.

Structure

Byers' resignation also resulted in the break-up of the DTLR. Local government and transport were separated, leaving Alistair Darling as Transport Minister in a government department that was smaller, but had major problems to resolve. John Prescott, who lost control of a big department (DETR) in June 2001, was appointed head of a new

Figure 13.1 Paul Boateng
In May 2002, Paul Boateng became the first black person to be appointed as a Cabinet minister.

ministry - Office of the Deputy Prime Minister - which took over local government and the regions. Consequently, Prescott moved out of the Cabinet Office. Gus MacDonald was appointed Minister for the Cabinet (ie was given the role of 'Cabinet enforcer'), with a brief to report directly to Tony Blair.

Conclusion

The reshuffle can be seen as a sign of weakness in the sense that the timing was forced and happened very early in the life of the Parliament. It reduced the likelihood of many more reshuffles before the next general election. The fact that DTLR was broken up suggests that 'super ministries' are judged to have failed. The new Cabinet ministers who have been appointed, Alistair Darling and Andrew Smith, are there because they are regarded as having a 'safe pair of hands' to run departments effectively rather than imaginative appointments in their own right.

Figure 13.2 The break-up of the DTLR
This cartoon suggests that John Prescott (the dog) and Alistair Darling were being handed a poisoned chalice in the reshuffle of May 2002.

Adapted from the *Guardian*, 29 and 30 May 2002.
See also *British Politics in Focus*, Second Edition, pp.436-37.

4 Successful ministers

Figure 13.3 shows that the personal poll rating of Stephen Byers had plunged to minus 49 points by May 2002. This made him more unpopular than Margaret Thatcher ever was in office. The fall in support was dramatic. A year earlier, he had a plus 11 points rating. A week after this survey, he resigned. Gordon Brown's popularity, however, was soaring in May 2002. At that time, he was by far the most popular leading member of the Cabinet. Tony Blair's rating, on the other hand, had dropped to the same level as in March 2001. During the autumn of 2001 while the war against Afghanistan was being fought, it had grown to plus 42.

The chart in Figure 13.4 shows that some departments respond to MPs' questions more speedily than others. This raises the question of whether the variable performance in answering MPs' questions is a legitimate sign of ministerial ineptitude. At present, there are no objective measures of how well a minister heads a department, delivers policy targets or sustains Cabinet government.

Unsuccessful ministers

The reasons why ministers leave their posts vary. In some cases, it is because the Prime Minister has made a judgement that they are not performing well. In other cases (Peter Mandelson and Geoffrey Robinson, for example), it is because of scandal. Occasionally, there are ideological reasons for leaving. For example, Peter Kilfoyle left his post as junior Defence Minister because he felt Labour was in danger of ignoring its core voters in industrial areas.

Adapted from the *Guardian*, 14 February 2001 and 21 May 2002. See also *British Politics in Focus*, Second Edition, pp.442-46.

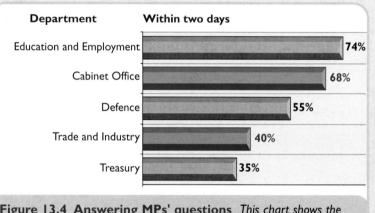

	Satisfied	Don't know	Dissatisfied	Net rating	Previous ICM rating	
Tony Blair	49	8	43	6	42	(11/01)
Gordon Brown	67	11	22	45	28	(05/01)
John Prescott	39	14	47	-8	-11	(05/01)
Robin Cook	37	29	34	3	8	(01/00)
Jack Straw	45	17	38	7	0	(05/01)
David Blunkett	52	18	32	20	27	(05/01)
Estelle Morris	35	29	35	0	n/a	
Tessa Jowell	34	43	23	11	n/a	
Stephen Byers	18	14	67	-49	11	(05/01)
Alan Milburn	37	18	45	-8	-14	(06/00)

Figure 13.3 The public's view
This table shows the results of a survey published on 21 May 2002.

Department	Within two days
Education and Employment	74%
Cabinet Office	68%
Defence	55%
Trade and Industry	40%
Treasury	35%

Figure 13.4 Answering MPs' questions *This chart shows the percentage of MPs' questions answered within two days.*

5 Civil service – top jobs

While, in April 2002, there were approximately half a million civil servants in total, it is the senior civil servants who have the crucial role in Whitehall. There were 3,429 senior civil servants in April 2002.

One of the key features of the senior civil service has been the sense of permanence, with a career path stretching from post-university recruitment to retirement. While this is still a common pattern for civil servants appointed a decade or more ago, there are an increasing number of new civil servants who have been recruited from outside the civil service later in their lives. This has particularly been the case in the recruitment of Next Step Agencies' Chief Executives. Of the 138 Agency Chief Executive appointments made by September 1998, 92 had been made by open competition and 31 had been recruited from outside the civil service. This is important as over 75% of the civil service now work in the executive agencies. Outsiders have also have been recruited to specific top posts within the civil service. For example, Michael Barber, who was a special adviser to David Blunkett, has become a career civil servant and Head of the Prime Minister's Delivery Unit.

Permanent Secretaries

Among the top ranks of the Permanent Secretaries, however, relatively little has changed. Rhodes claims that the typical senior civil servant in each government department is a white man, over the age of 50, with an Oxbridge degree in the humanities who has worked in the civil service for 25 to 30 years. He will have served in a central as well as a functional ministry and will retire at 60 after five to ten years in the top job.

The Head of the Home Civil Service

In September 2002, the Head of the Home Civil Service fitted all of the criteria listed by Rhodes above. Andrew Turnbull took over the role as Head of the Home Civil Service in 2002. He joined the civil service in 1970, beginning in the Treasury, but later working in the Prime Minister's Office. He was educated at Cambridge and is a keen cricketer and sailor. He has been a career civil servant all his life and is expected to remain in post until his retirement. When Turnbull was appointed to the post by Tony Blair, the position was not externally advertised and the other contenders for the post who held senior civil service positions had similar backgrounds.

Adapted from Greenwood 1999, Rhodes 2001 and the *Guardian*, 15 March and 9 April 2002. See also *British Politics in Focus*, Second Edition, pp.452-56.

6 The civil service under Labour

Under Labour, there has been both continuity with the previous Conservative administration and some elements of change.

Continuity

Three Conservative initiatives have remained substantially unaltered. First, the Next Steps programme continued. By 2000, over 75% of civil servants worked in executive agencies managed by Chief Executives, accountable to their ministers and senior departmental officials (see Figure 13.5). Second, the Citizens Charter programme remained in place, though it was renamed 'Service First' in 1998. And third, the Private Finance Initiative, renamed as the Public-Private Partnership, has been retained and expanded as a way of building new hospitals and schools.

Change

Change was signalled in the 1999 White Paper *Modernising Government* which had as its objective: 'better government to make life better for the people'. The intention was to reform the civil service by providing incentives to provide innovation and excellent service delivery. In addition, there were plans for high-quality and efficient public services, more outsiders to be brought in to Whitehall, public services to be available 24 hours a day where there was a demand and more 'joined up' government.

The Wilson Report

The civil service response to the White Paper is known as the 'Wilson Report' because it was written by the Cabinet Secretary and Head of the Home Civil Service, Richard Wilson. It was published in 1999 with the stated goal of creating a more open, diverse and professional civil service. There were a number of themes:

- greater leadership particularly at the top of the civil service
- better business planning
- improvement of performance management
- bringing in outsiders and developing existing staff
- improving diversity by setting targets for numbers of women, ethnic minorities and people with disabilities
- improvements for staff.

Critics

Critics argued that these changes would end the traditional basis of the civil service for three main reasons.

1. The injection of business values was inappropriate in the public sector.
2. The concern for value for money did not take sufficient account of public service ethos.
3. The unified civil service and its career base would be undermined which, in turn, would threaten its impartiality.

Implementation of reforms

Despite criticism, the changes suggested by the Wilson Report have been implemented. A year after the report, there had been an increase of nearly 50% in the number of appointments to the senior civil service from open competition, with almost 66% of the posts being filled by outsiders. It should be noted, though, that these percentages start from a low base point and that there is still resistance to change. At times, relations between New Labour and the civil service have proved difficult. One policy adviser complained about civil servants' old-fashioned approach ('they don't even carry mobile phones').

Labour ministers hoped that civil servants would accept change with enthusiasm. But civil servants have clung to the conventions

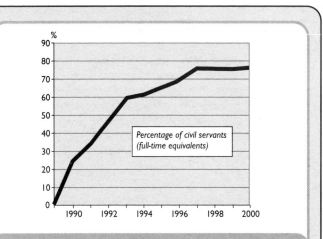

Figure 13.5 Civil servants and Next Steps *This graph shows the percentage of civil servants working in executive agencies under the Next Steps programme.*

of neutrality. Figure 13.6 shows the number of knowledge specialists (as opposed to traditional 'generalists') in Whitehall in May 2001.

Before Wilson retired from his post as Cabinet Secretary in 2002, he called for a Civil Service Act to protect the neutrality of the civil service. He expressed concern that civil servants were being drawn into the political arena and argued that an Act was needed which would: 'clarify the grey boundaries between what is and what is not acceptable, as well as the boundaries between government and party'. Hugo Young, writing in the *Guardian*, claimed that the Blairites had wrecked the best of the civil service and that Whitehall 'must restore its impartiality or kowtow to ministerial liars'.

New Cabinet Secretary

Andrew Turnbull, the new incoming Cabinet Secretary, announced a change in his role. There is to be a strengthened Cabinet Office with a new 'reform and delivery team' of civil servants under his leadership. This will change the role of units and advisers working around Number Ten. The intention is to allow the civil service to focus on administration while politicians focus on policies. Turnbull told his fellow Permanent Secretaries that he would hold them 'to account for delivering the government's agenda - and cut their bonuses if they failed'.

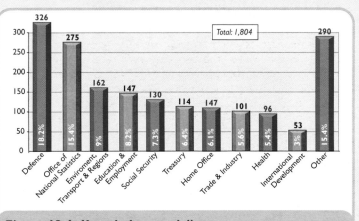

Figure 13.6 Knowledge specialists
This chart shows the number and percentage of knowledge specialists (ie economists, statisticians, social and operational researchers) in government departments in May 2001.

Adapted from HMSO 1999, Pyper 2000, Rathbone 2000, Cabinet Office 2000, Chapman 2001, Butcher 2002 and the *Guardian*, 2 March, 27 March, 9 April and 25 June 2002. See also *British Politics in Focus*, Second Edition, pp.447-50.

7 Political advisers – an overview

Between May 1997 and March 2002, the number of special advisers grew from 38 to 83. By March 2002, the cost to the taxpayer was £4.6 million a year. The relevant minister or Prime Minster brings special advisers into departments or Downing Street to gain advice from specialists who share their political outlook but who are separate from their civil servants. Unlike civil servants, special advisers:

- are not permanent employees
- are appointed personally by the Secretary of State or Prime Minister
- may not be anonymous
- serve their minister and the party, not the Crown.

According to Andrew Rawnsley, 27 special advisers were working for Tony Blair in 2000 (out of a total Downing Street staff of 149) and two of them - Alastair Campbell (Director of Communications) and Jonathan Powell (Chief of Staff) - were the most powerful people in Downing Street after the Prime Minister. Special Orders in Council had to be passed to allow Campbell and Powell to give orders to civil servants.

Concern about the influence and growth in the numbers of special advisers led to Lord Neill's Report *Reinforcing Standards*, published in 2000. This recommended that the number of special advisers should be limited and that their activities should be subject to a code of conduct backed by law. Concern about special advisers has not abated since then, however, especially after controversy involving a

Ministry of Agriculture, Fisheries and Food	2
Ministry of Defence	2
Department for Education and Employment	5
Department of the Environment, Transport and the Regions	5
Foreign and Commonwealth Office	2
Department of Health	2
Home Office	2
Departmnt of Social Security	2
Department of Trade and industry	2
Treasury	8

Figure 13.7 Special advisers
This table shows the number of special advisers in selected government departments in 2000.

number of them, notably Jo Moore who sent the notorious e-mail on 11 September 2001 saying that the terrorist attacks on the USA provided a good opportunity to bury bad news. Put simply, special advisers are often accused of putting a political spin on information for party political gain rather than telling the truth or providing useful advice.

John Birt

As well as special advisers paid for by the taxpayer, other experts (including business leaders, management consultants, academics and even seconded officials from other governments) work for Tony Blair and other government ministers. An example is John Birt, former Director General of the BBC, who was appointed in 2001 to provide advice on long-term transport strategy, working in the Forward Strategy Unit of Number Ten Downing Street (see Figure 13.8). Since advisers like Birt are not paid by the taxpayer and many work part-time, their position and status are hidden from MPs and even from Whitehall ministries. The Transport, Local Government and the Regions Select Committee, with a Labour majority, claimed: 'Never in peacetime has a prime minister gathered about himself such an assemblage of apparatchiks unaccountable to parliament'. One reason for the select committee's concern was the refusal of Birt to testify before it, but members also felt that the proliferation of advisers and policy units generated meddling and confusion.

Task groups and advisory groups

In addition to the special advisers are the 238 or so task forces, advisory groups and reviews set up between 1997 and 2002. By mid-2002, there were some 1,500 people employed on these task forces. The Department for Education and Skills topped the list, with some 60 reviews including one on citizenship, one on nutritional standards in schools and another called the Gifted Pupils Advisory Group. Critics have argued that civil servants could have carried out this work and that the creation of task forces is a way of avoiding decisions.

Figure 13.8 John Birt
This cartoon mocks the appointment of John Birt, the former Director General of the BBC, who was appointed to work as a part-time special adviser in the Forward Strategy Unit in Number Ten Downing Street in August 2001. His appointment was criticised by some commentators on the grounds that he had no track record to suggest that he had the expertise to devise workable solutions to difficult policy problems.

Adapted from the *Observer*, 31 December 2000, Dargie & Locke 2001, Rawnsley 2001, Butcher 2002 and the *Guardian*, 13 January 2000, 13 March and 8 June 2001, 9 January, 5 March, 15 March and 3 May 2002. See also *British Politics in Focus*, Second Edition, pp.460-61 & 464.

8 Political advisers – the view from inside

According to Pat McFadden, the former Deputy Chief of Staff at Downing Street, civil servants asked special advisers to warn Tony Blair when a Cabinet colleague was about to explode. 'Private Secretaries did not feel it was their place to tell the Prime Minister when a policy change could lead to an explosion from another Cabinet minister. So they would ask us to do that', he told an independent inquiry on 1 July 2002. Although he did not name ministers, it apppears McFadden was referring to differences between Blair and Prescott, not Blair and Brown. McFadden made a spirited defence of the good relationships between the press office, special advisers and senior civil servants at Downing Street. Not only did special advisers brief the media, but he was often asked to brief journalists: 'It was more to give a journalist the background of how a minister felt about a particular issue'. McFadden painted a different picture to that of chaos at the Department of Transport under Stephen Byers, with special adviser Jo Moore and the Chief Press Officer, Martin Sixsmith at each other's throats. He described relations in Number Ten as 'harmonious' and could not see why the Standards and Privileges Committee (which was holding the inquiry) might want to introduce rules regulating the relationship between special advisers, civil servants and ministers.

Adapted from the *Guardian*, 2 July 2002.
See also *British Politics in Focus*, Second Edition, pp.460-61 & 464.

9 Do civil servants still have a policy role?

According to Dargie and Locke, in recent years, the civil service has stopped playing its traditional role because the delivery of policy advice has begun to be performed by other organisations and bodies. There has been a loss of functions in the following directions:

- **upwards** to ministers, to alternative deliverers of policy advice (increasing use of think tanks and policy advisers) and to the European Union
- **downwards** to Next Steps and the regions, especially to the Scottish Parliament and the Welsh Assembly
- **outwards** to interest groups and professional organisations as well as to the judiciary and the regulatory agencies
- **through** privatisation, with a consequent reduction in the numbers of civil servants.

As a result, the civil service's key function has changed from providing policy advice to managing areas of work.

The civil service's role was changing before 1997, Dargie and Locke argue, but the change has become more marked since then. One sign of this is the growth in special advisers and task forces described above. A second sign is the way in which at least some ministers treat their civil servants. In March 2002, for example, it was reported that Alan Milburn, the Secretary of State for Health, told his Permanent Secretary Nigel Crisp 'to do what he was told'.

Not all political scientists agree with this analysis, however. There is the counter-view that at least some Labour ministers have been 'captured' by their departmental civil servants and changed their minds on issues after civil service pressure. Task forces and even political advisers can be marginalised by astute and experienced senior civil servants. Attempts to change the civil service can be resisted by the 'forces of conservatism' - a phrase used by Tony Blair to describe the old guard of the civil service holding back reform. In other words, supporters of this viewpoint argue, civil servants still play a key role in policy-making.

The reality may lie somewhere between these two positions. Theakston agrees that, overall, the civil service now has less group self-confidence. Civil servants, he argues, are rarely policy initiators but they now have a higher public profile. Rhodes broadly supports this view, arguing that the civil service has lost its monopoly on policy advice. There has, he argues, been a change of emphasis from policy advice to management.

Adapted from Theakston 1999, Dargie & Locke 2001, Rhodes 2001 and the *Guardian*, 2 March 2002.
See also *British Politics in Focus*, Second Edition, pp.456-61.

References

Butcher (2002) Butcher, T., 'The civil service under New Labour', *Politics Review*, Vol.11.3, 2002.
Cabinet Office (2000) *The Civil Service Reform Programme: Annual Report 2000*, Cabinet Office, 2000.
Chapman (2001) Chapman, R., 'Ethics in Public Service', *Politics Review*, Vol.10.3, 2001.
Dargie & Locke (2001) Dargie, C. & Locke, R., 'The Senior Civil Service: policy making, politics and government' in *Lancaster (2001)*.
Greenwood (1999) Greenwood, J., 'Tradition and change in the civil service', *Talking Politics*, Vol 12.2, 1999.
HMSO (1999) *Modernising Government*, Cm 4310, 1999.
HMSO (2000) *Committee on Standards in Public Life - Sixth Report: Reinforcing Standards*, Vol.1, HMSO, Cm 4557-1, 2000
Lancaster (2001) Lancaster, S. (ed.), *Developments in Politics*, Vol.12, Causeway Press, 2001.

Lancaster (2002) Lancaster, S. (ed.), *Developments in Politics*, Vol.13, Causeway Press, 2002.
Pyper (2000) Pyper, R., ' The civil service under Blair', *Politics Review*, Vol.9.3, 2000.
Rathbone (2000) Rathbone, M., 'The Wilson Report and the future of the civil service', *Talking Politics*, Vol.3.1, 2000.
Rawnsley (2001) Rawnsley, A., *Servants of the People*, Penguin, 2001.
Rhodes (2001) Rhodes, R., 'The civil service' in *Seldon (2001)*.
Seldon (2001) Seldon, A. (ed.), *The Blair Effect - The Blair Government 1997-2001*, Little Brown and Company, 2001.
Thain (2002) Thain, C., 'The core executive under Blair: the first term' in *Lancaster (2002)*.
Theakston (1999) Theakston, L., *Leadership in Whitehall*, Macmillan, 1999.

1 Peers in government

Taking the government as a whole (including Chief Whips in the Commons and Lords but excluding other government whips), there were 92 ministers in the government (including 23 Cabinet ministers) following the reshuffle after the general election in June 2001. Of the 69 non-Cabinet ministers, 15 were members of the House of Lords (see Figure 14.2). This was 50% up on the number in Tony Blair's first government in 1997.

Information from http://www.parliament.uk/commons/lib/hmg.htm, 30 June 2001. See also *British Politics in Focus*, Second Edition, p.471.

Figure 14.1 Lord Irvine and Lord Williams of Mostyn *Lord Irvine (the Lord Chancellor, left) and Lord Williams (Leader of the House of Lords) were the only two members drawn from the House of Lords in Tony Blair's new Cabinet appointed after the general election of 2001.*

Name	Position
Lord MacDonald	Minister of State at the Cabinet Office (appointed as Chancellor of the Duchy of Lancaster)
Sally Morgan*	Minister of State at the Cabinet Office
Baroness Blackstone	Minister of State at the Department for Culture, Media and Sport
The Lord Bach	Parliamentary Under-Secretary of State at the Ministry of Defence
Baroness Ashton of Upholland	Parliamentary Under-Secretary of State at the Department for Education and Skills
Lord Whitty	Parliamentary Under-Secretary of State at the Department for Environment, Food and Rural Affairs
Baroness Symons of Vernham Dean	Minister of State for Trade
Baroness Amos	Parliamentary Under-Secretary of State at the Foreign & Commonwealth Office
Lord Hunt of King's Heath	Parliamentary Under-Secretary of State at the Department of Health
Lord Rooker of Perry Barr	Minister of State at the Home Office
Lord Goldsmith	Attorney General
Baroness Scotland of Asthal	Parliamentary Secretary in the Lord Chancellor's Department
Lord Sainsbury of Turville	Parliamentary Under-Secretary of State at the Department of Trade and Industry
Lord Falconer of Thoroton	Minister of State at the Department for Transport, Local Government and the Regions
Baroness Hollis of Heigham	Parliamentary Under-Secretary of State at the Department for Works and Pensions

*In July 2002, Sally Morgan was still waiting to be admitted to the Lords.

Figure 14.2 Peers in government

2 The House of Commons' daily timetable

Westminster Hall Sittings

Since November 1999 and on an experimental basis, the House also sits in an additional chamber in the Commons called Westminster Hall. 'Non-controversial' issues are debated. The timetable for these sittings is:

- Tuesdays & Wednesdays 9.30am - 2.00pm - Private Members' adjournment debates
- Thursdays 2.00pm - 5.30pm - debates on select committee reports and other general items of business.

Information from House of Commons Factsheets - Procedure Series No 4, October 2001, www.parliament.uk/commons/lib/fs28.pdf
See also *British Politics in Focus*, Second Edition, pp.472-74.

Mondays-Wednesdays 2.30-10.30pm
2.30pm   Prayers☐
    Preliminary business -such as motions or new writs ☐ for by-elections, or unopposed private Bills
2.35-3.30pm **Question Time** - questions to ministers from MPs
3.30-4.00pm (Wednesdays only) **Prime Minister's Questions (PMQs)**☐
3.30pm   ☐(Mondays and Tuesdays) **Public business** - the main ☐ debates of the day, including those concerning new laws
10.00pm   Public business ends*☐
    Adjournment debate - on a topic raised by backbench MPs

(* If the House fails to complete its business by 10 pm it may continue to sit. ☐ All-night sittings are not uncommon.)

Thursdays 11.30am-7.30pm (still experimental)
11.30am-12.30pm **Question Time**
12.30pm   **Statements/PMQs**
       Public business
7.00-7.30pm   **Adjournment debate**
Fridays 9.30am-3.00pm
For ten Fridays each session, the House does not sit.

Figure 14.3 The House of Commons daily timetable

3 The Speaker

In October 2000, the Labour MP Michael Martin was elected as the 152nd Speaker, replacing Betty Boothroyd who had decided to retire. By electing Martin, MPs defied pressure from senior ministers who supported Tory ex-Cabinet minister, George Young. The election was supervised by Edward Heath because he was Father of the House (the longest serving MP). He rejected pleas for a straightforward ballot to choose from the 12 candidates, preferring instead the traditional method of selection, with each rival's name being added one by one as an amendment to the motion. To the dismay of Westminster modernisers, this cumbersome procedure took over six hours as even no-hopers took their turn, leaving the once crowded chamber almost deserted. Martin was never fewer than 76 votes ahead of his 11 rivals and in no danger of defeat. As tradition demands, he was dragged to the Speaker's chair to take up the post. Martin, the 55-year-old MP for Glasgow Springburn, is the first Speaker to be an authentic representative of the industrial working class, the child of an impoverished broken home who met his wife in a factory. He is also the first Catholic Speaker since Henry VIII's Protestant Reformation. Heath resisted calls from all sides to use his power to tear up rules not devised for a multi-candidate contest, instead offering his version of a compromise. That was to set out the order in which he intended to call the candidates, who would be voted on two at a time. Unexpectedly, he started with Martin. Equally unexpectedly, he let the contest run to the bitter end.

Adapted from the *Guardian*, 24 October 2000.
See also *British Politics in Focus*, Second Edition, pp.472-74.

Figure 14.4 The Speaker's election, October 2000
This cartoon satirises the election of Michael Martin as Speaker. The MP in the foreground is the then Father of the House, Edward Heath.

4 Statutory instruments

By no means all regulations come from statutes (Acts of Parliament) passed after deliberations by MPs and peers. Many are pieces of 'delegated legislation'. Parliament passed 3,412 pieces of delegated legislation in 2000. While Parliament gets to 'see' all pieces of delegated legislation, all but a handful go through on the nod. Few have even the faintest chance of being debated, let alone defeated. There is nothing new about the government's use of statutory instruments, even if, as Figure 14.5 shows, the number has been rising over recent years. Annual records began in 1895. Delegated legislation can only be made under a pre-existing Act of Parliament. They are laws made by civil servants. A minister, usually not the Secretary of State, does see and approve them, but the crucial decisions about what should be in regulations, their timing and, indeed, whether they should be made at all are taken in Whitehall. As citizens, we would probably object to our MPs spending too much time on the Thames Estuary Cockle Fishery Order 1994 or the Baking and Sausage Making (Christmas and New Year) Regulations 1985, but they are not all a matter of routine. The issues behind other regulations make headline news - such as the Sierra Leone [UN sanctions] Order 1997 which banned the selling of arms to Sierra Leone or the Beef Bones Regulation of 1997 which banned the selling of beef on the bone. Many regulations are drawn up in response to EU directives (such as the regulation banning the weighing of goods in pounds and ounces). At other times, civil servants respond to public pressure. The Wireless Telegraphy (Control of Interference from Videosenders) Order 1997, for example, banned the plugging of mini-transmitters into the back of videos after a videosender owner used his machine to beam hardcore pornography to his bedroom on a Sunday night during *Songs of Praise*. People in the neighbourhood complained when freak atmospherical conditions meant that the pornographic signal drowned out the religious worship.

Adapted from the *Guardian*, 20 January 2001. See also *British Politics in Focus*, Second Edition, pp.475-78.

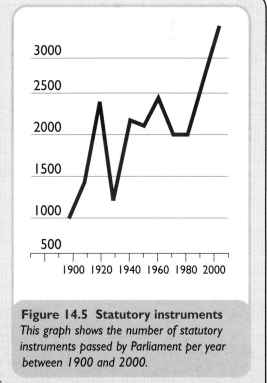

Figure 14.5 Statutory instruments
This graph shows the number of statutory instruments passed by Parliament per year between 1900 and 2000.

5 Select committees

Much has been heard, in recent years, about the 'modernisation' of Parliament. Issues such as 'family-friendly hours' have attracted much attention. But, the truest test of Parliament's effectiveness is its ability to call the government to account. The apparent impotence of the official opposition in the House of Commons in the 1980s and since 1997, has led to renewed criticism of Parliament's capacity to scrutinise the executive. Critical attention has focused particularly upon the departmental select committees (see Figure 14.6). The Chairs of all select committees comprise the Liaison Committee. Between 1999 and 2001, this Liaison Committee published three significant reports on the relationship between select committees and government. These reports highlighted the following problems:

- the whips' role in the appointment of select committees and their Chairs
- the committees' lack of resources
- the committees' inability to persuade the Prime Minister to appear before them
- the reluctance of some committees to criticise the government
- the leaking of select committee reports
- the time ministers take to respond to reports.

In February 2002, the House of Commons Modernisation Committee published a report making 22 recommendations which, according to the Leader of the House Robin Cook, amounted to the most fundamental overhaul of select committees since they were set up in 1979. These recommendations directly addressed the concerns of the

Culture, Media and Sport	Home Affairs	Transport, Local Government
Defence	International Development	and the Regions
Education and skills	Northern Ireland Affairs	Treasury
Environment and Rural Affairs	Science and Technology	Welsh Affairs
Foreign Affairs	Scottish Affairs	Work and Pensions
Health	Trade and Industry	

Figure 14.6 Departmental select committees in 2001
This table shows the departmental select committees in existence in July 2001.

Liaison Committee. The most important were:

- to limit the influence of the whips by placing responsibility for making appointments to committees in the hands of a new, independent committee
- to provide various kinds of additional resources and staff
- to pay committee Chairs additional salaries
- to make it possible for MPs and peers to be required to give evidence
- to enhance the committees' ability to pressure ministers to provide timely responses to their reports.

The publication of this report was followed by an announcement from Downing Street that, for the first time, the Prime Minister would give evidence twice a year to the Liaison Committee - the first time a Prime Minister had ever agreed to be questioned by an investigative committee. In May 2002, however, Labour whips ensured that a plan to create a backbench committee of nomination to choose MPs to sit on select committees was defeated. As a result, whips are still responsible for choosing members and Chairs of committees. Since Chairs are now paid an additional salary, that means that, in effect, whips decide who should receive the extra money.

Adapted from Alderman 2002 and the *Guardian*, 15 May 2002.

See also *British Politics in Focus*, Second Edition, pp.478-83.

6 The Parliamentary Commissioner for Standards

The Parliamentary Commissioner for Standards (see also Chapter 11, Section 7) is the only independent watchdog that can investigate allegations of sleaze and corruption against MPs. Yet, when the job was advertised in November 2001, it was downgraded in terms of both hours and salary. Whereas Elizabeth Filkin was appointed in 1996 to work a four-day week and was paid £76,000, in February 2002 her successor, Philip Mawer, was appointed to work a three-day week at a lower salary. This is despite the fact that the number of cases remained the same as three years' earlier and many were far more complicated than before. Although Elizabeth Filkin was appointed to work a four-day week, she regularly worked five days to keep pace with the number of complaints reaching her office. She had one secretary to assist her and was also responsible for:

- giving confidential advice to MPs concerning their entry on the Register
- providing induction courses for MPs on conduct and standards
- maintaining the Register.

Philip Mawer has the same responsibilities. In February 2002, he said that he would begin in March by working a one-day week and work up to a three-day week by May. Mawer is a former General Secretary of the Church of England Synod. He pointed out that: 'Parliament may appoint me and pay my salary, but they do not own my mind'. Some MPs were angry because they felt that Elizabeth Filkin had been bullied into not reapplying for her job because she had been prepared to take on high-profile investigations into the affairs of senior politicians.

Adapted from the *Guardian*, 12 November 2001 and 15 February 2002. See also *British Politics in Focus*, Second Edition, p.487-90.

Figure 14.7 Philip Mawer
Philip Mawer began work as Parliamentary Commissioner for Standards in March 2002.

7 House of Lords reform – the first stage

In November 1999, the House of Lords Act entered the statute book. This Act, intended as the first stage in a process of reform of the upper House, removed the automatic right of hereditary peers to sit and vote in the House. As the result of negotiations between the government and Viscount Cranbourne, then Conservative Leader in the Lords, a transitional arrangement was made, allowing 92 hereditary peers (about 10%) to remain in the House until the second stage of reform was introduced. A further ten hereditaries were also given life peerages.

The decision as to which hereditary peers should remain in the House was taken as follows:

- 75 were elected by their own party or cross-bench group within the House (42 Conservatives, 28 cross-benchers, three Liberal Democrats and two Labour peers)
- a further 15 were elected as Deputy Speakers or Committee Chairs
- two hereditaries were royal appointments (the Earl Marshall and the Lord Great Chamberlain).

The elections were held towards the end of 1999. Figure 14.8 shows the composition of the House of Lords before and after the first stage of reform was carried out.

Adapted from Norton 2001 and Baldwin 2002. See also *British Politics in Focus*, Second Edition, pp.490-99.

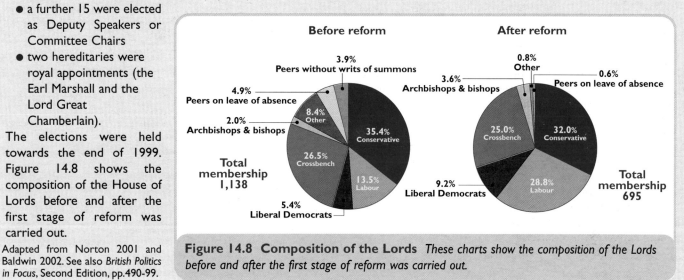

Figure 14.8 Composition of the Lords *These charts show the composition of the Lords before and after the first stage of reform was carried out.*

8 The Wakeham Report and White Paper

In 1999, the government appointed a Royal Commission on Reform of the House of Lords under the Conservative peer, Lord Wakeham, to make recommendations for the second stage of Lords reform. The commission was asked to complete its work by the end of 1999 and, to the surprise of many, managed to keep to this tight timetable, delivering its report on 28 December 1999 (it was published in January 2000). The Wakeham Report made 132 wide-ranging proposals on the recruitment of peers and changes to the procedures of the House. The main recommendations included:

- a new second chamber of about 550 members, largely appointed
- regional elections (using proportional representation) for the elected minority
- an independent Appointments Commission to ensure party, gender and ethnic balance
- the continuation of the role as the highest court of appeal
- a reduction in the number of Church of England bishops to allow for appointments representing other Christian denominations and non-Christian communities
- a 15-year fixed term of office.

The report offered three options for the number of peers to be elected - 65, 87 or 195 - the preferred option being 87.

In November 2001, the government introduced a White Paper announcing its plans for the second, and final, stage of the reform process. In broad terms, the plans follow the recommendations of the Wakeham report. Under the proposals presented in the White Paper, no new functions would be given to the new second chamber. Its role would still be to act as one of the constitutional checks and balances. Only one change to the powers of the House was proposed - a veto over secondary legislation would be replaced by the

power to delay for three months the passage of statutory instruments.

The main proposals, however, were concerned with the composition of the new House. The main recommendations included:

- removal of the remaining 92 hereditary peers
- the House to be reduced, over a 10 year period, to a maximum of 600 members - the political balance of the membership to be based on the share of the vote at the preceding general election, but no party able to have an overall majority
- 20% of the House to be directly elected - by proportional representation in large, multi-member regional constituencies
- 80% of the House to be appointed - 20% to be appointed by a statutory independent appointments commission accountable to Parliament, 60% to be nominated by the political parties
- the introduction of quotas for appointees, ensuring a minimum of 30% men and women and a broad representation of ethnic minority and regional groups
- existing life peers to maintain the right to lifetime membership
- fixed terms for new members, but the government to consult on the period
- Church of England bishops to remain (but reduced from 26 to 16)
- no automatic place for the leaders of other faiths.

Adapted from Wakeham 2000, Norton 2001 and the *Guardian*, 21 January 2000 and 8 November 2001.
See also British *Politics in Focus*, Second Edition, pp.490-99.

9 Reactions to the White Paper of November 2001

The White Paper on Lords reform published in November 2001 was the target of a great deal of criticism. Responses to the government's consultation on Lords reform revealed that 89% of MPs favoured a majority-elected second chamber. A report published by the Public Administration Committee in February 2002 called for a 60% elected second chamber in which peers served two- to five-year terms. In May 2002, the government agreed to set up a joint Commons-Lords committee. This joint committee had 24 members. It was charged with drawing up options for the future composition of the Lords (to be put to the vote in both Houses) and then with considering the powers of the second chamber. When the committee's membership was unveiled in June 2002, reformers'

optimism was dampened. They argued that the spread of opinion among those appointed to the committee leaned towards the traditionalist and did not reflect the substantial majority in the Commons who supported a move towards a majority of peers being elected. In addition, there was concern at the appointment of Jack Cunningham as the committee's Chair. He is a known opponent of election and a government loyalist expected to seek to produce a result Downing Street can support. Reformers fear that this committee will be used to kick Lords reform into the long grass.

Adapted from the *Guardian*, 20 June 2002.
See also *British Politics in Focus*, Second Edition, pp.490-99.

10 Impact of the first stage of reform of the House of Lords

The interim House of Lords has 695 members (compared to 1,138 previously), some 83% of whom are life peers (compared to 39% before reform). The rest are 89 elected hereditaries, 26 bishops and two royal office holders. By June 2000, Tony Blair had approved the creation of 202 new peers, an average of 66 per year. This is a higher appointment rate than that of any Prime Minister since 1960. Thatcher created 216 peers in 11 years in power while Wilson created 143 during his first government and 83 when he was in office between 1974 and 1976. The effect of these changes has, surprisingly, been to increase the average age of the Lords from 65 to 67 years. Before reform, there were 147 peers under 50. In 2000, there were just 51 peers under 50 and 17 over 90. By contrast, an MP's average age in 2000 was 52. One of the difficulties facing Labour before it reformed the Lords was that the party only had 47 peers under the age of 70, making it difficult to deliver a reasonable vote, let alone a majority on a daily basis. There was the danger that, without change, the government wouldn't be able to get its business through. The expulsion of the hereditaries reduced the direct influence of the Tory Party. Before, the Tories had 35.4% of votes, the cross-benchers 26.5%, Labour 13.5% and the Liberal Democrats 5.4%. In 2000, the Tories still made up the largest group, but their 232 peers then commanded 32% of the vote. Labour's voting power in 2000 was up to 199 or 28.8% of the votes. Cross-benchers had been reduced to 25% and the Liberal Democrats were up to 9.2%. The remaining 5% was made up of bishops and others with no formal party allegiance. Although the Lords' role as a 'revising

chamber' was often praised in the 1980s, there were far fewer government defeats under Thatcher than there have been under Blair (see Figure 14..9). This follows a trend set in the past. Whereas there were 26 defeats under Heath, there were 356 during the Wilson-Callaghan era. The contrast between the Major and Blair years is equally striking. In the last two years under Major, there were ten government defeats. In Tony Blair's first year, the number had soared to 39 and a further 31 were inflicted in 1998-99. This demonstrates a level of hostility not experienced under the Tories. In the six months following the removal of the hereditaries, there were 17 government defeats. It has been estimated that the government would not have lost seven of these votes if it had expelled all hereditary peers. The evidence suggests that the first stage of Lords reform may have removed the in-built Tory majority, but not the anti-Labour majority. The government is still operating in basically hostile territory.

Adapted from the *Guardian*, 29 June 2000.
See also *British Politics in Focus*, Second Edition, pp.490-99.

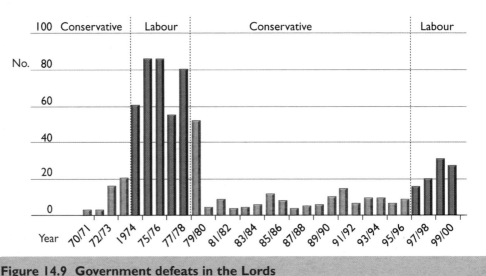

Figure 14.9 Government defeats in the Lords
This chart shows the number of government defeats in the House of Lords between 1970 and May 2000. The figures are percentages of divisions (ie contested votes).

11 Reform of the House of Commons

Reform of the House of Commons is important because it inevitably involves an attempt to define the relative powers of the Commons and executive and to formalise the relationship between the two. Critics have argued for most of the last century that the House of Commons has become progressively weaker in relation to the executive - so weak, in fact, that it has become a rubber stamp. All the signs are that this process has accelerated under Labour. Symbolic of the lobby fodder status of MPs was the vote in November 1997 when the government pushed through controversial legislation to reduce the amount of benefit paid to single mothers. Some backbenchers were in tears as they forced themselves through the division, voting for the government on an issue that was against all their principles. Since 1997, there has been a regular accusation, aimed at the government in general and at Tony Blair in particular, that the House of Commons has been sidelined and that, increasingly, we are moving towards a presidential style of government. Critics argue that reformers have not strengthened their case by focusing too much on creating a family-friendly House (ie concentrating on measures for the convenience of MPs) when the key issue should be the scrutiny of an over-mighty executive. The surprise appointment of Robin Cook as Leader of the House of Commons after the June 2001 general election gave a boost to reformers. In December 2001, Cook made a series of recommendations to the Commons' Modernisation Committee. These included:

- plans for shorter debates
- plans for morning sittings
- pre-legislative scrutiny of Bills by select committees
- switching Prime Minister's Question Time to midday on Wednesday
- Bills to be carried over to a second session rather than, as at present, killed off at the end of a parliamentary session
- MPs to give less notice of questions, allowing questions to be more topical
- ministerial statements to be made earlier in the day to give them wider broadcast and newspaper publicity
- the end of the long summer recess
- the possibility of electronic voting.

Cook also proposed more resources and powers for select committees (see Section 5 above). As a reform package, Cook's proposals were ambitious and represent the most significant attempt to strengthen the Commons since Norman St John Stevas introduced departmental select committees in 1979-80. Ultimately, it is up to MPs whether or not to accept the proposals. Cynics suggest that the guiding spirit of most MPs is self-interest and that not too much should be expected from the Cook proposals.

Adapted from Granath 2002.

See also *British Politics in Focus*, Second Edition, p.499-501.

Figure 14.10 Robin Cook
Robin Cook served as Foreign Secretary from May 1997 to June 2001. In June 2001, he was appointed Leader of the House of Commons.

12 Scrutiny

Whereas Congress in the USA can constitutionally block the President, the position of the Commons is one of critical support. The public has given the government a mandate, but at the same time expects it to be called to account. Finance is the historic check over the executive, but 'estimates' are given only three days of parliamentary time and departmental select committees have no input at this stage. The Budget has not been defeated since 1910. The Public Accounts Committee (PAC), assisted by the National Audit Office, checks that the £200 billion a year has been lawfully spent. But the PAC holds few public hearings and Parliament plays scant attention to its annual debate. The Leader of the Opposition is paid an additional salary to spearhead the exposure of governmental faults. The adversarial system, together with Question Time and 20 days on which the opposition can table a motion, provides opportunities. But the opposition lacks information, civil service support and the ability to initiate rather than to react. The departmental select committee system is central to the Commons' efforts to make government accountable. More reports have been issued under Labour than under the Conservatives and more ministers have given evidence, but the whips' ability to block Robin Cook's proposal for a nomination committee suggests that the government is unwilling to extend the committees' power much further.

Adapted from Ridsdill-Smith 2001.

See also *British Politics in Focus*, Second Edition, pp.499-501.

References

Alderman (2002) Alderman, K., 'Select Committees in the House of Commons' in *Lancaster (2002)*.
Baldwin (2002) Baldwin, N., 'Reforming the second chamber', *Politics Review*, Vol.11.3, February 2002.
Granath (2002) Granath, A., 'Constitutional reform: a work in progress', *Talking Politics*, Vol.14.3, April 2002
Lancaster (2002) Lancaster, S. (ed.), *Developments in Politics*, Vol.13, Causeway Press, 2002.

Norton (2001) Norton, P., 'Parliamentary reform in Labour's second term', *Talking Politics*, Vol.14.1, September 2001.
Ridsdill-Smith (2001) Ridsdill-Smith, C., 'Do we have parliamentary government?', *Politics Review*, Vol.11.1, September 2001.
Wakeham (2000) Wakeham, Lord, 'Lords reform', *Politics Review*, Vol.10.2, November 2000.

15 Management of the economy

1 Inflation

One of the reasons why Old Labour acquired a reputation for economic incompetence was that inflation had been very high under Wilson/Callaghan - it had reached 25% in 1975 (in large part due to the 1973 quadrupling of oil prices by the OPEC countries). Under Tony Blair, inflation has remained low. Based on the Retail Price Index, excluding mortgage interest payments, it fell from a rate of 2.5% in early 1999 to just 2% at the end of 2001. During the first four months of 2002, inflation was in the 2.2-2.6% range. It then fell to 1.8% in May, leaving the government well on course to hit its 2.5% per annum target again. Indeed, in only four months since the beginning of 1999 - January and March 1999, August 2001 and January 2002 - did the rate of inflation exceed 2.5% and, even then, the rate was only 2.6% or 2.7%, low enough to pose no real threat to the government's overall target for the financial year.

Adapted from ONS 2002a. See also *British Politics in Focus*, Second Edition, pp.518-21.

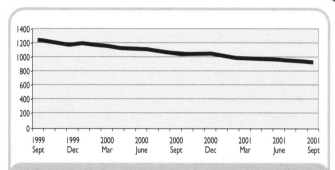

(i) Quarterly inflation rate, 1999-2001 (%)

1999				2000				2001			
1	2	3	4	1	2	3	4	1	2	3	4
2.5	2.3	2.2	2.2	2.1	2.1	2.1	2.1	1.9	2.3	2.4	2.0

(ii) Inflation rate January-May 2002 (%)

January	February	March	April	May
2.6	2.2	2.3	2.3	1.8

Figure 15.1 Inflation

2 Unemployment

Unemployment continued its downward trajectory during the period 1999-2002, as indicated by Figure 15.2. The official rate of unemployment was 4.3% at the beginning of 1999 and fell continuously. By the end of 2001, ministers were able to claim that Britain had virtually recreated full employment - something which it had widely been assumed during the 1980s and early 1990s was no longer attainable. Indeed, New Labour itself had originally confined itself to a goal of 'full employability', rather than full employment. The number of claimants in June 2002 was 952,400, up by 1,300 on May 2002 but down 14,900 on a year earlier.

Adapted from ONS 2002b.
See also *British Politics in Focus*, Second Edition, pp.518-21.

Figure 15.2 Unemployment *This graph shows the number of claimants receiving unemployment benefit in the period September 1999 to Septemeber 2001 (in thousands).*

3 Earnings

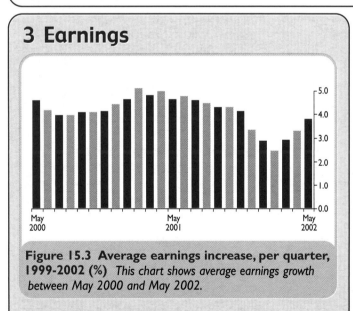

Figure 15.3 Average earnings increase, per quarter, 1999-2002 (%) *This chart shows average earnings growth between May 2000 and May 2002.*

The period since 1998 has witnessed a steady, sustained increase in average earnings, over and above the rate of inflation. Figure 15.3 shows that throughout 1999 and 2000, the increase in average earnings was consistently above 4%. With inflation throughout this period only once exceeding 2.5% (and usually rather lower), it is clear that for many, if not most, people in paid employment, incomes rose steadily.

Adapted from ONS 2002c.
See also *British Politics in Focus*, Second Edition, pp.518-21.

4 Property prices

One significant consequence of the combination of low interest rates and the steady increase in average earnings was a large increase in property prices. Average property prices increased from £66,385 in January 1999 to £102,886 in May 2002. This figure, of course, conceals marked regional variations. A property which would have cost £76,000 in the North-West of England (May 2002) would cost £171,500 in London.

While the overall increases in property prices have been welcome to many home-owners, some of whom find that their properties have virtually doubled in value during the last four years, the scale of the increase raises two concerns. First, some commentators are concerned that the property market is overheating and predict a collapse in house prices like that which occurred during the first half of the 1990s. Other commentators, however, believe that the more likely outcome is a slowdown rather than an outright fall in prices.

The second concern is that young people and key workers (for example, teachers, nurses, police officers) are being priced-out of the housing market, especially in London and Southern England, because their salaries are insufficient to afford to buy a house or a flat. Clearly, a booming, prosperous economy generates problems of its own, further widening the gap between the 'haves' and the 'have-nots'.

Adapted from Nationwide 2002 and the *Guardian*, 29 April 2002.
See also *British Politics in Focus*, Second Edition, pp.518-21.

5 The Monetary Policy Committee

Established almost immediately after Labour's election victory in May 1997, the Monetary Policy Committee is responsible for determining the level of interest rates. Composed of nine members - five from the Bank of England and four independent economic experts appointed by the Chancellor - who meet monthly, the Monetary Policy Committee sets the appropriate level of interest rates in the context of the 'monetary policy framework' drawn up by the government.

Under New Labour, the priority has been to promote economic stability (eradicating the previous tendency towards 'boom-and-bust'). Such stability is regarded as essential for the successful attainment of the government's other economic goals, namely high and stable levels of growth and employment. In determining its 'monetary policy framework' and associated objectives, the government declares its overall target for the annual rate of inflation (excluding mortgage interest payments). Since 1997, this has remained at 2.5%.

With inflation well below the 2.5% (maximum) target for virtually all of the 1999-2001 period, the Monetary Policy Committee has felt confident enough to keep interest rates at, or below, 6%. Indeed, by the end of 2001 interest rates had been reduced to just 4%. They remained at that level throughout the first half of 2002.

Adapted from Stephens 2001 and BoE 2002.

See also *British Politics in Focus*, Second Edition, pp.530-33.

6 The single European currency (the euro)

The question of whether Britain should join the single European currency (the euro) has remained a highly controversial and divisive issue in British politics since 1999. However, while polls have consistently shown that a majority of people are opposed to British membership of the euro, growing numbers of people seem resigned to the idea that Britain will join anyway, sooner or later. An ICM poll published in December 2001 revealed that 62% of British people believed that Britain would join the euro within the next 10 years, literally double the number (31%) who thought the same in September 2000.

The same poll also revealed that British opposition to joining the euro appeared to be softening somewhat, with 31% claiming that they would vote in favour of joining if a referendum was held and 58% saying that they would vote against. The same question asked back in November 2000 had revealed only 18% of British people claiming they would vote Yes, with an overwhelming 71% declaring that they would vote No. In the space of barely a year, therefore, the gap between supporters and opponents of British membership of the euro had halved, from 53% to 27%.

Supporters of British membership of the euro were quietly confident that opposition would further dissipate once the other EU countries phased out their own currencies completely in early 2002. British tourists, it was envisaged, would become accustomed to using the euro when on holiday and might also become aware of the lower prices which exist in much of Europe. Furthermore, in readiness for European tourists visiting Britain, a number of high street shops declared that they would accept the euro. The more people became familiar with the euro, so the argument went, the more opposition would weaken (a phenomenon often described as 'euro-creep').

Which of the following best describes your own view of British participation in the single currency?

Strongly support British participation	
February 2002	18%
April 2002	19%
Generally in favour of British participation, but could be persuaded against it if I thought it would be bad for the British economy	
February 2002	24%
April 2002	24%
Generally opposed to British participation, but could be persuaded in favour of it if I thought it would be good for the British economy	
February 2002	24%
April 2002	22%
Strongly oppose British participation	
February 2002	29%
April 2002	29%
Don't know	
February 2002	5%
April 2002	6%

Figure 15.4 Attitudes towards the euro *This table shows the results of a survey conducted in June 2002. A sample of 1,003 people were asked the questions. The percentages do not add up to 100% because of don't knows.*

As Figure 15.5 shows, polls conducted by MORI during early 2002 indicated that, while a majority remained opposed to British membership of the euro, 22-24% of those expressing opposition admitted that they might otherwise support membership if they were persuaded that it was in Britain's economic interest to join. This leaves those opposed as a matter of basic principle at less than 30%. This places the onus on pro-European politicians to present a more confident and convincing case to the British public before the referendum is held.

Adapted from www.mori.com/polls/2002/ft and the *Guardian*, 18 December 2001. See also *British Politics in Focus*, Second Edition, pp.521-25.

References

BoE (2002) Bank of England:
www.bankofengland.co.uk/mpc/decisions
Nationwide (2002) Nationwide Building Society:
www.nationwide.co.uk/Hps/historical/PDF/MPR0204
ONS (2002a) Office of National Statistics:
www.statistics.gov.uk/themes/economy/Articles/PricesandInflation

ONS (2002b) Office of National Statistics:
www.statistics.gov.uk/themes/labour-market/unemployment_claimant_count
ONS (2002c) Office of National Statistics: www.statistics.gov.uk/pdfdin
Seldon (2001) Seldon, A. (ed.), *The Blair Effect - The Blair Government 1997-2001*, Little Brown and Company, 2001.
Stephens (2001) Stephens, P., 'The Treasury under Labour' in *Seldon (2001)*.

1 Elected mayors

Much to the horror of the Labour leadership, though not to many ordinary Labour Party members in London, Ken Livingstone announced his interest in seeking the Labour nomination as candidate for London Mayor. Livingstone, a left-winger and rebel since his days as Leader of the Greater London Council, was regarded as unreliable. In order to prevent him obtaining the Labour nomination, the Labour leadership set up an electoral college with:

● one-third of the votes from party members
● one-third from London MPs, MEPs and Greater London Authority (GLA) candidates
● one-third of votes from London trade unions.

The ploy worked. Frank Dobson (who had been persuaded to resign from the Cabinet where he had been the Secretary of State for Health) won the Labour nomination by a narrow margin. Following this defeat, Ken Livingstone decided to stand as an independent candidate and was then expelled from the Labour Party.

The Conservative Party approach to the selection of its candidate was just as problematic. After internal disagreements and false starts, Geoffrey Archer won the selection contest by a majority of 9,300 votes over his rival, Steven Norris. However, shortly after his selection in 1999, the *News of the World* published an article accusing him of providing a false alibi before his 1987 libel trial. Archer stepped down to fight the case (he was later successfully prosecuted and sent to prison). The Conservatives decided to re-run the selection, much to the annoyance of Norris who thought he should be given the nomination as runner-up. Norris subsequently easily won another postal vote of Conservative Party members and became the Conservative Party candidate.

The voting system

The five million voters in London have two preferences under the Supplementary Voting system (which is used to elect the Mayor). A candidate who wins more than 50% of the first preference votes is immediately elected as Mayor. If nobody wins more than 50% of the vote the two candidates with the highest number of votes remain in the contest. All the others are eliminated and the votes of the losers distributed to the two remaining candidates. The candidate with the highest number of first and second preference votes is elected as Mayor.

The voting system for the GLA is a version of the Additional Member system. Some members are directly elected from the London Boroughs. Others are elected from the party lists, providing an approximate proportionality of seats to votes cast.

The campaign and election result

Livingstone held onto the support of many traditional Labour voters as well as picking up support from a broader audience who liked his style and policies for transport. Dobson's campaign suffered because of the selection process and because he was known to be reluctant to stand. He was also seriously weakened by a strong Conservative campaign. Steven Norris argued that the position of Mayor was primarily concerned with technical and managerial issues rather than party politics. He distanced himself from the Conservative Party and did not use the word Conservative in his election address. He also stressed the need for a social and radical agenda substantially to the left of the national Conservative leadership.

Livingstone's policy of opposing government plans for a partial sell-off of the tube proved popular with Londoners and, despite a late Conservative surge, Livingstone came top of the first poll and won when the second preferences were counted (see Section 2 below). However, the turnout in the election was only 34% which cast doubt on the claim that mayoral elections would be a new way to re-invigorate enthusiasm for local government elections in the UK.

Adapted from Game 2000 and Cole 2001.
See also *British Politics in Focus*, Second Edition, pp.538-44.

Figure 16.1 Labour's candidates for London Mayor *Following a referendum in London in 1998, the race began for the major parties to select candidates to stand as directly elected Mayor and as members of the Greater London Authority (GLA).*

2 The results of the election in London in 2000

Table (i): Mayoral election, first preference votes

Candidate	Party	Votes	% Vote
Ken Livingstone	Independent	667,877	38.96
Steven Norris	Conservative	464,434	27.09
Frank Dobson	Labour	223,884	13.06
Susan Kramer	Liberal Democrat	203,452	11.87
Ram Gidoomal	Christian People's Party	42,060	2.45
Darren Johnson	Green	38,121	2.22
Michael Newland	British National Party	33,569	1.96
Damian Hockney	UK Independent	16,324	0.95
Geoffrey Ben-Nathan	Pro-Motor	9,956	0.58
Ashwinkumar Tanna	Independent	9,015	0.53
Geoffrey Clements	Natural Law Party	5,470	0.32

Table (ii): Mayoral election, final result

Candidate	Party	Votes	% Vote
Ken Livingstone	Independent	776,427	57.92
Steven Norris	Conservative	564,137	42.08
Majority		212,290	15.84

The Greater London Authority, comprising the Assembly and the Mayor, has responsibility for:

- economic development and regeneration
- fire and emergency planning
- culture and tourism
- public health
- environment
- transport
- planning
- police.

Table (iii): The GLA, election result

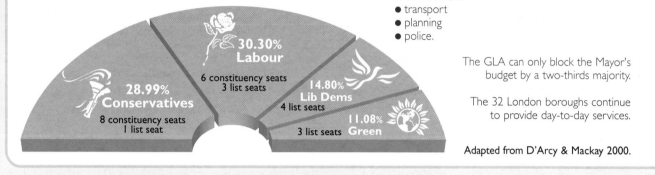

The GLA can only block the Mayor's budget by a two-thirds majority.

The 32 London boroughs continue to provide day-to-day services.

Adapted from D'Arcy & Mackay 2000.

3 The 2000 Local Government Act

While the 2000 Local Government Act has a number of elements (it requires stronger ethical standards from councillors and innovations in voting systems, for example), the key change has been the requirement for local authorities with a population of over 85,000 to change their policy-making machinery. Local authorities must choose one of three management structures:

- a directly-elected Mayor working with a Cabinet of not more than ten senior councillors, selected by the Mayor
- a directly-elected Mayor who appoints a council manager to run the council services
- a Leader elected by the council, working with a Cabinet of not more than ten councillors.

A decision by any local authority to opt for the directly-elected Mayor has to be ratified first by a local referendum. Also, a local authority is required to hold a referendum to decide whether to opt for a directly-elected Mayor if more than 5% of the local electorate petition for the change.

Evaluation

The new structures involve a separation of powers between the executive and the rest of the council. The whole council ceases to have a role in policy-making. Instead, its main function is to monitor the executive. As a result, the role played by many councillors will be reduced to that of 'backbencher'. Key decisions will be taken by the executive. Under the old arrangements, council decisions were taken either at full council or delegated to sub-committees whose composition had to reflect the political balance of the council. Under the new arrangements, it would be possible for the executive to be composed of one party, though, given the number of 'hung' councils, it is likely that many executives will be made up of councillors from more than one party. The full council will still have to approve the budget and the overall plans for the year,

but will not become involved in detailed policy decisions. The full council will, however, be able to create scrutiny committees which can require the executive to explain their actions.

The response of the local authorities

Most local authorities have chosen the third option - Council Leader working with a Cabinet. This involves least change as it is the system closest to that which existed before. However, in a small minority of local authorities there has been support for the mayoral concept and the issue has been put to the voters in local referendums. The outcomes of these referendums have been mixed. For example, in Middlesborough 84% of the voters were in favour of a directly-elected Mayor whereas 62% of people in Brighton voted against. Turnout in the referendums has also varied, with only 18% voting in Lewisham while 36% voted in North Tyneside. The first mayoral elections outside London were held in May 2002. Seven new Mayors were elected - three Labour Party candidates, two independents, one Conservative and one Liberal Democrat. In some local authority areas, there has been a grass-roots campaign to win support for a referendum against the wishes of the local council and, in some cases, the government has threatened reluctant councils that reserve powers could be used to force referendums. However, it is clear that government ministers are divided on the issue and, following the experience in London and the Labour Party's failure to win the mayoral contests in Hartlepool and Middlesborough in 2002 (independent candidates beat the Labour candidates), there may be a reluctance to push the concept, especially if it leads to a loss of political control in an area. A batch of elected independent Mayors is not what was anticipated when the idea was originally formulated.

Adapted from Leach 2000, Labour Research, February 2000, the *Guardian*, 15 October 2001 and 4 May 2002 and Chandler 2001. See also *British Politics in Focus*, Second Edition, pp.543-45.

4 Case Study – Oxford City Council and Oxfordshire County Council

In May 2002, Labour regained political control of Oxford City Council by winning 29 of the 48 seats. As part of the government plans for local government reorganisation, Oxford City Council had decided to opt for an executive (a Cabinet of councillors with a Council Leader). Labour took all the seats on the executive with each member of the executive being given a specific area of responsibility (for example, the Council Leader took responsibility for strategic finance). At the same time, scrutiny panels (made up of councillors not on the executive) were set up to examine the decisions made by the executive. If there is a disagreement on a budget or a policy decision, the executive can be overruled by a meeting of all councillors. This, however, is unlikely to happen as Labour has a majority in the council.

Local Government Commission

From 1 April 2001, the work of the Local Government Commission was transferred to the new Electoral Commission. The Local Government Commission had been responsible for the major changes in the structure of local government, particularly the introduction of unitary authorities. Once these major structural changes were completed, the Local Government Commission undertook periodic electoral reviews of local electoral boundaries.

Oxford provides a local example of the work undertaken. The Local Government Commission recommended that there should be 24 wards with two councillors elected from each ward instead of the current 17 wards with three councillors elected from each ward. This recommendation came into effect in time for the local elections in 2002.

Oxfordshire County Council

In Oxfordshire, there was a hung council between 1986 and 2002 with Conservatives, Labour and Liberal Democrats sharing decision-making. In the 2001 elections, the Conservatives won 26 seats, with Labour winning 24 seats. The

Liberal Democrats won 18 and the Green Party won seven. In November 2001, Oxfordshire County Council opted for a Cabinet of councillors with a Council Leader. The Cabinet has nine members and, in 2002, only included Conservatives and Liberal Democrats (five Conservatives, including the Leader, and four Liberal Democrats). The members of the executive have taken areas of responsibility including:

- corporate and community leadership
- corporate and community strategies and finance
- highways, parking, road safety and public transport
- community care and health
- strategic planning and waste management
- youth service, libraries, the arts, tourism and leisure
- education
- community safety, drugs, fire service and planning.

They are shadowed by five scrutiny committees all of which are chaired by Labour County Councillors.

Decentralisation of decision-making

The government has emphasised the need to increase public participation in local government. One way in which it hopes to achieve this is through greater decentralisation of decision-making in local government. An example of greater decentralisation can be seen in Oxford. Five Area Committees have been set up to serve different parts of the city. The committees are designed to provide a forum for local people and community groups to debate issues and form partnerships; and contribute to the debate on the council's plans for the future. The Area Committees meet in public. They are made up of ward councillors. Meetings allow members of the public to speak on issues which concern them, ask questions and suggest agenda items. Area Committees have been given powers set out by the executive to take some day-to-day decisions in their local area. In addition, each Area Committee has its own budget to implement. The intention is to devolve power and budgets giving ordinary members of the public real influence on decisions. However, the Area Committees have been criticised on a number of counts. First, they have power over very few decisions and have a very limited budget. Second, there is a fear that local pressure groups, rather than members of the public, will dominate them. And third, their decisions can be challenged if four councillors ask for a particular decision to be looked at again. If this happens, the full council or the executive can overrule the original decision.

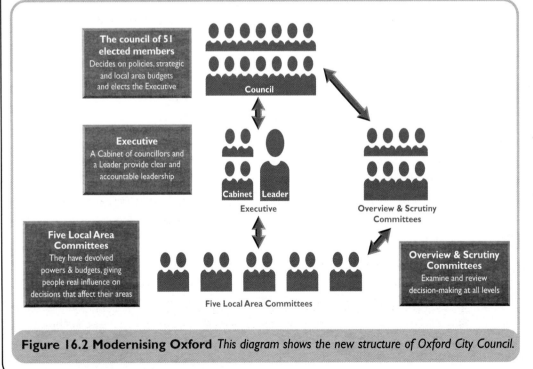

Figure 16.2 Modernising Oxford *This diagram shows the new structure of Oxford City Council.*

Adapted from information provided by Oxford City Council and Oxfordshire County Council, and Wilson 1999.
See also *British Politics in Focus*, Second Edition, pp.545-49.

5 Referendum in Bristol, February 2001

Faced with a shortfall in their budget, the Labour-controlled council in Bristol decided to allow the electors to make the decision about future finances for the city in a referendum. Electors were offered a choice which included no increase in the council tax (with a consequent cut of £4.5 million in education) and then a series of council tax rises with varying amounts of money then being available for education spending. The Labour council's preferred option was for a 4% increase in the council tax with a standstill in council spending. This would have amounted to around a £75 per year increase on the average band D property which already costs £1,000 annually for the council tax payer.

George Micklewright, the Labour Leader of the council, said that the referendum would be an important step for local democracy in Britain: 'We have been looking for ways to give Bristol people more say over important council decisions'.

There had already been a referendum in the Hengrove area of the city. The 30,000 residents of this area were asked whether they wanted a football and sports stadium built in their neighbourhood. Just over 10,000 residents voted in that referendum and they rejected the plan by two to one.

Central government has promoted the use of referendums as a way of involving local people in local decisions. In 1997, a government paper, *Local Democracy and Community Leadership*, suggested a large range of ways of seeking and responding to the views of the citizen. These included: citizen juries; focus groups; visioning conferences; deliberative opinion polls; citizens' panels; community forums or area-based neighbourhood committees; interest and user group forums as well as referendums.

Critics of the council, however, argued that the referendum was an abdication of responsibility by the council leaders. Barbara Janke, the Leader of the Liberal Democrats on the council, said: 'Labour has used the referendum to get themselves off the hook of having to make a hard decision'. Critics also suggested that the referendum was being used to prevent a split in the ranks of the ruling Labour group, which only had a majority of two on the council. Several Labour councillors had earlier rebelled against their own party and voted against plans to close two primary schools.

In the event, the turnout for the referendum was 40%, compared to a turnout of 30% in local elections in Bristol. However, of the 270,000 electors who voted, only 18% supported the council's preferred option for a 4% tax increase. Over half of the electorate backed the no increase option, even though the Labour council had warned that this would lead to cuts of £4.5 million in the education budget.

Labour councillors described the vote as a useful exercise in local democracy, but admitted that the result was not one that they had wanted. The local *Bristol Evening Post* suggested that it was 'now left to the city council to pick up the pieces of a vote which had badly misfired'.

Adapted from DETR 1997 and the *Guardian*, 16 February 2001.

6 Powers of the Scottish Parliament

The powers transferred from Westminster to the Scottish Parliament are considerable. It has full legislative powers over a wide range of matters and can vary income tax. In addition, the Parliament produces an executive - in effect the Scottish government - which it then holds to account. The executive largely determines the legislative programme and is responsible for implementing policies. Whenever there is a division of powers between different levels of government, there is the potential for disputes over who does what. To avoid this, a joint ministerial committee was set up, comprising UK government and Scottish executive ministers. The devolution legislation also provided that in the event of a conflict, the Judicial Committee of the Privy Council would make a binding decision.

Adapted from Denver 2001.

Reserved powers *(not devolved)*	Areas not reserved *(responsibility of Scottish Parliament)*
Common market for UK goods and services	Agriculture, fisheries and forestry
Constitution of the UK	Economic development
Defence and national security	Education
Employment legislation	Environment
Fiscal, economic and monetary system	Health
Foreign policy, including Europe	Housing
Health (in some areas); medicine	Law and home affairs
Media and culture	Local government
Professional regulations (in certain cases)	Research and statistics
Protection of borders	Social work
Social security	Training
Transport safety and regulation	Transport

Figure 16.3 Powers of the Scottish Parliament
This table shows the powers that have been devolved to the Scottish Parliament and those that have not.

7 Best Value

The 'Best Value' initiative brought in by central government means that, by 2005, all local authorities must have reviewed all their services to make sure they are providing cost-effective, high-quality services which are focused on the needs of local people (see Figure 16.4 for the management framework). Best Value reviews must:

● challenge why and how services are provided
● compare performance with the performance of other councils, and with private and non-profit holders who provide similar services and monitor customer satisfaction
● consult local people and local stakeholders to find ways of improving the services
● show that in-house council services are the most cost-effective by subjecting them to external competition (if in-house services are more expensive, councils may have to contract the work to a private firm or to the voluntary sector).

The government's aim in introducing Best Value was to ensure that, within five years, all council services achieved performance levels that were only achieved by the top 25% of councils at the start of the five years. The Audit Commission carries out inspections which are then published. A star rating is provided, ranging from no stars for poor performance to three stars for excellent performance. If performance does not improve, the government has the power to switch control of a service away from the poorly performing council.

The Audit Commission

The Audit Commission has provided a bleak picture of many local council services, calling into question the speed at which Best Value can boost performance. More than 60% of services inspected between September 2000 and September 2001 were given poor or fair ratings. The Audit Commission controller noted: 'There are stark differences in how well councils are coping with Best Value. Many councils have yet to get to grips with the most challenging aspects of Best Value...Almost two-thirds of councils are either coasting or performing badly'.

The government view

Sources within the Labour Party have described Best Value as the last chance for local government. While this may be an exaggeration, if Best Value fails, other patterns of delivery of local services might be introduced.

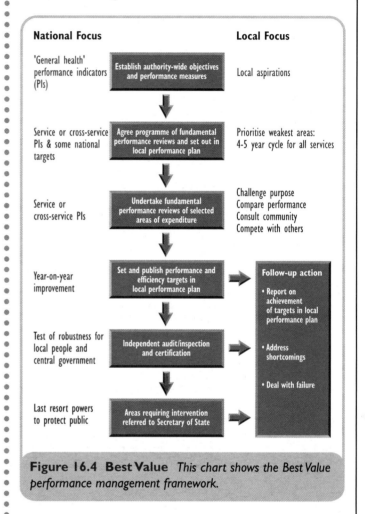

Figure 16.4 Best Value *This chart shows the Best Value performance management framework.*

Adapted from McNaughton & McNaughton 1999, Audit Commission 2001, the *Guardian*, 12 March, 29 May and 19 September 2001. See also *British Politics in Focus*, Second Edition, pp.565 & 570.

8 White Paper on the future of local government

The key proposals in the White Paper *Strong Local Leadership - Quality Public Services* (2001) can be summarised as follows:

● comprehensive performance assessments for all councils will be introduced - councils will be classified as high-performing, striving, coasting and poor performing
● high-performing councils will not be subject to such strict controls from central government
● coasting and poor performance councils will have their performance monitored against an action plan
● where a council is failing, its functions could be transferred to other providers
● regulation by central government will be reduced
● there will be a reduction in 'ring-fenced' grants (ie grants which are provided by central government only if the

money is spent on services determined by central government).

In his statement to the House of Commons on the White Paper, Stephen Byers claimed that he wanted to stop the trend towards central prescription and interference which dominated central-local relations in the 1980s and 1990s. He argued that local authorities are often best placed to respond to local needs. He also announced that there would be new proposals for grant distribution to local councils, abolishing the standard spending assessment. Finally, he placed an emphasis on the need for stronger community leadership by local Council Leaders.

Adapted from DETR 2001 and the *Guardian*, 10 December 2001. See also *British Politics in Focus*, Second Edition, pp.567-72.

9 Regional assemblies

Following the moves to devolved government in Northern Ireland, Scotland, Wales and London, the Labour government has expressed its support for forms of regional government in England. In 1999, eight Regional Development Agencies (RDAs) - business-led quangos - were set up to drive regional economic development. Initially, they were given a budget of £1 billion between them, but in July 2000 they were given a spending boost - an extra £500 million by 2003. They were also promised greater freedom to operate outside Whitehall's tight control, with the promise of a single budget drawn from three main departments, giving them the ability to tailor policies to particular regions.

The establishment of the RDAs was followed by the creation of eight Regional Chambers, made up of councillors, religious leaders, trade unionists and business leaders. These are supposed to pave the way to full-blown regional assemblies. Full-time staff have been appointed and, in some cases, the chambers have even been called 'assemblies'. However, these bodies, at present, are not elected bodies.

Labour's promises

Labour stated, in its 2001 election manifesto, that where there is no demand for regional government in England, none would be set up. But, where there is a stronger sense of regional identity and a demand for a political voice, referendums could be held and, if positive, directly elected assemblies set up.

The first timetable for English devolution was announced by Nick Raynsford (the Regions and Local Government Minister) in November 2001. Noting the growing discontent in the North, he said that it was no longer possible to restrict devolution: 'We see no reason why there should not be...one regional assembly in at least one region before the next general election. A White Paper was published in May 2002 giving details of plans for a referendum in one area and an indication of the responsibilities of any assemblies established. To counter the charge of increased bureaucracy, the government made it clear that, if assemblies were established, then, in areas where there were already county and district councils, a tier of local government would have to be abolished. Any assemblies that are established, therefore, are more likely to be in areas where there are unitary local authorities.

Adapted from the *Guardian*, 13 March and 26 July 2000, 30 November 2001 and 5 May 2002 and Labour Party 2001.
See also *British Politics in Focus*, Second Edition, pp.571-72.

10 Quangos

In opposition, Labour criticised the Tories' failure to cull quangos. In power, the Labour government has been an enthusiastic creator of executive and advisory bodies which stand at arm's length from Whitehall departments. The reason is simple. Ministers, for the most part, lack managerial experience and so, usually, do their senior civil servants. They 'talk' management but have no experience of it. Officially, there are some 1,000 quangos. The biggest are shown in Figure 16.5. The Higher Education Funding Council dispenses grants to universities. It is thought offensive to the ideal of academic autonomy for the money to be handed out directly by the Department of Education. Lower down the list, English Partnerships give grants for the physical regeneration of, for example, former coalfields. There are also c.500 NHS trusts, authorities and boards. Since John Major created the office of Commissioner of Public Appointments, quango jobs have been inspected to ensure successful candidates are deserving. On arriving in power, Labour promised to improve gender balance and diversity. Studies show that it has, at the expense of a large influx of party members into

Figure 16.5 The top five quangos in 2000 *This table shows the top five quangos in 2000 by staff numbers and by spending.*

NHS appointments (party members being, in some measure, black and female). Quangos are accountable. Their spending is monitored by the National Audit Office on behalf of the Public Accounts Committee.

Adapted from the *Guardian*, 4 September 2000. See also *British Politics in Focus*, Second Edition, pp.538-44

References

Chandler (2001) Chandler, J.A., 'The Blair administration and local government' *Talking Politics*, Vol.3.3, April 2001.
Cole (2001) Cole. M., 'The crowning of Red Ken: the battle for London in 2000', *Talking Politics*, Vol.13.2, January 2001.
D'Arcy & Maclean (2000) D'Arcy, M. & Maclean, R., *The Race to Become London's Mayor*, Politico's, 2000.
Denver (2001) Denver, D., 'The devolution project', *Politics Review*, Vol.11.1, September 2001.
DETR (1997) Department of the Environment, Transport and the Regions, *Local Government and Community Leadership*, 1997.
DETR (2001) Department of the Environment, Transport and the Regions, *News Release 535*, 2001.
Game (2000) Game, C., 'Local government modernisation: much more than just elected Mayors' in *Lancaster (2000)*.

Labour (2001) *Ambitions for Britain*, Labour Party manifesto, Labour Party, 2001.
Labour Research (2000) *Labour Research* 'Is municipal mutiny brewing?', February 2000.
Lancaster (2000) Lancaster, S. (ed.), *Developments in Politics*, Vol.11, Causeway Press, 2000..
Leach (2000) Leach, S., 'Democratic Renewal', *Politics Review*, Vol.10.2, November 2000.
McNaughton & McNaughton (1999) McNaughton, N. & McNaughton, R., 'Best Value: a fresh start for local government', *Politics Review*, Vol.8.3, February 1999.
Wilson (1999) Wilson D., 'Threats and promise: New Labour and Local Government', *Politics Review*, Vol.9.4, April 1999.

17 Citizenship and redress of grievances

1 Asylum seekers

Rarely has a week gone by in recent years without the media reporting a new influx of asylum seekers entering Britain. The regularity of such reports, and their often alarmist or sensationalist tone, has transformed the issue of asylum seekers into something of a 'moral panic' and placed the Blair government on the defensive, susceptible to allegations of allowing Britain to become 'a soft touch', and of failing to 'stem the flood'.

In fact, during the period 2001-02 there were somewhere between 60,000 and 80,000 applications for asylum in Britain, a figure which actually represents a decline in numbers because, in 2000, Britain received 97,860 applications for asylum (compared to 78,760 for Germany, 38,590 for France, 18,000 for Italy, and 10,920 for Ireland). Since 2000, the decline in the number of applications for asylum to Britain has been matched by an increase in applications to other European countries, most notably France and Germany.

Something that tends to get overlooked in reports which allege Britain is being 'swamped' by asylum seekers is the fact that only about 10% of applications for asylum are actually granted and a further 10% given 'exceptional leave to remain'. There is often also a misconception about the amount of social security paid to each asylum seeker. A poll conducted by MORI (for *Reader's Digest*) in 2000 discovered that many British people thought that asylum seekers received well over £100 per week in social security payments. In fact, social security payments are generally set at 70% of Income Support rates. In 2002, a couple without children would receive £59.26 per week while a single person would receive £37.77 if they were 26 or over or £29.89 if 18-25. It should be noted that, from April 2000 to April 2002, asylum seekers' social security was paid in the form of vouchers which could only be used to buy food and other goods at specified shops and outlets (only £10 could be exchanged for cash). It should also be noted that asylum seekers are invariably reliant on social security because Home Office regulations prohibit them from working for the first six months.

Citizenship and asylum seekers

One government response to the growing public anxiety over asylum seekers was to call for ethnic minority groups to display greater sensitivity to traditional British norms and values. In December 2001, for example, the Home Secretary, David Blunkett, stated that the practice of enforced marriages for (some) Asian girls was incompatible with integration into

Figure 17.1 Citizenship tests *This cartoon was produced in December 2001.*

British society. 'We don't tolerate the intolerable under the guise of cultural difference', he said. 'We have norms of acceptability, and those who come in…should accept those norms'. In the same speech, Blunkett picked up on an idea floated in August 2001 by Lord Rooker, a Home Office Minister with special responsibility for immigration, and suggested that immigrants applying for British citizenship might be required to demonstrate proficiency in the English language, as well as other 'norms of acceptability'.

Such ideas were reflected in the White Paper *Secure Border Safe Haven* which the Home Office published in February 2002. This suggested that immigrants seeking permanent residency in Britain would be required to attend 'citizenship courses' at which they would be taught not just English language, but aspects of British culture, politics and traditions. The successful completion of such a course would be marked by a ceremony at which an oath would be sworn, pledging to 'respect the rights and freedoms of the United Kingdom…uphold its democratic values…observe its laws faithfully and fulfil my duties and obligations as a British citizen'.

Such initiatives were clearly intended to reflect New Labour's 'Third Way' emphasis on 'rights and responsibilities', the clear implication being that while the government was keen to tackle racism and associated socio-economic deprivation, black and Asian immigrants had to do more to help themselves, while, at the same time, avoiding behaviour or practices which alienated the indigenous or 'host' population.

Adapted from the *Observer*, 19 August 2001, the *Independent on Sunday*, 9 December 2001 and www.Homeoffice.gov.uk/rds/immigration.

2 The Auld Report and trial by jury

The Auld Report into the future of Britain's criminal justice system was commissioned by Lord Irvine, the Lord Chancellor, in 1999 and published in October 2001. The 686-page report contained 328 recommendations for the reform of Britain's criminal courts, but the proposal which caused most controversy was that which sought a change in a defendant's right to opt for trial by jury in a Crown Court (rather than being tried in a Magistrates' Court). The Auld Report recommended, instead, that a new intermediate court - to be known as the 'District Division' - be established. This would have a judge and two lay magistrates instead of juries and would hear cases where the sentence, if the defendant was found guilty, was likely to be two years imprisonment or less. It was also proposed that the defendant would no longer have the right to choose where their case was heard. Instead, the decision would be taken by the magistrates themselves.

The recommendations relating to juries were widely condemned - by politicians, by many sections of the legal profession (including the Bar Council, the Law Society and Lord Woolf, the Lord Chief Justice) and by civil liberties campaigners. The Chair of the Bar Council (which represents 9,000 barristers), Roy Amlot, was among those who implored the government not to sacrifice justice and juries 'on the altars of cost and efficiency'. Indeed, such was the breadth and depth of opposition that, by the beginning of 2002, the government was forced to backtrack. When the *Guardian* finally saw a draft of the White Paper *Justice for All* in July 2002, it was able to report that the jury reform contemplated was limited. The White Paper did envisage cutting the number of jury trials, but only a few defendants would lose the right to a jury trial if they wanted it. Judges would be able to try complex frauds without a jury. But the Serious Fraud Office completed only eight such trials in 1999-2000. In addition, magistrates' sentencing powers would be increased from six months to one year, to encourage them to keep more of the cases they previously sent for jury trial. Even so, defendants would still be able to insist on a crown court jury trial if they wanted one. Apart from complex fraud, legislation would allow the handful of cases 'where the jury actually is being intimidated' to be tried by judge alone. Consideration would be given to extending judge-alone trials to other complex cases, but no legislation was promised. In addition, a formal, US-style plea bargaining system, with the defendant being told in advance the sentence discount for pleading guilty was also expected to produce more guilty pleas and reduce the number of cases going to jury trial. This was the third occasion since 1997 that the Blair governments had been obliged to back down, due to trenchant opposition, from an attempt to curb a defendant's right to choose trial by jury.

Adapted from Morris 2001, the *Independent*, 16 October 2001 and the *Guardian*, 22 January and 15 July 2002.

3 The Parliamentary Commissioner for Administration (the Ombudsman)

Department/organisation complained about	New cases opened	Total caseload	Department/organisation complained about	New cases opened	Total caseload
Ministry of Agriculture, Fisheries & Food	25	35	Home Office	95	121
Charity Commission	7	12	Inland Revenue	214	266
HM Customs & Excise	24	32	HM Land Registry	20	23
Ministry of Defence	15	15	Legal Services Commission	73	107
Department of Education and Employment	55	69	Lord Chancellor's Dept	79	99
Environment Agency	12	13	Department of Social Security	720	986
Dept of Environment, Transport & Regions	97	123	Department of Trade & Industry	36	44
Foreign Office	13	16	The Treasury	38	39
Department of Health	20	24			

This table shows the main cases being investigated by the Parliamentary Commissioner for Administration 2000-01. If all complaints and cases are considered, the Ombudsman's complete caseload for 2000-2001 comprised 1,721 new cases and 507 ongoing cases, yielding an overall total of 2,228 (compared to 2,055 in 1998).

Adapted from www.ombudsman.org.uk

References

Morris (2001) Morris, T., 'Crime and Penal Policy' in *Seldon (2001)*.

Seldon (2001) Seldon, A. (ed.), *The Blair Effect - The Blair Government 1997-2001*, Little Brown and Company, 2001.

1 Reform of policing in Northern Ireland

Inextricably linked to the peace process in Northern Ireland is the reform of policing there. With 90% of members of the Royal Ulster Constabulary (RUC) being drawn from the Protestant/unionist community, many Catholics/nationalists have viewed it with distrust and suspicion, believing that it was biased against them.

Following the Good Friday Agreement, former Conservative Party Chairman, Chris Patten, was invited by Tony Blair to chair an inquiry into the future policing of Northern Ireland. The Patten Report, published in the autumn of 1999, offered 175 recommendations in order to ensure that:

- future policing in Northern Ireland facilitated 'parity of esteem' between the communities
- there was 'rigorous impartiality' in accordance with the principles of the Good Friday Agreement.

Of these 175 recommendations, the main ones are displayed in Box 18.1.

In response to the Patten Report, the government drew up its Police (Northern Ireland) Bill, which was given its First

1. New name, the Northern Ireland Police Force, to replace that of the Royal Ulster Constabulary.

2. The Union Jack and portraits of the Queen not to be displayed at police stations in Northern Ireland, in accordance with the principle that symbols should be 'free from association with the British or Irish states'.

3. Parity of recruitment between Catholics and Protestants within ten years.

4. Creation of a Police Board, comprising political representatives and appointees, but without either unionists or nationalists having overall control.

5. Officers in the new police force to be given lessons in human rights as part of their training, while the oath of service to include a commitment to 'respect the traditions and beliefs of people'.

Box 18.1 Main proposals in the Patten Report

Reading in May 2000, and received the Royal Assent in November that year. Some commentators are highly critical of this Act on the grounds that it fails to implement fully the recommendations in the Patten Report. O'Leary, for example, points out that Patten wanted a police force rooted in both communities, not one. That is why he recommended that the name of the service be entirely new. The Act, though, because of a government decision to accept an amendment tabled by the Ulster Unionist Party, styles the service 'The Police Service of Northern Ireland (incorporating the Royal Ulster Constabulary)'. Patten unambiguously recommended that the police's new badge and emblems be free of association with the British and Irish states and that the Union flag should not fly from police buildings. The Act postpones these matters. The government left it to local parties to reach agreement. Since the Secretary of State, Peter Mandelson, had already ruled that only the Union flag, albeit on specified days, should fly over the buildings of the devolved administration, nationalists lacked faith the government would deliver on cultural neutrality and impartiality. Not to follow Patten's recommendations has spelled a double message - that the new police is the old RUC retouched and it is linked more to British than Irish identity. Patten recommended an Oversight Commissioner to 'supervise the implementation of our recommendations'. Under pressure, the Labour government put the Commissioner's office on a statutory basis (the original Bill did not do so - it required an amendment). But, the Commissioner's role is confined to overseeing changes 'decided by government'. Had Mandelson and his colleagues been committed to Patten, they would have charged the Commissioner with recommending legislative and management changes necessary for the full implementation of the Patten Report. That they refused to do so speaks volumes. Patten recommended that the Ombudsman should have significant powers and should 'exercise the right to investigate and comment on police policies and practices', whereas in the Act the Ombudsman may make reports but not investigate (so it is not a crime to obstruct the Ombudsman's work).

Adapted from O'Leary 2001. See also *British Politics in Focus*, Second Edition, pp.612-17.

2 Crime statistics 2002

Offence	2001-02	Headline change (%)	Difference due to recording changes (%)	Real change (%)
Violence against the person	569,327	8	13	-5
Sexual offences	38,054	11	21	-8
Burglary of a dwelling	365,437	7	3	3
Burglary other	386,743	3	-2	5
Robbery	115,577	28	1	27
Vehicle theft	903,145	1	1	1
Non-vehicle thefts	1,122,476	9	3	6
Criminal damage	952,981	11	9	3
Other notifiable offences	516,934	3	6	-2
Total crime	**4,970,674**	**7**	**5**	**2**

The above figures are based on returns from 37 of the 43 police forces in England and Wales

(i) Crime in England and Wales, 2001-02
This table shows the estimated impact of recording changes on the recorded crime statistics of 2001-02.

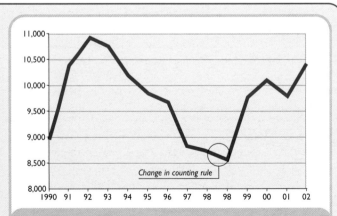

(ii) Recorded crime
This graph shows the number of violent, property and vehicle-related offences per 100,000 population in England and Wales, 1990-2002.

Adapted from the *Guardian*, 12 July 2002. See also *British Politics in Focus*, Second Edition, pp.624-28.

3 Crime in 2001–02: the *Daily Mail*

Official figures published on 12 July 2002 showed that crime in England and Wales rose in the previous year by the greatest margin for a decade. At the same time, the proportion of crimes solved fell to an all-time low. The most startling revelation was that the number of muggings increased by 28%. The Home Office's Recorded Crime Figures, published on 11 July 2002, also show that sex offences rose by 11% and murder and manslaughter by 4%. Burglary was up 7% and theft from cars 4%. In general, crime rose by 7%, the largest annual increase since 1991. This follows a drop of 2.5% last year. Every previous year since 1993 also saw a fall, except for a 3.7% rise from 1999 to 2000. Ministers sought to play down the dismal figures, blaming part of the increase on changes in the way in which police forces keep their records and insisting that levels of crime in general were 'stable'. Officials said that of the 7% rise in crime, 5% was down to the new way of compiling data, meaning crime only rose by 2%. But they could not deny the soaring level of robberies and the Home Secretary, David Blunkett, pledged to make the fight against street crime a priority for the police. The Home Office tried to offset the bad news by publishing another set of figures, the British Crime Survey, which showed crime in general falling by 2%. However, that survey - an annual questionnaire of 33,000 adults who are asked to record their experience of crime - found that robbery had soared by 17%. There were also warnings that the British Crime Survey might be less reliable in terms of recording a drop in crime because of the small size of its sample. Nor does it include the experience of those aged under 16, crimes against businesses or drugs offences.

Adapted from the *Daily Mail*, 12 July and 15 July 2002. See also *British Politics in Focus*, Second Edition, pp.624-28.

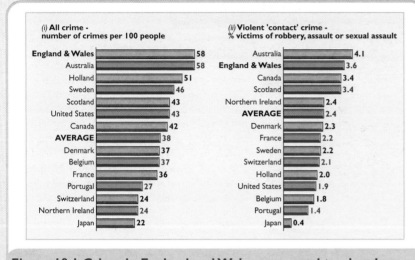

Figure 18.1 Crime in England and Wales compared to elsewhere *These charts compare levels of crime in England and Wales to that elsewhere. The figures were based on a survey of 2,000 people in each country, carried out by the United Nations Crime and Justice Research Unit in 2000.*

4 Crime in 2001–02: the *Guardian*

The annual police recorded figures, published on 12 July 2002, show that the sustained drop in the crime rate in England and Wales over the past six years appears to be over, with a 2% rise in the annual police recorded figures, including the first increases in burglaries and thefts for ten years. The simultaneous publication of the results of the more reliable British Crime Survey, which estimates crime to have fallen by 2%, led the Home Office to report that 'crime appears to have been stable over the last year, following a period of consistent decline'. This year's publication of crime statistics has included two big changes. For the first time, the British Crime Survey and the official police figures have been published on the same day and there has been a major reform of the way the police record crime. The Home Office said that the change in recording practice had reduced the overall 'headline' figure of a rise of 7% in the police figures to 2%. Among the detail of the figures, 'real increases' of around 5% in thefts and burglaries in the 12 months to March 2002 will alarm ministers. They are the first increases in these types of crime for ten years. The government has a target to reduce domestic burglary by 25% over the six years 1998-2004. These figures show that, after three years, it has fallen by 14% and may now be starting to rise. The Home Office says there is a link between the fall in burglaries in recent years and the fall in unemployment among young men. Government statisticians also point to a similar link between car crime and falling general unemployment rates.

Adapted from the *Guardian*, 12 July 2002. See also *British Politics in Focus*, Second Edition, pp.624-28.

Figure 18.2 The problem with crime statistics *This cartoon was published on 12 July 2002, the day after the 2001-02 crime figures came out and a few days after the WorldCom scandal had broken in the USA (corrupt accountancy led to the corporation's collapse).*

References

O'Leary (2001) O'Leary, B., 'The Belfast Agreement and the London government' in *Seldon (2001)*.

Seldon (2001) Seldon, A. (ed.), *The Blair Effect - The Blair Government 1997-2001*, Little Brown and Company, 2001.

1 Press ownership

Under the current rules governing newspaper ownership, there has to be a referral to the Competition Commission if the total circulation of the titles being bought by another newspaper group is more than 500,000 (unless the company making the purchase is not involved in the selling of newspapers). The Competition Commission then has to consider if the purchase is in the public interest before passing the matter to the Trade and Industry Secretary for a final decision. If, however, the papers are not making money, there is provision in the rules for the Secretary of State alone to make the decision.

The only significant change in national press ownership in the period between the summer of 1999 and the summer of 2002 came in 2000 when Northern and Shell bought the *Daily Express*, *Sunday Express* and the *Daily Star* from Lord Hollich. The purchase caused a major stir because the owner of Northern and Shell, Richard Desmond, had major financial interests in the publishing of pornography. However, as Northern and Shell was not involved in the publishing of newspapers, there was no need for an inquiry by the

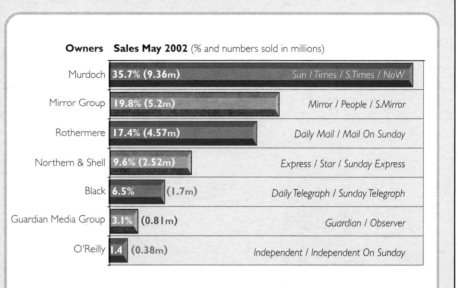

Owners	Sales May 2002 (% and numbers sold in millions)	
Murdoch	35.7% (9.36m)	Sun / Times / S.Times / NoW
Mirror Group	19.8% (5.2m)	Mirror / People / S.Mirror
Rothermere	17.4% (4.57m)	Daily Mail / Mail On Sunday
Northern & Shell	9.6% (2.52m)	Express / Star / Sunday Express
Black	6.5% (1.7m)	Daily Telegraph / Sunday Telegraph
Guardian Media Group	3.1% (0.81m)	Guardian / Observer
O'Reilly	1.4 (0.38m)	Independent / Independent On Sunday

Figure 19.1 National newspaper ownership and circulation

Competition Commission and the sale went ahead. This left the concentration of ownership of the press unchanged with the 19 major national daily and Sunday newspapers owned by just seven different owners (see Figure 19.1).

Adapted from the *Guardian*, 17 June 2002.
See also *British Politics in Focus*, Second Edition, pp.650-52 and 660-61.

2 Broadcasting

Government ministers have described the media ownership rules, which limit who can own broadcasting outlets in this country, as 'outdated, inconsistent and inflexible' and so have sought to introduce reform. In December 2000, a White Paper (and then a consultation paper) was published on media ownership. These documents set out different options for future television and radio ownership. There were conflicting responses to this initiative from the media industry. Part of the problem is the fast changing world of the media which now includes the internet and telecommunications as well as

traditional broadcasting. There is a fear of further concentration of ownership and cross-media ownership while at the same time there are commercial pressures for ever larger media conglomerates. In particular, Rupert Murdoch and News International have plans to expand their media empire into terrestrial television in this country. Current media ownership rules prevent that from happening, but this position looks set to change (see Section 3 below).

Adapted from HMSO 2000, HMSO 2001, Jones 2001 and the *Observer*, 2 December and 27 June 2001.
See also *British Politics in Focus*, Second Edition, pp.650-52 and 660-61.

3 Draft Communications Bill (2002)

The draft Communications Bill introduced in May 2002 outlined the rules that the government proposes to scrap. These are:
- rules that prevent single ownership of ITV
- rules that prevent ownership of more than one national commercial radio licence
- rules that prevent the joint ownership of TV and radio stations
- rules that prevent large newspaper groups from

acquiring Channel 5, or radio licences
- rules that prevent non-European ownership.

If this Bill becomes law, it will mean that the global media companies will be able to buy British television and radio companies. The *Guardian* suggested that it will mean that 'Mr Murdoch will tighten his grip on Britain's media'.

Adapted from the *Guardian*, 8 May 2002.
See also *British Politics in Focus*, Second Edition, pp.650-52 and 660-61.

4 Privacy and the Press Complaints Commission (PCC)

Between 1991 and 2002, the Press Complaints Commission (PCC) examined some 23,000 complaints made by members of the public. Among the high-profile rulings was that against the *Mail on Sunday* in 1999 for intruding into the privacy of the Prime Minister's daughter. This ruling was regarded as particularly important as it set a precedent for the protection of the privacy of children of all public figures. It was followed by another ruling by the PCC against the *Telegraph* and the *Mail* in January 2002 when they were found guilty of invading the privacy of Euan Blair by publicising the fact that he had applied for a place at Trinity College, Oxford.

In January 2002, after seven years as Chair of the PCC, Lord Wakeham resigned, following the collapse of Enron (a company with which he was involved). Critics argued that this made the future of the PCC uncertain. Professor Robert Pinker, Wakeham's replacement, did not carry Wakeham's political weight, they claimed, and was not a public figure. He might, therefore, not have the authority to deal with outraged editors and complainants. This was of particular concern because some lawyers were arguing that the Human Rights Act offered a way of securing more effective guarantees of privacy for people than the PCC and editors were becoming alarmed at the possibility

of facing two hurdles when people complained (ie the PCC and the courts). Newspaper owners, it was argued, might decide that it was not worth continuing to fund the expensive machinery of self-regulation if the courts gradually took over the role of the PCC. The case of Gary Flitcroft, the footballer who attempted to prevent the *Sunday People* naming him in an article which made revelations about his sex life, may have worked in the PCC's favour, however. In March 2002, Lord Woolf, a Judge in the Court of Appeal, ruled that the injunction banning the press from naming the footballer could be lifted. If the judge had not ruled this way, it would almost certainly have meant the end to the 'kiss-and-tell' stories which are so popular with the tabloid press. The judge made it clear that he believed that, had he ruled in favour of Flitcroft, it would have meant an end to many tabloids and this, he argued, would have harmed freedom of speech. In the judgement, he said it was right to lift the injunction 'irrespective of whether a particular publication is desirable in the public interest'. This suggests a big push towards freedom of speech and a recognition for the first time that celebrities are not automatically entitled to wholesale privacy.

Adapted from Jones 2000 and the *Guardian*, 19 July 2001 and 28 January and 1 February 2002.

5 The media and Number Ten

After the general election of June 2001, it was decided that Alastair Campbell should relinquish his role as Press Secretary and, instead, become the Director of Communications. This meant that he would focus more on the strategic plans of the government rather than on day-to-day issues. Campbell had been under increasing criticism from MPs. In a report from the Public Administration Select Committee just before the 2001 general election, the claim was made that Campbell and Jonathan Powell (the Prime Minister's Chief of Staff) were influencing the promotion of civil servants and should lose their powers to issue orders to civil servants.

In May 2002, Campbell announced changes in the lobby system of parliamentary briefing. Now, any journalist is able to attend a morning question and answer session with government ministers and civil servants, though a closed afternoon briefing continues to be held (for lobby correspondents only). Such is the cynicism about Campbell, however, that this has been interpreted as an attempt to gain greater control over the media (since a large gathering of the press is easier to manipulate than a small group of specialist lobby correspondents).

Adapted from the *Guardian*, 13 March and 8 June 2001 and 3 May 2002. See also *British Politics in Focus*, Second Edition, p.680.

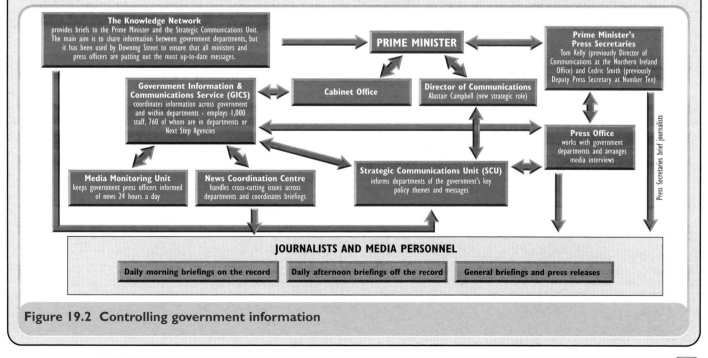

Figure 19.2 Controlling government information

6 Freedom of information

Labour finally published its long heralded revised Freedom of Information Bill in May 1999. It contained many changes, compared to the earlier White Paper. The main changes were as follows:

1. The White Paper's requirement that ministers should demonstrate that substantial harm would come from publication had been replaced by the far weaker test of prejudice.

2. The Security and Intelligence Services were subject to a complete exemption from the terms of the Bill.

3. Information that related to the formulation or development of government policy was also exempted, whereas the White Paper had proposed that such information could only be withheld if ministers could show that substantial harm to the public interest would result.

Pressure groups like the Campaign for Freedom of Information argued strongly that the Bill was a deep disappointment as it would do little to improve openness in government departments. When the Home Secretary, Jack Straw, presented the final version to Parliament in October 1999, he made minor concessions. But, Maurice Frankel, Director of the Campaign for Freedom of Information, claimed that: 'an overriding defect [of the Bill is] the several blanket exemptions which allow authorities to withhold information without evidence of harm'.

As the Bill passed through the Lords, the government made further concessions, namely:

- acceptance that, if the public interest for and against disclosure was equally balanced, the information would be disclosed
- the placing of a statutory obligation on public authorities to help applicants seeking information.

MPs, from all parties, tabled 118 last-minute amendments in an attempt to improve the legislation, but the Home Secretary imposed a guillotine to force the measure through and the Bill received the Royal Assent on the 30 November 2000.

Delay in implementation

The Act was expected to come into operation in 2002. Elizabeth France who was appointed Information Commissioner and will, therefore, be responsible for enforcing the Act argued, in a leaked letter, that it would be 'sensible and realistic' to implement it in 2002, as first planned. She had wanted the government to introduce a phased implementation, starting with government departments from October 2001, followed by local councils from April 2003, NHS bodies by October 2003

and schools and universities from April 2004. But, Tony Blair has argued that all 70,000 public bodies affected by the Act must be ready to implement it at the same time. The result is that the Act will only come into force in January 2005, four years after Parliament approved it.

In July 2002, it became known that Tony Blair created a precedent for secrecy in Whitehall by refusing for the first time to accept the findings of the parliamentary ombudsman on release of information under the 'Open Government' code. Richard Wilson, the Cabinet Secretary, told the Commons Public Administration Committee that a political decision at the highest level of government had been made to block the release of information on ministers' declarations under the Prime Minister's code of conduct. Wilson defended the government, saying: 'Even an insignificant piece of information can be highly damaging. The concern that the government has is that it is very important not to constrain the relationship which exists between ministers, permanent secretaries and their colleagues. You would find ministers feeling that everything they did might become the subject of public speculation'.

In opposition in 1996, Tony Blair claimed that freedom of information was fundamental to bringing about a new relationship between the government and the people who would be 'stakeholders in running the country'.

Figure 19.3 The Blair government and freedom of information
This cartoon was published in February 2002, shortly after the Enron scandal broke in the USA. Freedom of information is enshrined in the American constitution.

Adapted from Gore 1999, Rathbone 2001 and the *Guardian*, 11 October 1999, 10 November 2001 and 12 July 2002.
See also *British Politics in Focus*, Second Edition, pp.681-84.

References

Gore (1999) Gore, P., 'Freedom of information under Blair', *Talking Politics*, Vol.12.1, Summer 1999.
HMSO (2000) *A New Future for Communications*, CM5010 (DTI/DCMS), HMSO, 2000.
HMSO (2001) *A Consultation Paper on Media Ownership Rules*, (DCMS/DTI), HMSO 2001.

Jones (2000) Jones, B., 'The media and democracy: Part 1: the press', *Talking Politics*, Vol.13.1, Summer 2000.
Jones (2001) Jones, B., 'The media and democracy Part 2: broadcasting and democracy', *Talking Politics*, Vol.13.2, January 2001.
Rathbone (2001) Rathbone. M., 'The Freedom of Information Act', *Talking Politics*, Vol.13.2, April 2001.